The
Hitler
Book

THE HITLER BOOK

SCHILLER INSTITUTE

Edited by Helga Zepp-LaRouche

New Benjamin Franklin House
New York
1984

Contents

Acknowledgments

My thanks to all those in the USA and Europe whose research work made this book possible, and especially to the writers Dr. Helmut Böttiger, Andreas Buck, Thierry Lalevée, Michael Liebig, Laurent Murawiec, and Angelika Raimondi.

I also extend my thanks to John Sigerson, President of the Schiller Institute in the United States, and to Susan Parmacek Johnson, for supervising preparation of this English edition of *Das Hitlerbuch*, which is being published by the Institute in West Germany. Thanks also go to John Chambless, Edward Carl, and Caroline Sulzer for their translations from the German.

Helga Zepp-LaRouche
June, 1984

HELGA ZEPP-LAROUCHE

Introduction:
He Who Does Not Learn
From History Is Forced
to Repeat It

This book is a contribution to understanding the
current political situation in the Federal Republic
of Germany. Its publication has become necessary
because processes now at work within the German
population are to a large extent unknown to that
population, and to such an astounding degree that
we must not only draw upon the history of the
twentieth century; we must proceed from the fact
that Germany has never come to terms with its past.
This has been all the more difficult because there
exists no competently written history of Germany
in the twentieth century. Between the official histories and actual experience, there exists an all too
gaping chasm, and Germans have had little chance
of recognizing themselves within this mass of literature, let alone using it to achieve some clarity
about their past.

The most distressing aspect of the German tragedy is that the citizens of the Federal Republic are
once again on the brink of plunging into disaster.
Seemingly without a history of their own, and yet

shackled by that history, in the 38 years since the end of the Second World War the Germans have not been able to define a positive national identity. And now they are once again chasing after the chimera of a supposed national interest. Their lack of historical awareness and self-knowledge comes into bold relief in the German's largely unconscious fear reactions to the looming war danger. This danger is hard to ignore; the Soviet Union and Warsaw Pact states are currently preparing for war. Reorganization of their military command structure, mobilization of all units into the highest state of preparedness, militarization of the civilian economy, and indoctrination of the population are but some highlights, along with the recently much-publicized preparations for committing acts of sabotage in the West through so-called spetsnaz groups—specially trained units totalling around 30,000 agents with instructions to paralyze key sectors of energy, transport, and communication shortly before the outbreak of war.

Even though this threat to the Federal Republic comes unmistakably from the East, large parts of the population are nevertheless steeped in anti-Americanism, and are, to various degrees, becoming swayed by the seductive tones of Soviet assurances of the U.S.S.R.'s unbounded love of peace. On the one hand, the Soviets are extending their carrot, tempting West Germans with the chance to have a nuclear-free zone in Central Europe and a possible reunification into a neutral German state. But at the same time they are waving their stick, claiming in the Soviet media that the policies of the U.S.A. and the Federal Republic are identical to those of the Nazis, that there is a revival in the army of old Prussian militarism, and so forth. Coming at the present moment, such characterizations are primarily aimed at mentally preparing the population of the Warsaw Pact countries for a "just war" against an alleged resurgence of fascism. The Federal Republic's population, knowing about this mobilization in the East, is to be put into such a state of fear and terror that it will, so to speak, voluntarily run into the Soviets' open arms. And if it does not, everything is already in place for a military intervention.

Is President Reagan a new Hitler? Is the Federal Republic under Chancellor Kohl pursuing a Nazi policy? Is the Bundeswehr a conspiracy of revanchists, dripping with Prussian-Hitlerian militarism? Such claims are quite obviously absurd, and could hardly be taken seriously even in the Soviet Union.

In the recent past, accusations of fascism have often been used as justification for political power-plays, but never were there more dangerous implications than today: the result could be a new world war. Without a doubt, there does exist a new danger of fascism. Fascism will, however, come from a different quarter than the Soviet writers claim. In fact, leading circles of the still-powerful Western oligarchy are attempting to respond to the current world economic crisis with economic proposals identical to those which Hitler's Economics Minister and former Reichsbank President Hjalmar Schacht carried out during the last Great Depression.

The danger of a new fascism exists in the inhuman brutality with which the International Monetary Fund forces its infamous conditionalities upon the developing countries, knowing full well that this will cause millions of human beings to die by starvation. In Africa alone, the IMF's policy threatens to kill off more people than Adolf Hitler did in the course of the Second World War. The danger of a new fascism, however, is also embedded in the racism of the Club of Rome, an organization which considers the white Anglo-Saxon race to be under siege, and which has de facto written off the black, brown, and yellow peoples of the earth as "useless eaters." This club of technology-haters is promoting each and every irrationalist cult which might serve as a nurturing environment for fascism. The danger of fascism also results from the coincidence of mass unemployment with a mood of cultural pessimism, as well as the so-called peace movement's constant undermining of governmental authority through its use of violence and terror.

But all these dangers are not what the Soviet Union is referring to. Where is their anti-fascist resistance movement to fight this old evil in its new garb? Or is the anti-fascist resistance perhaps not working very hard after all? The reality is that the Communist phase within the Soviet Union has more or less come to an end. To the extent that the ideology of Marxism-Leninism—never fully embraced by the East bloc population—loses its appeal, the much more deeply rooted mentality of czarist Russia rears its head again. Dostoevsky and Tolstoy are resuming their former positions as spokesmen for the so-called Russian soul and the idea of the "holy Russian race," the brotherhood of the blood and soil of "Mother Russia," of "Holy Moscow," and finally, the medieval idea of Moscow as the third and final Rome, the capital of a future world empire.

Anyone who has followed the recent proliferation of such ominous ideas in Soviet publications or in speeches from leading Soviet military figures, can be left with little doubt that the Soviet Union is currently in the midst of a decisive molting process. The comparatively rational phase of communism is yielding to an irrational and violent fundamentalism, whose highest aim is no longer even the progress of the socialist state, but rather lies in the protection of the holy soil of Mother Russia, from which the Russian soul is supposed to derive its power. This impulse has now been elevated to the status of a national mythos, feeding into Moscow's dream of a world empire.

This metamorphosis taking place within the Soviet Union is likewise moving in the direction of fascism; at the same time, however, it signifies a return to the murkier side of Russian history and mentality, an aspect closely associated with the name of Dostoevsky. This morbid cultural pessimist's world outlook was one of the most crucial sources of all national socialism. The fact that this is usually covered up in most historical research, makes it no less true. The point of departure for investigation along these lines would have to be the German-language translator of Dostoevsky, Moeller van den Bruck, the man who coined the term "Third Reich" and who introduced Dostoevsky's world outlook into German thinking.

The Soviet Union has long ceased claiming it supports the world's "progressive movements." With increasing unabashedness it has been utilizing old and new Nazi networks, such as the Green movement—that new vessel for fascist world outlooks—or the old Nazi structures operating out of Switzerland, or even the Islamic fundamentalist Sufis and Shi'ites. These curious alliances of Moscow all proceed not only from their desire to promote anything which weakens the West, but are also based on their epistemological affinity. This affinity is the cement uniting the left and right wings, whose common denominator consists of rabid anti-Americanism, the idea of a neutralized central Europe and a reunified Germany. From the New Right around Alain de Benoist to the so-called left—so called by such people as Social Democratic leader Oskar Lafontaine out of historical ignorance—the unifying link is a new wave of the old National Bolshevism which kept on surfacing during the Weimar Republic.

Behind the current policy of appeasement in the West, there lurks a singular longing to join with the Russians in reversing the defeats suffered by Germany in the last war—a hope many sought to fulfill following the defeat of World War I. That defeat constituted the fertile soil for the National Bolshevist tendencies of that time. The peace movement, which then as now consists almost exclusively of the ecology and counter-culture movement, is still preoccupied with the watchwords of an "anti-capitalist longing" now surging throughout the German people. This at any rate was the term used by Gregor Strasser, leader of the National Bolshevist wing of the Nazi Party. Such a historical parallel is by no means accidental, as is clearly shown by recent positive evaluations of the Strasser brothers appearing in the peace-movement literaure, e.g. in the West Berlin terrorist-connected newspaper *taz*.

Not openly, but with voices hushed as if in fear of ghosts, circles in the peace movement are muttering about "Weimarization"—the key notion behind that evil phrase, the "ungovernability" of the Western democracies in general and the Federal Republic of Germany in particular. During the parliamentary vote on the stationing of Pershing missiles in Europe, the Greens clearly demonstrated who their teachers have been on the subject of unhinging the parliament through violence and terror; namely, the Nazis. The worst danger here is that the so-called established parties and institutions themselves are disintegrating under the pressure of events. Probably the most terrifying example of this is the degeneration of the Social Democratic Party since the departure of Helmut Schmidt.

Weimarization—and then what? Is it possible to conceive of a new phase of fascism in Germany? Unfortunately, just as in 1931, the question must be answered in the affirmative. And today, the danger of war is all too evident. Yet we cannot dismiss the fact that the threat of a new fascism is not confined to the Federal Republic, but this time extends over the entire world. The threat could become reality if oligarchical financial circles succeed in enforcing their Malthusian economic policies, or if the West capitulates to Russian-Orthodox hegemonic claims. The irrationalism of Khomeini and his terrorist commandos also pose a serious threat to Western civilization, if we are unable to put an end to this monstrosity.

Humanity today probably faces the gravest crisis in its entire history. It is all the more urgent to achieve epistemological clarity concerning the roots of fascism. Otherwise, what will happen when it appears in different garb? This book differs substantially from other publications on this theme, in that it documents the continuity of fascist networks through to the present, and shows how they operate today.

There is no other way to give a true account of fascism. In this respect we must agree with Friedrich Schiller's thesis, that the historian must retrieve from the entire sum of events, those circumstances "which have had a crucial, undeniable and easily traceable influence on the shaping of the world today and on the condition of the generation now living. In gathering materials for universal history, therefore, we must look to the relation of an historical datum to the state of the world at present."

None of the published books on this theme have met this criterion, with the result that, in spite of their wealth of detail, they are simply wrong. Although a few works here and there stand out from the general mass of publications by having unearthed important aspects of the history of National Socialism and fascism, no presentation exists which significantly concentrates on this "relation of an historical datum to the state of the world at present." Such a presentation must not only trace how Nazi networks have survived to the present day, but must also show the fate of all the various ideological strands leading into National Socialism—the ideological jumble out of which Hitler's particular brand of National Socialism was merely the most successful. All these currents, from Theosophists and Anthroposophists, Eugenicists and Pan-Europeans, National Revolutionaries and National Bolshevists, through various Conservative Revolution tendencies, to the Strasser and Hitler wings of the NSDAP—a total of perhaps 4,000 to 5,000 different tendencies—have significant overlapping areas with respect to content and practice.

Among these tendencies, Hitler's National Socialism, with its practice of eliminating competitors through violence and terror, was certainly the most successful. This, however, does not mean that the less successful currents were free from guilt, or that their policies would not have led to equally genocidal results, had they won the upper hand instead.

One of the worst blunders, therefore, in all previous historiography has been the attempt to lend some of these other groupings an aura of antifascist resistance, simply because they succumbed to internal rivalries. Such groups, were they to be overlooked now, could continue to exist undisturbed and could under the right conditions increase in influence.

The new world economic crisis contains within it all the dangers of a resurgence of fascism. But just as the emergence of the Nazis and Hitler's seizure of power were by no means "sociological phenomena," so there is nothing "organic" about developments today; now as then, the formation of such movements has been consciously guided and artificially orchestrated.

Certain oligarchical circles have for some time been whispering about a "new Hitler project," and about how they could find a more appropriate Führer figure, educate him in rhetorical skills and supply him with the necessary "charisma." It is easy to see how, in this television age, such a figure could be created out of the most lowly material—Jimmy Carter being a case in point. Our pursuit of this discussion was an important motivation to the writing of this book.

The old "Hitler model" is, of course, outmoded in its exact original form. A new version of fascism would probably be more oriented toward Strasser's wing of the NSDAP. This, at any rate, seems to be the direction indicated today: fanatical hatred of technology, mystification of nature mixed with regionalism, and the all-pervasive National Bolshevist groundwork, based on dreams of an independent Central Europe as a "third power" with a reunified, neutral, but armed Germany.

Here lies the crux of the matter. A "new Hitler project," which currently has crucial momentum in German politics, does not simply mean a shift into overtly fascist policies. What is required are deftly formulated and cleverly executed "intelligence-chessboard moves."

In order to better understand such operations, we must consider the fact that, as early as 1977, the Warsaw Pact held a large maneuver in the German Democratic Republic and other states under the code name "Operation Polarka." This operation was kept secret not only by the East, but by NATO as well; it would have caused quite a stir if, during the chancellorship of Helmut Schmidt, it had been revealed that the object of these maneuvers was a surgical strike into the Federal Republic, with the aim of removing Nazis who had supposedly taken state power.

We must also recognize that the Soviet Union was the only one of the four victorious powers which never agreed to the formulation of the United Nations Charter of 1948, and therefore still defines the subsequently founded Federal Republic as merely a successor to the fascist aggressor. The Soviet Union therefore officially regards the Federal Republic as a potential opponent, a nation against which military operations are perfectly legitimate.

Although the Polarka maneuver seemed at first to be solely political in nature, its true content was only first revealed in a series of speeches and articles issued by Moscow following the West German Parliament's November 22, 1983 decision to install the Pershing missiles. The Soviet military newspaper *Red Star* charged that the Bundeswehr was encouraging a revival of the old Hitler-Prussian revanchism. East German party chairman Erich Honecker accused the Kohl government of seeking a reunified Germany and a return to the borders of 1937. Soviet Politburo member Grigorii Romanov told the German Communist Party congress in Nuremberg that the same country which was responsible for starting two world wars (an insupportable argument with respect to World War I), is now engaged in preparations for a third, as evidenced by the stationing of the Pershing II and cruise missiles as first-strike weapons on its territory. Numerous Soviet publications have described Reagan as the "new Hitler," emphasizing that the Federal Republic shares this responsibility. Such accusations, of course, are patently absurd in light of the actual balance of military power in both the strategic and intermediate areas. Their real purpose, however, is to mobilize the population within the East bloc for war, and to legitimize a possible military incursion against the Federal Republic.

Now, one might object that such an argument could not possibly hold water; who could imagine Helmut Kohl as a new Hitler? No one in his right mind could possibly accuse Mr. Kohl of planning to emerge as a new powerful Führer!

So then, where are these Nazis which Moscow succeeds in puffing up into credible bogeymen? Even though the hard core of the "Green" so-called peace movement has been engaged in countless terrorist acts in the best tradition of the SA, we would be quickly disappointed if we expected the Soviet Union to describe those people as Nazis. No, on the contrary, Moscow has been providing these actual Nazis with generous financial support.

Instead, the pretext for Moscow's accusations is the new "Republican Party" in West Germany, formed in Munich five days after the missile stationing, and named in order to induce the public to read "x" whenever they see "y." Before its foundation, this party had already been assured financing from oligarchical circles in southern Germany, and its ranks include members so outspoken about their uninterrupted admiration for Hitler that one has good grounds for suspicion. Indeed, it almost seems as if this party wants to send a loud and ringing message: "See, there *is* a resurgence of Nazism in the Federal Republic!" With central roles played by such prominent persons as Franz Schönhuber (*I Was There*), who in turn is said to maintain close friendly relations with the current head of the Nazi International, Swiss banker François Genoud, then our suspicions can only increase. Genoud himself is considered to be not only at the hub of Nazi-Communist activities worldwide, but is also well known through the European press for his ties with the internationally sought terrorist Carlos and with East Berlin. Is it conceivable, then, that the East has had some hand in the formation of such a blatantly right-wing party as this "Republican" Party professes to be? We must at any rate ask the question, "cui bono?" and watch its development carefully.

Historical truth can never be discovered from the initial appearances of events. This is doubly true for the history of Nazism; never has there been a field more thoroughly and frequently plowed and cultivated by both East and West as this one, and many events which appear on the surface to be "political," are in fact nothing more than secret service operations.

The loser in this game of power is the German people themselves, because such games deprive them of all sense of cause and effect and lawfulness in the real world. Our only remedy here is to remove these events from the shadows and expose them to the light of day, with the goal of leading the Germans into a true consciousness of their own history. Their knowledge of their own share of responsibility, as well as the responsibility of others, is the Gordian knot which must be cut if there is ever to exist real sovereignty for the Germans. We must overcome the self-righteous hypocrisy found so often abroad, the prejudice that all Germans were Nazis and that the Nazis were only in Germany. In reality, Germany is one of the most tormented nations in the world, even considering all the poverty and suffering this world harbors.

Anyone with a precise knowledge of Germany cannot doubt that it was Germany itself which suffered most at the hands of the Nazis. The price for the Nazis' crimes must be reckoned not only by the number of dead; the nation also seems to have lost its soul, and it is still uncertain whether it will ever be able to regain it. In order to understand the miserable situation of the Federal Republic today—its inability, during the 38 years following the war, to either become a nation or to produce a national republican elite which could espouse our country's vital interests—we must include in our considerations the entire span of the last 200 years.

Why and how could Germany have sunk from the highest cultural level of its classical period with its humanistic conception of mankind, down into the depths of Nazi bestiality? This question still needs to be answered; indeed, it represents the key to locating the German identity. Precisely because classical Germany had attained such a pinnacle of humanistic culture, it had made itself into the target of the international oligarchical forces of the Conservative Revolution. What took place in the Germany of Schiller, the Humboldts, and Beethoven, was indeed a true classical period, rooted in Greek classicism and the Italian Renaissance, elevating the conception of mankind to new, hitherto unattained heights. The concept of the American Revolution, the "ideas of 1789," transmitted by the works of poets and composers of that era, penetrated more deeply and more lastingly into the conscience of the population, and educated a greater portion of the population in republican ideas, than ever before or ever after.

Whoever desires to understand the collapse of the German people must learn to comprehend the reasons for this transformation of Weimar classicism's unlimited cultural optimism into the cultural pessimism of the Weimar Republic—a pessimism which in turn made National Socialism possible, and which is still running rampant today.

This transformation is symbolized by three dates in Germany's history: 1815, 1918, and 1945. Each of these years had ramifications for Germany which at the time were scarcely comprehensible to individual citizens; they were the products of extremely complex international constellations. For the individual, the events of those years brought deep disappointed expectations, and produced the fissures in national identity which paved the way for cultural pessimism.

The Congress of Vienna in 1815 had an indisputable and decisive influence on the Germans' decline. Had this assembly never taken place, National Socialism would probably have never come into being. Never had the Germans been closer to conducting a republican revolution on the American model, and never had they reached a higher moral level, than they were during the 1812–15 Wars of Liberation. These wars were not merely a republican uprising against Napoleon's imperialist occupation of the greater part of Germany; above all else, they were spearheaded by a flourishing constitutional movement.

The movement was led, of course, by the Prussian reformers vom Stein, Humboldt, and Scharnhorst, but it drew its vitality from the countless common citizens who were filled with patriotism and inspired by Schiller's dramas and other republican writings. Even at the Vienna Congress itself, vom Stein still cherished hopes that the negotiations would result in a united, sovereign German nation. But that was precisely what the international oligarchy conspired to prevent. With the intrigues and machinations of the English, French, Venetians, the Russian nobility, and especially the wretched Metternich (the man whom, not surprisingly, Henry Kissinger admires the most) arrayed against them, the German republicans did not stand a chance. Cloaked in hypocritical fundamentalism, the Holy Alliance snuffed out each and every shining idea, introducing instead an era of brutal oppression and surveillance. The German population, unable to understand why their heroic and victorious struggle against Napoleon had not led to a nation-state, lapsed to an ever greater degree into an other-wordly Romanticism during the years following the Restoration, drifting later on into outright demoralization. It is only from this standpoint that the influence wielded by Nietzsche and the other demagogues of cultural pessimism becomes comprehensible.

As for 1918, standard historical research has long

since rejected the thesis that Germany bears sole responsibility for World War I. If the Congress of Vienna signified the end of a period of hope in Germany's history, then the Treaty of Versailles marked the beginning of the subsequent disaster. Out of the colossal injustice embedded within this treaty, the terms of which the population was never in a position to fulfill, all of the later calamities flowed. Hitler made good use of the justified outrage felt by the population, a large portion of whom had been uprooted through four and a half years of senseless, brutalizing trench warfare.

Hitler, however, was by no means the charismatic loner whose personality might enable us to understand the "National Socialist phenomenon." Hitler's entire personal career was, after all, but one product of the oligarchy's cultish world outlook, and it was this same oligarchy which, on the urging of Hjalmar Schacht, decided to raise Hitler onto its shield in 1932. The same oligarchy, therefore, which had passed judgment over Germany at Versailles and had set reparations payments at such an absurdly high level that any economic recovery was rendered out of the question, now looked for the strong man who could carry out a policy of austerity according to their specifications and with the required ruthlessness. Hitler was their man!

But Hitler alone did not give the Weimar Republic its final death blow. This was done by that curious "action alliance" of Communists and National Socialists, both of whom were intent on destroying the constitutional "system." Later memories of the destruction wrought by the Nazis against the Soviet Union during the Second World War, have largely blotted out these earlier memories of the astonishing affinity which existed between "right" and "left" during the Weimar period.

On the one hand there was the Strasser wing of the NSDAP, openly preaching for an alliance with the East. But even within the Hitler wing, the methods used by the SA and SS to construct a totalitarian one-party state and to deploy a terrorist apparat, were remarkably similar to those of the post-Lenin Bolsheviks, who themselves had never broken with the old traditions of czarist Russia.

From the Soviet side, Stalin and the Comintern forced the German Communist Party (KPD) to support the Nazis—a move which unleashed considerable turmoil among the German Communists, who were more representative of the direct legacy of Karl Marx than the specifically Russian strain of Bolshevism. Stalin and Georgii Dmitrov, head of the Comintern's Western Secretariat, ordered the KPD to fight against the "social fascist" Social Democratic Party (SPD), and to form an action alliance with the Nazis "in order to hasten the dissolution of the dwindling democratic block governing Germany." Stalin thought Hitler was a useful tool for weakening the West, a pawn who would soon discredit himself, at which point Germany would be ripe for Communist takeover.

At play here were the same considerations which later moved Stalin to conclude the Hitler-Stalin pact. The frequent if sporadic collaboration between Nazis and Communists against the SPD—which continued well after the start of the emergency government under von Papen!—was grounded on the Soviet side upon the the same philosophy which today permits them to collaborate with the Green "peace movement." Moscow itself, we can be assured, has no illusions about this movement's National Socialist character, but it sees its anti-Western orientation as an asset in Moscow's own struggle against "capitalism." The Soviets have apparently still not learned the lesson that one can always sponsor a National Socialist movement, but one cannot necessarily prevent such a monster from eventually striking back against its master. Today the Federal Republic is threatened once again by the same Nazi-Communist alliance as it was during the Weimar Republic.

Financial circles in Zürich, London, and New York not only financially supported Hitler before his seizure of power; through the pages of the *New York Times* they lavished public praise on him well into 1939. And at the 1932 Conference on Eugenics at the Museum of Natural History in New York City, not only were leading Nazi racialists present, but they were flanked by representatives of the so-called Eastern Establishment, headed up by Averell Harriman's mother and the infamous William Draper, who soon thereafter was to participate in the terror bombings of German cities. (Following the war, Draper came to Germany in order to "re-educate the Germans.")

Today it would have a liberating effect on the German population if more knew these facts, and if they could experience rage that the same political circles which helped Hitler to power, later had the arrogance to impose upon the Germans their own queer idea of democracy. Access to such knowledge is generally blocked by a prejudice that National Socialism is a strictly German matter; we therefore recommend that such prejudices be dissolved, and that National Socialism should instead be regarded as only an extreme form of the oligarchical world outlook, which is locked in battle against the opposing philosophy of humanism and progress.

One instrument in the oligarchs' armamentarium has been the thesis of so-called collective guilt. Its inventors, Hugh Trevor-Roper and John Wheeler-Bennett, intended to use this thesis to extinguish any glimmerings of humanist culture which might have lingered on within the German population following the Nazis' campaigns of psychological terror.

Everyone who lived through the years following World War II knew that the thesis of German collective guilt was designed to break the back of the German people once and for all. To be sure, Germans were conscious that they were at fault, and that their resistance against the Nazis obviously could have been stronger, especially on the part of large organizations such as the SPD and the trade unions, who were in a position to put up effective resistance. But few could have accurately predicted what was in store for Germany after the Nazis arrived, since there were no examples to draw upon from recent history. After the seizure of power, the reign of terror set into motion with such brutality and efficiency that the predominantly individual resistance of a very considerable number of courageous people was quickly wiped out. "Shot while escaping," the newspapers would report laconically whenever the SA or the SS had to cover up another cold-blooded murder.

We must see the Germans' behavior following Hitler's seizure of power in its proper proportions. Their reactions differed little in this respect from the way people behaved abroad. Were we not also, just recently, in grave danger of a Third World War set off by the incompetent Jimmy Carter—a danger already evident before his inauguration, and against which presidential candidate Lyndon LaRouche warned in a half-hour television broadcast in November 1976? If we had had a Third World War then, would people be talking afterwards—assuming there were survivors—of the Americans' collective guilt? And the "resistance" against Jimmy Carter in 1976 was not very great.

The problem was not that all Germans had become Nazis or even Nazi sympathizers. The problem was rather that, once again, a momentous historic moment had found a "little people," as Schiller once put it concerning the French Revolution. Most people at the time preferred to turn to their private affairs, just as they are doing today. "Yes, sure, the violence of the Nazis is upsetting, but I have to look after my family and my career; and anyway, they'll discredit themselves once they've gained power," was the common reply. And the Nazis certainly did discredit themselves; unfortunately, the Second World War had to be fought before they did.

The victims, then, were these "little people" who thought they could remain aloof from politics; many of these became the men who bled and froze to death on the Eastern Front, or crawled home after the war with shattered limbs and withered hearts. It was these "little people," women and children, who night after night, year after year, ran to hide in their cellars, whose lives were destroyed and who will never, despite all subsequent efforts, be able to blot out the terror of those years.

While the population was still paying for the Nazi leaders' insanity, while the Allied terror bombing was still destroying German cities—to no military purpose, but solely in order to study the population's reactions—the post-war world was already being divided up. The Bretton Woods monetary system was essentially based on a draft proposal by Hitler's Economics Minister Walther Funk, though for the sake of politeness the name of a Churchill collaborator was placed on it. From its very inception, Bretton Woods contained all the seeds of destruction which were to lead to the second world economic crisis of the 1980s. And while the soldiers were being ground up in a war which, since Stalingrad, had increasingly lost any prospect of victory, the leading Nazis were busily shipping their collected booty into Switzerland, where they could count on tender support from the Dulles brothers. Here, long before the war's end, it had already been decided who among the Nazi bigwigs would be permitted to re-emerge with a clean record—as did Messrs. Schacht and Skorzeny, for example—who would be spirited off abroad, and who would be quietly incorporated into the Anglo-American secret service, as exemplified by SS officer Klaus Barbie, along with many others.

No, the course of German history has never been as black and white as the movies would have us believe, with the good Anglo-Americans lined up against the nasty Germans. There never was any new beginning, never some sort of zero hour; there was only a regroupment of forces. A few were justly condemned, many criminals both in and outside Germany got away scot free, and the entire German population was made into the scapegoat for the unsuccessful Hitler project. Even though two world wars fought and lost went a long way toward breaking the backs of the Germans as a nation, it was the Allied occupation which accomplished the rest. All the pacifism, anti-Americanism, hatred of technology and irrationalism so evident today in the West German population can be directly credited to this misguided occupation policy, and now the bill is being presented. Unless the United States recognizes its past mistakes, and substitutes a new, positive policy, the German-American relationship will never truly heal.

Where the Occupying Powers Failed

Perhaps the best way to gain insight into the mistakes made by America in occupied Germany, is to compare the policies of John J. McCloy and Gen. Lucius Clay in Germany with those of Gen. Douglas MacArthur in Japan. These two completely contrasting approaches are in turn expressions of the fact that McCloy and MacArthur represent two poles within American policymaking.

MacArthur, whose thought and actions were embedded in the spirit of the American Revolution, guided his policy toward conquered Japan with a true concern for its future, and acted to strengthen republican tendencies within the country in order to win Japan as a long-term friend. McCloy represented the opposite outlook. He remained a typical representative of the treasonous Tory clique which became known as the Eastern Establishment, whose entire efforts, over the 200 years since the American Revolution, have been tirelessly directed toward reversing the gains of this revolution. The immeasurable wealth held by this clique derived largely from trafficking in slaves and drugs.

McCloy, true to his tradition, acted toward occupied Germany as would an arrogant colonial lord. The idea of formulating a policy for Germany which would also meet U.S. national interests could not have been further from his mind; he dedicated himself single-mindedly to carrying out the policies of his own faction. Even if the Japanese today are correct in criticizing the American pragmatism embedded within MacArthur's educational reforms, and preferring to change them. MacArthur's policies are the true exemplar of the art of statecraft. Faced with a situation which could have easily fallen into total chaos, he succeeded in creating a certain degree of stability, while at the same time paving the way for a truly new start in Japan.

MacArthur had instructed all of his officers and soldiers that they should not under any circumstances do anything to injure the pride of the Japanese. Soldiers were under strict orders to respect the Imperial Palace and other temples and shrines. As a result, the thousands of American soldiers stationed in Japan behaved like "gentlemen," and quickly gained the population's respect and friendship. MacArthur had recognized that it was necessary to keep the institution of the imperial court, in order to maintain continuity for the Japanese nation. On the other hand, he actively engaged the Japanese in carrying out his own reforms. All this took place in a predominantly friendly atmosphere, producing a cross-pollination of ideas fruitful for occupier and occupied alike.

The reconstruction of Japan would never have been as successful as it was, were it not for the cooperative and attentive manner in which MacArthur proceeded in the best interests of both Japan and his own nation. MacArthur allowed the Japanese to keep their identity within the context of their own culture, while at the same time he fostered freedom-loving, republican "American" elements, as exemplified by MacArthur himself. This explains the difference between Japan today, with its much smaller share of problems, and the Federal Republic of Germany.

McCloy's policies were quite different. Not only did he conspire with the Dulles brothers to leave the Nazis' Swiss headquarters untouched, along with the funds they had squirreled away there. Under McCloy, the old Nazi secret service networks were smoothly transferred into well-paying Allied positions. In this so-called new order, the American occupying powers actively sought opportunistic "re-educated" Nazis whom they could hoist into leading positions as so-called "unknown quantities," so as to better control these people through blackmail material from their dossiers.

McCloy made no secret of his intention to create a political vacuum within the occupied areas. Every autonomous democratic organization was suppressed, and all efforts went instead into building up "American assets." And so it came to pass that every institutional structure, whether of a private or a public nature, was interwoven with these "U.S. assets" which could be brought back into line at any time merely by referring to their past. This was also the case with the parties (especially the Free Democratic Party), as well the communications media, trade unions and, above all else, the legal system.

The fact that the Anglo-American occupiers discouraged existing republican tendencies in favor of their own controllable "assets," has turned out to be a great liability for these same circles today. Not only have these "assets" produced what astonishes us about the "green" movement, but faced with a crisis these ostensibly faithful allies of the

United States will once again turn against their masters. Willy Brandt's career is a case in point.

Americans should not be amazed that the old Nazis whom they believed they could use, are now steering a course toward National Bolshevism. Only if this mistake is immediately corrected, can we still prevent the Federal Republic from drifting out of the Western Alliance.

These Anglo-American policies had terrible consequences for all well-meaning people in post-war Germany—all those who had actually put up resistance, whether Christians, old Social Democrats, members of the Reichsbanner organization, humanists or simply people who, lacking any visible prospects, went into a so-called internal emigration in order to preserve at least some remainder of personal integrity. All these people had waited and hoped for the American liberators.

For the sake of these people, such artists as Wilhelm Furtwängler and Heinrich Schlussnus stayed behind in Germany, doing so with the knowledge that, with all the suffering the German population had been subjected to, no one could deprive them of their humanistic culture. These people made up the enthusiastic audiences for hastily organized concerts immediately following the war, some of which were held in empty factory buildings. It was these so-called simple people who took into their own hands the resumption and organization of production, and proceeded to build new parties. Many brave men and courageous "rubble ladies" (*Trümmerfrauen*) took it as obvious that those who had had nothing to do with the Nazis would now be the ones with a chance to prosper.

But they had to look on with increasing disappointment while the same people who had gotten along so well with the Nazis were now succeeding with the Allies as well. The process of political self-organization was abruptly halted, and new political leaders were hoisted into place, among them many exiles selected according to psychological profile. Efficient officials from the Nazi regime, equipped with their new *Persilschein* (whitewash certificate), once again sat in their offices as judges and administrative advisors.

And once again, just as in 1815 and in 1918, the world became incomprehensible to the normal citizen. Events had no rational explanation, and justice seemed nowhere to be found.

But most absurd of all was the collective guilt thesis aggressively promulgated by the occupying powers. Under the pretext of re-educating the population, perhaps more damage was done than had been accomplished by everything which had come before. What went on within the British re-education camp, Wilton Park, was nothing short of brainwashing; the idea was bludgeoned into detainees' heads that there was no such thing as absolute and unconditional values and truths to guide one's actions; instead, everything had to be done pluralistically, democratically, and pragmatically. If a relatively widespread pacifism is on the rise in the Federal Republic today, then the cause and the blame lies almost exclusively with the coordinators of Wilton Park and associated "de-Nazification programs."

The re-educators had little interest in eliminating fascist tendencies; at best, they went after some of the more exotic types who could cause public embarrassment. Wilton Park was aimed instead at eliminating what remained of humanistic culture, and attempted to equate German classicism with the philosophy of National Socialism. Everything Germans had ever believed in was denigrated, irrespective of whether these were convictions, illusions, and prejudices stemming from the Nazi period, or ideas and concepts from Germany's earlier, positive history.

The result was a classic shock reaction; following such a confession of collective guilt, the victim was left with no choice but to forget or suppress the past as quickly as possible. And thus we had the birth of the German without a history. It is still not uncommon today to meet representatives of the war generation who can only respond to concrete questions about this period by going into a confused and disoriented state; one can always be sure that such people have no Nazi skeletons in their closet. Real Nazis, on the other hand, have quite good memories.

Once every institution had been seeded with "Anglo-American assets," there was no way for a national republican elite to develop; consequently, since then there has not existed a single institution which has been in a position to espouse national sovereignty for the Federal Republic. Re-education had put a stigma on the very notion of nationhood, and West German citizens were given no chance to develop into a normal nation within the world community.

The Federal Republic has, at best, played the role of a flourishing business concern during the post-war years. But when the world economic crisis of the late 1970s began to fracture this economic underpinning, even this superficial identity began to totter, and the seemingly stable Federal Republic suddenly began to collapse with breathtaking speed.

The initially higher morale of the reconstruction period was soon replaced by massive repression; in retrospect, the 1950s were indeed the best and most optimistic years since the war's end.

During the 1960s no one wanted to talk about the Nazi period or how it came about. The order of the day was: succeed, don't take risks. Parents were too concerned with material things, or did not trust themselves to transmit to their children humanistic values which, perhaps, they themselves had once believed in. They passively looked on while the subversive rebellion of 1968 prepared the groundwork for today's wave of National Bolshevism. They passively accepted the 1970 school reforms, which robbed the younger generation of any chance to obtain a comprehensive education.

West Germany's population thus seems to be divided into two groups: the war generation, whose sense of history has been extinguished; and the younger generation, which has received far too little scientific education, far too little German-language instruction, and far too little education in history, and which can therefore be easily swept up by the same onrushing wave of National Bolshevism which already brought disaster upon Germany once before. In the Weimar Republic, the lack of any institutions representing national interests in a positive sense, enabled Hitler to use Germans' justified outrage against the injustices of the Versailles Treaty to his own ends. So today, we are faced with the danger that the denial of the right to shape a national identity will be utilized once again.

Faced with a military, economic, and social crisis, some sort of national interest is indeed emerging. It is, however, based not upon the citizen's identification with a national, sovereign republic, but upon mystical yearnings for a homeland and the ideology of blood and soil, as we can easily observe today.

Though the predicates might be different, the dynamic upon which these events are based remains the same. The well-founded suspicion that the Federal Republic may not be defensible under the prevailing military doctrine of "Mutual and Assured Destruction" (MAD), along with the certainty that the Federal Republic would cease to exist in the event of a nuclear war, have contributed much to the spread of today's cultural pessimism. It is this cultural pessimism which spawns the old "anticapitalist yearnings," along with the hope that Germany's problems could be solved jointly with the East.

Is there any way out of the crisis overtaking us? At present, this is still an open question. One thing is sure: whoever refuses to learn from history is condemned to repeat it.

There are two essential preconditions to be met before the Federal Republic—and one hopes, sometime in the future, all of Germany—can develop into a truly sovereign republican nation. A republican movement must emerge within the Federal Republic itself, while the United States must create a new, republican basis for its own policy toward the Federal Republic.

With a sense of urgency, we must now make up for what we failed to do in the post-war period; we must give birth to a republican force, firmly based upon German history's best traditions, upon the philosophy of the first great German humanist and founder of modern scientific inquiry, Nicolaus of Cusa, and upon Kepler, Leibniz, Schiller, Beethoven, Humboldt and the great scientific tradition of the nineteenth century. We must finally achieve the Prussian reformers' aim of educating common citizens into informed citizens of the world, citizens actively involved in the shaping of the affairs of state.

In short, we need a revolution—a republican revolution which must begin in the minds of our citizens and must lead to the successful establishment of a republic. Owing to its historical and geographical situation, the Federal Republic cannot do this by itself. Only if the United States corrects its political mistakes of the occupation era, is a durable positive change possible. President Reagan has indicated the way out of our military-strategic dilemma, proposing to replace the doctrine of MAD with the doctrine of Mutual and Assured Survival. Under this new doctrine, the Federal Republic would once again become militarily defensible.

But as indispensable as military measures are, they do not in themselves represent the positive solution. The cultural crisis now shaking the Western world has brought about the circumstance, that only a tiny handful has any concrete notion of the so-called values of the free West they are committed to defending. This must be changed.

The United States and Germany must return to their respective traditions of the American Revolution and the cultural optimism of our humanist classicists. In the spirit of Friedrich Schiller we must respond to the present challenge with these words:

Man is greater than his fate. We can learn from history; we can retrieve our own soul. We must only cease, right now, thinking like "little people."

Helga Zepp-LaRouche

1

The Philosophical Roots of National Socialism

The voluminous literature on fascism and National Socialism is dominated by two opposing views: are we dealing here with a "sociological phenomenon," or with a specific form of a historical tendency whose spiritual predecessors can be identified in past centuries?

Proponents of the first version attempt to portray fascism and National Socialism as the more or less accidental emergence of an extraordinarily "charismatic" Führer figure, who seduced the masses with his demagogic and rhetorical skills. These masses' susceptibility to the "charismatic figure" is then usually explained psychologically, i.e., by referencing various aberrant forms of behavior within that population. This in turn leads to the assertion that Hitler was made possible by a specific "German national character."

Labeling Nazism a genuine German product is, of course, a mental trick which allows us to maintain a moral distance—we see a Nazism with no past and no future. We are relieved of the burdensome responsibility to measure our present political currents against those standards which, at least in principle, had already been established at the Nuremberg trials.

Until now we have lacked a historically verifiable explanation of the actual characteristics of Nazism and fascism. This lack has made it possible for political forces vaunting themselves as the anti-fascist resistance to flaunt their own, verifiably fascist, policies, while their opponents' contrary policies are often denounced as fascist.

In this case as well, we can arrive at truth; as Nicolaus of Cusa correctly observed long ago, mere opinion is what blocks us off from recognition of our opinions. The major problem is that many writers are unconscious of the basis upon which they arrive at their own knowledge; hence what they present as judgments are often nothing but opinions.

We place the major blame for this dilemma on the artificially introduced separation between the sciences and the so-called humanities, between *Naturwissenschaft* and *Geisteswissenschaft*. This separation, dating from the period following 1815, has blotted out the necessary criteria for arriving at adequate knowledge. Absurd theories such as Max Weber's "value-free science" or the pluralism of the Jesuits, found their way into scientific thought. It is therefore virtually impossible to provide modern readers with the conceptual geometry which would enable them to adequately explain Nazism and fascism.

Schiller's Contribution to Historiography

Perhaps the best point of departure for investigating recent historical developments is that portentous turning point in modern history, when the American Revolution coincided with the birth of German classicism and the inception of the industrial revolution. This is because, in the final analysis, every political precursor of Nazism happens to have been directed against the after-effects of these three events. But we must extend the scope of our investigation still further, and it is no accident that it is Friedrich Schiller, the finest representative of that era, who points us in the right direction.

Schiller's work as a historian set new absolute standards for historiography. In his essay "The Legislation of Lycurgus and Solon," Schiller described two contrasting models for a state, models which shaped the outlines of every state during the succeeding 3,000 years. The Athens of the wise Solon, formulator of the first written republican constitution, was taken as the exemplary model for all subsequent conceptions of the state, and celebrating its brilliant triumph in the American Revolution. The Sparta of the tyrant Lycurgus, on the other hand, bore all the characteristics of a fascist state, and through the centuries has remained the oft-cited point of reference for everything which might be considered a precursor of Nazism. It was no accident that Hitler's opponents saw the "Third Reich" as the fulfillment of this essay of Schiller, and recognized that the Nazi regime was only a modern version of Lycurgus' Sparta. These people had hoped that, following the long-awaited collapse of the "Third Reich," Solon's Athens would become the guiding model for the reconstruction of the German nation.

Using this conflict between forces representing Sparta and those in the tradition of Athens as our conceptual yardstick, we are now in a position to understand the history of the past 3,000 years—and probably the history of the previous millennia as well. This conflict epitomizes the bitter warfare between oligarchism and republicanism. The arrival of the Nazis on the political scene therefore in no respect represents a break with the past, as some historians of the first school would have us believe. For an explanation of Nazism, we can turn directly to history.

The Oligarchical System

In the oligarchical system, the idea of the state is identical with that of the empire. This is true not only for Sparta, but for its closely related predecessors such as the Assyrian Empire, Babylon, and Persia, as well as Rome, Byzantium, the Ottoman and Austro-Hungarian Empires, and the British Empire. A small oligarchical elite rules over a mass of subjects who are deliberately kept in a state of backwardness. The elite claims for itself the right to plunder this population, whether it be through the arbitrary setting of ground rent, control of a usury-based credit system, the mechanism of state power itself, or through the ruthless extraction of the last ounce of labor from their subjects, be they slaves, serfs, or other inferior beings whose death through exhaustion is viewed as a normal event.

Combing the works of most so-called scholars of fascism, one searches in vain for this central economic aspect, which runs like a red thread through every oligarchical empire and system. This economic aspect is in fact the primary and most crucial distinguishing characteristic of Nazism. Such systems are always dominated by extreme forms of monetarism, utilized by an autocratic and scornful oligarchical elite to maintain at all costs their usury-based, economically bankrupt monetary system.

From this perspective we can discern clear parallels with the Egypt of the pharaohs, who had no scruples about wearing out their slaves on the pyramids; Sparta's bloody exploitation of the helots; the practices of the British East India Company; and the Nazis' economic exploitation of forced laborers and concentration camp inmates. For the leading financiers in Switzerland, London, and New York, it was Hjalmar Schacht's argument which clinched the matter: only a drum-beater like Hitler would be capable of imposing the necessary drastic austerity and making it palatable to the masses. This was the principal reason for the massive financial support flowing into Hitler's movement from abroad.

Whenever the maintenance of a currency and credit system is put before the maintenance of human life, we have the clearest evidence that we are looking at a fascist system. Whoever sanctions the policies of the International Monetary Fund (IMF), which today is deliberately condemning millions of human beings to death with its infamous credit conditionalities, is morally no better than the Nazi war criminals who were condemned to hang at Nuremburg.

The oligarchical system views the world as a series of great, eternal cycles of birth and death, of construction and destruction. Death and destruction are considered highly desirable, since they have a purifying effect, killing off the weak and enabling the strong to survive. There is no place in this system for scientific and technological progress; indeed, such progress is viewed as the real enemy threatening the eternal cycle.

This corresponds to a conception of man as a creature incapable of change, whose "nature" is fundamentally inclined toward evil. Hence, the rule of men over men is derived not from an ontological natural law, but merely from the ability of this or that oligarchical elite to force its will upon its underlings. Law has no objective basis in this system; all that counts is the power to avoid responsibility for one's own acts.

Such a system is workable, of course, only if the popular masses accept this state of affairs and the ostensible superiority of the oligarchical elite, and conceive of themselves as objects, not as subjects, of events. It is for this reason that the oligarchical system requires more precise and more ingenious mechanisms of mass control in order to protect itself against unwelcome surprises. The preferred mechanism of control is a web of mythology for the masses to believe in. These myths are carefully cultivated and applied by the elite itself, or by a designated caste of priests. Such mythologies, in harmony with the cyclical world outlook, have been interwoven with every pre-Christian "regional" deity—Cybele, Isis, Shakti, Mother Siva, Mithra, Thor, Wotan, to name a few. The dominant figure in these prevailing myths was usually a goddess who symbolized "Mother Earth" and which thus provided the basis for an ideology of "blood and soil." In northern ideologies, for example, this role was played by the so-called world ash tree, Yggdrasil.

The Republican System

Solon of Athens' republican concept was quite another matter, and through Plato was passed on to the entire succeeding humanist tradition. In the republican state, all individuals are endowed with equal, inalienable rights founded upon natural law. The state is not an instrument of power, but rather serves the exclusive purpose of permitting the maximum unfolding of the potentials of each of its citizens, who, as citizens, are vitally concerned with development of the state as a whole. In the republic, leadership's primary task is not to act as a parasite on the population, depriving it of its livelihood. Its task is to exert leadership on the basis of its acquired wisdom, on the basis of its fully developed understanding of law, and, above all, because of its readiness to assume political responsibility and to act accordingly.

By its very nature, the republican system is the political expression of the physical universe as a negentropically developing continuum, as has been proven by modern science. Whereas scientific and technological progress represents a grave threat to any return to an eternally unchanging state of affairs—the characteristic feature of the oligarchical system's cyclical world view—this progress from a republican standpoint is the absolute precondition for the existence of the universe, as it is for human society.

The lawfulness of the universe, its negentropic evolution, is knowable and accessible to human reason and knowledge. Such knowledge, however, is not passive. Man, by virtue of his ability to think the higher hypothesis and make his knowledge increasingly correspond to universal law, is capable of altering this law itself, and in a lawful manner. Scientific progress is only another expression for this interaction between reason and the physical universe; the hypotheses formed by reason are efficient in the real world, and this allows us to conclude that there exists a correspondence between the macrocosm and the microcosm.

A republican state is therefore vitally concerned with the scientific progress of all its citizens, and with the improvement of their standard of living. This especially includes improvements in education and training, which raise the productivity of labor and thereby enrich the source of all social wealth.

For the oligarchical system, the sole source of wealth is the ownership of land and physical resources, the right to extract ground rent, and the ability to lend at usurious rates of interest. The system ultimately depends on maintaining the areas under its control in a state of permanent backwardness, in order to seize raw materials at the cheapest price. The scribblings of the "evil Parson Malthus" are but one of the numerous attempts to provide a rational justification for the oligarchical faction's policies, and to give them at least the veneer of legitimacy.

Anyone who thinks of the land as the only source of social wealth is apt to feel threatened by the arrival of every new individual into the world; such a person fears that the newcomer will want to share these resources with him, thereby decreasing what belongs to the ruling elite. This is the origin of the so-called overpopulation theory, which in turn supplies the oligarchical vision of a fixed system with a corresponding zero-growth ideology.

It is virtually impossible to distinguish any qualitative difference between Malthus's silly "law of population"—his rationalization for the practices of British colonialism—and the Nazis' classification of so-called "inferior races" as "useless eaters," and the Club of Rome's recommendation that the al-

leged population problem in the developing countries be solved by "natural means" such as denying
them technology transfers or "raising the death rate"
through hunger, epidemics, and deliberately in-
cited regional warfare. Human life has no value in
this system, and its proponents consider it their own
privilege if they wish to practice genocide, whether
it be against Sparta's helots, the Jews, the Slavs,
political opponents, three million people in Cam-
bodia, or the 150 million people in Africa who have
been "written off" by the IMF.

The republican system does not share this utter
disregard for human life. The land and the soil,
taken by themselves, have no significance. The sole
source of wealth is the rise in the productivity of
human labor effected through technological progress. Every newborn child, when viewed in this way,
represents a potential enrichment of society, provided that that society develops all the potentials
residing within that child. This in turn requires not
only a high nutritional level, but a basic education
which promotes character formation and a potentially never-ending higher education.

It has been entirely due to the work of republicans over the millennia that the earth's population
potential has grown from approximately five million at the introduction of agriculture, to about four
and a half billion today. The earth could easily have
a population potential of several dozen billions, if
currently existing technologies were vigorously applied.

This long chain of qualitative technical innova-
tions has repeatedly enabled mankind to overcome
limitations imposed by so-called natural resources.
Human reason has conceived of new sciences and
new technologies, defining and developing new raw

materials, taking a little piece of dirt and turning it first into iron ore, and then into a transmitter of energy.

Republican society therefore puts the highest premium on that side of man which absolutely distinguishes him from the beasts; no beast has ever independently altered his "natural resources." Within this progress-oriented climate geniuses have developed, men and women whose unique contributions have extended the limits of existing knowledge, and through whose individual accomplishments humanity as a whole has attained a bit of immortality.

This emphasis on the creative faculties of the individual, as was embedded in the legislation of Solon, has been a constant source of irritation to the leadership of the oligarchical faction, and they have always perceived it as a grave threat. It goes without saying that any efforts to instruct the so-called masses in reason calls into question the continued dominance of the oligarchical elite in the medium term. This was the reason for the murder of Socrates, whom his opponents hypocritically accused of seducing the youth of Athens, whereas his sole intention was to encourage them to use their own minds, as Plato reports to us in the Apology of Socrates.

Plato's dialogues contain everything which constitutes the essence of the republican system and European humanist culture: natural law, based on the ordering of existence and permanently guaranteeing the individual's God-given rights to life and personal development, and a cosmology which explains the development of the universe to the present day, along with a corresponding republican constitution which holds the rule of "philosopher kings" to be the prerequisite for social well-being.

But it was Augustine who stated in his famous letter to Marcellinus, that only with the appearance of the person of Jesus Christ was Platonic philosophy able to assume unassailable authority over all other teachings. Christ, by becoming the perfected embodiment of the divine within man, laid the unshakable foundation for the inviolability and dignity of human life. It might seem tautological to state that without the person of Christ, 2,000 years of European Christian civilization would not have been possible; this, however, is of crucial significance for any historical investigation.

Through the idea of Man-become-God, from this time onward every human being participates in God (*capax dei*), on condition that he, as the Image of the Living God, strives to replicate on earth His most noble quality as God-the-creator. Creation is not understood as a single event—a "big bang"—but is rather is a continuous process of creation, in which man's creative capacity can be considered the arm of God.

Man, so understood as the image of God, must by his nature be fundamentally disposed toward the Good. From this flows his obligation to perfect himself. A refusal to develop all the creative faculties residing within him is therefore defined as sin.

Christian philosophy is therefore in perfect harmony with the republican system, and it should therefore come as no surprise that it was bitterly opposed by the oligarchical camp. The most blatant example of this was the Roman Empire itself which, boasting all the characteristics of a fascist state, used the most brutal methods in its attempt to exterminate the Christians.

What followed historically, to oversimplify a bit, were merely variations on either model. It is nonetheless fascinating to observe how conscious the protagonists of each side were of their respective predecessors. To be sure, such information cannot be found in the usual history textbooks; original sources must be drawn upon.

The Italian Renaissance was buoyed by Plato and Greece; Jean-Jacques Rousseau, godfather of the Greens, praised the customs of Sparta. And the dark minions of the British imperialism have always sung exalted paeans to the empire of the Romans.

The American Revolution

The American Revolution was a decisive historical turning point. The emergence of the Nazis and all other current political trends must be understood from the standpoint of this event. Our modern history books usually reduce this ground-breaking event to the trivialities surrounding the Boston Tea Party. In reality, it represented a decisive republican victory over the oligarchic system.

America's Founding Fathers were not the backwoodsmen Hollywood would have us believe. Benjamin Franklin's networks in America and in Europe represented a republican and scientific elite, and it was not without reason that Franklin was called the "Prometheus of the Eighteenth Century." The European republicans set great hope on the New World, where individual freedom and prosperity for the industrious, without regard to status or birth, were written on every flagstone. The revolution was triggered by England's refusal to grant the American colonies the unlimited right to build its own manufacturing industry; this finally brought the American republicans to realize that their own economic development could be secured only by separating themselves from the mother country and fighting for independence.

A perusal of the writings of the America's Founding Fathers makes it quite evident that their aim was nothing less than victory of the republican economic system over the oligarchs' system. Examples of this were Alexander Hamilton's "Report on Manufactures" and the later writings of Mathew and Henry Carey. To this day, the U.S. Constitution remains the best republican constitution ever written, because it was of one metal, containing within it the spirit of the entire European humanist tradition.

But not only in America did the oligarchical camp suffer a painful defeat; their system seemed to be under assault on many fronts. Not only was the initial phase of the French Revolution threatening to follow America's example, but simple citizens were becoming scientifically educated in such institutions as the École Polytechnique. The largely uneducated oligarchs saw this as a brazen challenge, especially since the simultaneous flowering of the industrial revolution was threatening to shatter their old structures.

From a cultural standpoint as well, humanity was soaring to its most exalted heights, reaching a new pinnacle of development. Through its composers and poets, German classicism produced a breathtaking wealth of works of art, whose impact on the public had the effect of ennobling the individual as never before. A better ability to distinguish subtle shadings of emotion, coupled with a Promethean boldness of spirit—these were by no means contradictory, but were expressions of a perfected human character. Large sections of the population were especially swept up by the influence of music and poetry, as evidenced by the rapid spread of "house music" and the mass enthusiasm for the dramas of Schiller and others. It was understandable if the best minds of the age were convinced that humanity had arrived at the threshold of the Age of Reason.

The Oligarchy Strikes Back: The Conservative Revolution

The oligarchical camp, however, did not leave the field in defeat, but moved on all fronts to reverse these unpleasant developments. In America the British Tories stepped up their campaign of treason against the young republic, a campaign extending from the War of 1812 to the machinations of today's Eastern Establishment, which still spares no effort to unhinge the U.S. Constitution.

In France, agents of the British, Swiss, and French oligarchy took control of events in the French Revolution and crushed the republicans' initiatives during the Jacobin Terror. Robespierre's famous remark on the decapitation of France's humanist elite—"The Revolution does not need any scientists"—shows him to be an agent of the oligarchy. The fact that the employers of Danton and Marat sat in England; that Jacques Necker had ruined the French economy for the sake of Swiss financial interests; that the Duke of Orléans had organized the storming of the Bastille; and that Napoleon was manipulated into wanting to rule over a new world empire—all are testimony to the bitter counterattacks launched by the oligarchy, which under no circumstances was going to allow a repetition of the American Revolution on European soil.

The German republicans' resistance to Napoleon's imperialist ambitions managed to produce the best and most fruitful period in Germany's history. The actual impetus to this development, however, did not come from Napoleon's invasion. Even before Napoleon's troops had dealt the Prussian armies a humiliating defeat at Jena and Auerstadt—opening the way to the intervention of the Prussian reformers around vom Stein, Scharnhorst, and von Humboldt—humanist ideas had already become widespread. Friedrich Schiller, through his direct influence on vom Stein and von Humboldt, left a deep impression on this epoch. During the subsequent liberation struggles, above all others it was this beloved "poet of freedom" who lifted the spirit of the soldiers and the entire population.

Never had Germany been closer to becoming a sovereign, republican national entity. These Wars of Liberation, whose immediate goal was the defeat of Napoleon's tyranny, in fact represented a much deeper and broader constitutional movement within the population. The great ideal of republican freedom, in which a monarch would be "king among millions of kings," was their guiding star, as is attested to by the voluminous, impassioned personal correspondence of the period. Schiller, in his letters on *Don Carlos,* had described the American Revolution as the "favorite subject of the decade." Conversations inevitably dwelled upon "the spread of a more pure, more gentle humanity, the greatest possible freedom for the individual within the greatest flowering of the state—in short, humanity in its highest state of perfection, as this is attainable within its nature and powers." A quarter century later, this ideal was given new life.

Without question, the course of German history would have been immeasurably more positive, and we would have never experienced the horrors of the twentieth century, had the population's hopes for a victory over Napoleon and the creation of a German nation come to fruition. Herein lies the great tragedy. But it is also an historical point of reference to which we must return, if we are to raise the question of a positive German identity today.

The Vienna Congress marked the end of republican turmoil in Germany. The oligarchy of England, Russia, France, Switzerland, Venice, and Austria had regrouped their forces, and were determined to leave no openings for the German negotiator, vom Stein. Following 1815, and with a vengeance in the wake of the Carlsbad Decrees of 1819, there began a long phase of gloomy reaction, with devastating effects on the population. Most citizens were unable to reconstruct in their minds precisely why and how they had been robbed of the fruits of their struggle. As the bigoted narrowness of the Holy Alliance increasingly made itself felt, the clear mind of the world citizen and patriot shrank into the limited purview of the *Burschenschaften* (student dueling societies) and maudlin German chauvinism. Clear conceptions yielded to romantic *Schwärmerei*, and the disappointed hopes lapsed into latent cultural pessimism.

This paradigm shift from classicism to Romanticism, however, was no more a "sociological phenomenon" than was West Germany's turn from a belief in progress during the "economic miracle" of the 1960s, to the 1970s' zero-growth ideology and hatred of technology. The subversion, sabotage, and final defeat of the hopeful republican freedom movement at the start of the nineteenth century was the result of the same shift; and all the weapons directed against the humanist conception of man can be summed up under one modern concept: the "Conservative Revolution."

Under that title, Armin Mohler wrote the standard work on this theme—first published in 1949—in defense of the Nazi regime. According to Mohler, the Conservative Revolution has been an ongoing process ever since the French Revolution. He explains that:

> Every revolution brings along with it a counter-force which attempts to reverse the revolution. And with the French Revolution's victory came a world which the Conservative Revolution regards as its mortal enemy. For the time being we would like to describe their world as one which revolves not around that which is unchangeable in man, but which believes it can alter man's nature. It therefore proclaims the possibility of stepwise progress, considers all things, relations and events to be accessible to comprehension, and attempts to consider every object in isolation and understand it in and of itself alone.

Mohler's book is only worthwhile reading for clinical purposes. He leaves no doubt about his constituency for the Conservative Revolution, frankly admitting—in 1949!—that this notion is synonymous with fascism. (His description "conservative" is actually ill-chosen, since with its implied notions of "preserve" and "maintain," it is always associated with the idea of influencing the whole, whereas for the Conservative Revolution the whole always remains the same.) The implicit notion in all ideas of progress, that man is fundamentally good, that he can gradually perfect himself unless hindered by aversive circumstances, is entirely foreign to the thinking of the Conservative Revolution. The idea that man is equally disposed to good and to evil lends it a decidedly gnostic and Manichæan character, a feature which later made its way into Nazi ideology.

Mohler describes the paradigm shift in the following terms: "In a broad sense, the term 'Conservative Revolution' includes the common basis of all completed or incipient transformations in all areas of life, in theology as well as in physics and music, or the planning of a city, structuring a family, or the care of the body or the building of a machine." It is therefore an "alternative movement," with all the essential features of thate movement today.

The reversals in Germany were only one part of a trend which swept through virtually every European country and permeated all areas of life—a trend represented by Dostoevsky and the Aksakovs in Russia, Sorel and Barres in France, and Pareto and Evola in Italy, to name a few examples.

In theology, the Bishop of Mainz, von Ketteler, developed the counterrevolutionary idea of solidarism as a bludgeon against the Augustinian tradition; in physics, Cauchy and Laplace sabotaged the work of Monge, Carnot, and Legendre at the École Polytechnique, breaking with the Leibnizian tradition in mathematics (especially the calculus) and re-establishing mathematics along Cartesian lines.

In music there was a break between those composers who had been educated in the pre-1815 tradition of Bach, and whose compositions were based on the necessary progressions of well-tempered counterpoint—the first generation of Mozart and Beethoven, the second generation of Schumann and Schubert, and Brahms in the third generation—and those trained after 1815, who dwelled on the instability of chaotic progressions, such as Wagner or Hugo Wolff, not to speak of our present so-called modern composers.

Romanticism was consciously promoted by the European oligarchy as a movement which advocated the total rejection of reason and humanism, upon which Weimar classicism was based. One of the oligarchy's most influential agents, who supported the young Romantics with body and soul, was Madame de Staël, daughter of the Swiss banker Jacques Necker, who as French finance minister had ruined France for the sake of the Swiss banks. Heinrich Heine has pointedly described how Madame de Staël and her circles were angered that the "republican" culture found in the Weimar classics, in musical soirées at home, or in the great theater houses had begun to spread through large portions of the population. In a blue rage, she attempted to regain her own control of culture by luring young artists into her own salon. These recruits threw themselves into action with the same abandon as today's "beautiful people" or the nobility's "jet set." Not only did this romantic movement produce the organized terrorism of Giuseppe Mazzini's "Young Europe," but it also spawned the tendency stretching from the turn-of-the-century youth movement to today's counterculture "alternative" movement, along with its ideologues Friedrich Nietzsche, Paul de Lagarde, Julius Langbehn, Alfred Rosenberg, and so forth. The Nazis too drank out of this "alternative" trough.

Three of the most serious attacks, however, came in the areas of philosophy, history, and law. Schiller's grand conception—the study of universal history as a method of education to reason—had to be destroyed. The aim was therefore to deny the unity of the sciences and the humanities—of *Naturwissenschaften* and *Geisteswissenschaften*—and to reject the validity of natural law.

Barthold Niehbuhr, who hated Schiller's and Humboldt's humanism, glorified Rome as the "perfect state" and established his so-called modern science of historiography (which is not really all that modern), incorporating within it all the elements of the feudalistic interpretation of history.

Savigny stormed against natural law as it was laid down by the philosophy of German Idealism, and campaigned for the historical relativity of law, claiming that law had "organically" developed in tandem with the the "changing *Volksgeist*"—a theory designed to justify the existence of every regime contrary to law and every form of rapacious and arbitrary rule. From there to the *volkisch* idea was but one short step.

The most devastating oligarchical attack on the republican spirit, however, was led by the philosopher G. W. F. Hegel in Berlin, who is proven by "check-stubs" to have been a paid agent of Austria's Metternich against the Prussian state, and was therefore working directly for the sinister reaction of the Holy Alliance. It is a sad commentary on the level of our universities, that the holy aura surrounding Hegel has remained intact down to the present day.

When one considers that Hegel finished his *Phenomenology of Mind* in the year 1806, in the midst of the intellectual climate of the Weimar classics, we can only conclude that his ostensibly dialectical method was nothing but a Jesuitical distortion of the Socratic method so gloriously evident in the dramas of Friedrich Schiller. Hegel's idea of the world-historical individual was indeed drawn from the classics; his "philosopher kings" or "philosophical minds," however, tended to degenerate into mere power-mongers (Napoleon, for Hegel, was the World Spirit on horseback!), and were much closer to the master-race concept of Nietzsche and Hitler. Worst of all, toward the end of his teaching career Hegel not only engaged in the corrupt practice of blocking or spoiling the studies of many young and hopeful students, but also—in his *Philosophy of Right*—he provided the perfect justification for the totalitarian state, which served as source material for Europe's reactionary oligarchical circles, as it did later for the Third Reich.

We could name many more figures and fields which were involved in the Conservative Revolution's attempt to reshape the population's conscious values. In all these cases it can be proven, often in great detail, that these were not "sociological phenomena" or mysterious transformations in the *Zeitgeist,* but were developments initiated or financed by the oligarchy.

In spite of passing rivalries, the oligarchy's efforts after 1815 were closely coordinated, and they often succeeded in setting into motion movements which crossed national borders, such as Young Europe and the Anthroposophist movement. The direct successors of these movements today are tied to the activities of such supranational institutions as the Trilateral Commission, the Club of Rome, and the Aspen Institute.

The republicans, who could look back upon the American Revolution as their proudest victory, were seriously weakened following 1815 and were later eliminated as a political force. At best, republicans worked on as dispersed, humanistically inclined individuals, who had lost consciousness of the great historical weight of their task. Such individuals reacted to humanist culture solely on the basis of their own personal moral disposition.

The oligarchy's Conservative Revolution did not succeed equally well in all fields and in all parts of the world. Lazare Carnot, who had to flee from France along with Alexander von Humboldt, organized in Berlin a spirited opposition against Hegel and Savigny; under Carnot's and von Humboldt's protection the spirit of Weimar lived on in the natural sciences and in classical philology. The center of scientific work was later moved to Göttingen, which produced such pioneering scientists as Bernhard Riemann and Georg Cantor. Through the work of Felix Klein, this tradition was kept alive into the beginning of the present century.

While Hegel was providing the totalitarian state with a frightening ideological justification, pointing the way to the Nazis' "everything is permitted" rule, Romanticism was at the same time softening up the general population. The Holy Alliance slowly but surely stifled Germany's soul, and encouraged the emergence of such romantic philosophers as Schopenhauer, who began to deny the power of reason. For Schopenhauer, egoism was the natural disposition of mankind, and life as such was not an adequate affirmation of life. Thus the republicans' cultural optimism yielded to an irrational, immoral pessimism.

The Case of Friedrich Nietzsche

The absolute height of Romanticism, or rather the nadir of general culture, where raving folly and emotional infantilism turned into aggressive mania, the welding point between the Romantic muddle-heads and the Nazis—this was the world of Nietzsche, whose works can only be described as the mind running amok.

This self-hating, joyless psychotic could not tolerate the idea of reason; he hated Socrates, Schiller, Beethoven, and Humboldt. In his confused writings he attempted, if incoherently, to rewrite history, emphasizing not the classical and Renaissance periods as the Weimar classics had done, but the Dark Ages, the dionysian and bacchanalian orgies, the dances of St. Vitus and the flagellants. He regarded the scientific mode of questioning as man's arch-enemy, just as the Greens do today. Everything the Nazis later made into reality was already lurking within Nietzsche's tormented brain, darting about with increasing frenzy: the *volkisch* idea, a deep hatred of industrial progress, the "biological world outlook" of "blood and soil," the idea of a master race, the mystically inspired hatred of Christianity, and its final and ultimate form, the *Ecce Homo*, where Nietzsche cries out: "Have I made myself clear?—Dionysus against the Crucified. . . ."

Nietzsche, celebrated along with Dostoevsky as the prophet of the Conservative Revolution, was the spiritual pathfinder for the nihilism of the National Socialists and the existentialist philosophers.

The most extreme form of nihilism is the recognition that every belief, every notion of truth is necessarily false, since a true world does not exist. It is thus an illusion of perspective. . . . Let us think this thought in its most frightening form: Existence, such as it is, without purpose and without aim, but ineluctably returning, without end, into nothing—this is the only return. This is the extreme form of nihilism: nothingness ("purposelessness"), eternally!

Nietzsche's sick cultural pessimism has had many variants, from Lagarde, Langbehn, and Oswald Spengler through to Jean-Paul Sartre, but he has never been outdone. The Nazis, Pol Pot, and Khomeini have seen to the practical application of his world outlook. An equally devastating effect was inflicted on German intellectual life by the works of Wagner and Dostoevsky. The latter was translated by Moeller van den Bruck, who in a fit of inspiration coined the name for the "Third Reich." By this expression he meant a third historical empire to follow the Holy Roman Empire of German Nations and Bismarck's Empire; but his primary aim was a final empire, where "right" and "left" would be transcended in a single synthesis.

The Republic Is Carried to its Grave

In order to counter the widespread mythos surrounding the meaning of "right" and "left," let us cite a representative of the "Black Front":

The Black Front can be clearly situated if we dispense with the bourgeois-democratic schema of "left" and "right." Let us imagine the German parties and political currents to be shaped like a horseshoe, whose bend represents the Center and at whose end-points are the KPD and NSDAP respectively; the space occupied by the Black Front lies inbetween those two poles of Communism and National Socialism. The opposites of "left" and "right" are dissolved by their entering into a kind of synthesis, while strictly excluding the "bourgeois." This position between the two poles is the best characterization of the tensile nature of the Black Front. . . .

The idea here is no different from the West German Green-peace leader Petra Kelly's "fundamental opposition": the Conservative Revolution's deeply rooted enmity against the ideas of European civilization.

If individual predicates might have changed in the meantime, the substance nevertheless remains the same, whether it be the Romantic movement, the *Burschenschaften*, the youth movement, or our modern Greens and "alternative movement" activists.

In Germany, one of the first phenomena to develop out of the European Conservative Revolution was the so-called German Movement. In contrast with their promising name, this movement strove not to realize a republican nation imbued with the spirit of Weimar classicism, but rather embraced the ideas of Germanness preached by the likes of Father Friedrich Jahn, picking up later on Friedrich Naumann's idea of a "social Kaiserdom" or the Great Empire fantasies of the old German *Bund*.

Armin Mohler, in his above-cited book, distinguishes between two wings of the German Movement: the reformed wing, under which he classifies the various political tendencies, e.g., the Christian-Social and anti-Semitic movement of Adolf Stöcker, Friedrich Naumann's National Social Movement, the old German League, the solidarist movement initiated by von Ketteler, and the German nationalists within the Austro-Hungarian monarchy; and a broader, more "theoretical" grouping which Mohler considers to have a much more lasting influence. This second group includes Nietzsche, Lagarde, Langbehn, Moeller van den Bruck, Ernst Niekisch, the two Jüngers, K. O. Paetel, and Otto Strasser.

Both groupings shared a fundamental hostility toward the industrialization of Germany. Even though the cultural life of the Wilhelmine era had already lapsed into decadence, it was the cultural pessimism of such writers as Lagarde and Langbehn, with their not inconsiderable effect upon the youth movement, which dealt the final death blow to morality.

But not until the terrible experiences of World War I was the population made ready for the events that followed. The still-barren soil at Verdun speaks volumes about these four and one-half years of bloody carnage, which uprooted large portions of the population, especially the youth, depriving them of any hope for a normal life. The "rain of steel," the senselessness of the trench warfare, extinguished any nobler motivations dwelling within the common soldier, who in many cases had already been under the influence of the youth movement before the war. In this climate of meaninglessness, a dangerous anarchistic ferment began spreading throughout the population. Many who never found their way back into normal lives after spending their formative years in the trenches began to organize themselves into paramilitary groups, seeing these as their only prospect for survival. It was from these strata that the Freikorps, the "alliances" of the postwar youth movement, the Communist armed units and the National Socialists' Sturmabteilungen (SA) recruited their cadre.

The young Weimar Republic was, from the very start, bitterly opposed by all those sides of the political spectrum grouped around the Communists, the numerous tendencies within the Conservative Revolution, and the oligarchical camp, as represented by the Thule Society, for example, and, later on, by National Socialism. During the five years immediately following the war, conditions in Germany bordered on a state of civil war, with over 20 attempted coups from both right and left. Various armed units—from the Rotfrontkämpferbund, the SA, and the Stahlhelm, to the "Vikings" of Capt. Hermann Erhard and the "Oberland Alliance," the Wehrwolf, or the Reichsflagge—began to unleash violent political confrontations. The specific ideology of each of these organizations played only a subsidiary role in these conflicts. "Rightists" and "leftists" rubbed shoulders as a matter of course, and members often migrated from one side to the other. It was not uncommon for people to switch from the Communist Party (KPD) to the NSDAP; the most famous example of this was Hitler's criminal judge Roland Friesler, who originally came from the KPD. Organized political murder as an instrument of policy—just as we know it with today's international terrorism—was a common practice in this period.

The bitter opposition between KPD and NSDAP in the Weimar Republic is well known; meeting-hall battles and terrorist attacks were a daily occurrence. But from the very beginning there ex-

isted within each camp a National Bolshevist
tendency, whose influence fluctuated from year to
year. Here we must also distinguish between the
surges within the general population and the "theoreticians" of the Conservative Revolution, who considered themselves an intellectual elite. In spite of
a certain following of their own, this elite remained
aloof from events, disdainfully voicing the opinion
that the National Socialists had watered down the
pure theory of the Conservative Revolution, as had
all the other 500 groupings and tendencies within
the Weimar Republic.

The totally unrealistic reparations payments demanded by the Versailles Treaty contained the seeds
of the Weimar Republic's destruction. Its fate was
sealed by the same imperialistic circles within the
victorious nations, which had been no less guilty of
starting World War I than were the Germans. Just
as the brutal credit conditionalities of the IMF today
are choking off all development within the so-called
Third World, the Versailles conditions rendered
any German economic recovery an impossibility,
and led directly to the Great Depression.

The victorious powers' financial and economic
strangulation of Germany first made possible the
"success" of the KPD and NSDAP, both of whom
benefited from the ferment against the Versailles
Treaty. From the outset, both parties sought to
destroy the "system," the young Weimar Republic.
The de facto collaboration between Nazis and Communists in this endeavor, repeatedly took on a very
practical form, and was the ultimate cause of the
Weimar Republic's collapse.

National Bolshevist Dreams

Whenever the National Bolshevist tendency was on
the rise within the Nazi movement, discussion

quickly moved to the necessity for an alliance between Germany and Russia as the key to defeating the "West," perhaps even leading to eventual world domination by both states. Many German military people, still laboring under the shock of the outcome of the war, cherished hopes that with the aid of the Russians, their humiliating defeat might be reversed. This hope was nourished by the Russian Army's advances in connection with the 1920 Russo-Polish war. Even though the advance was soon halted at Warsaw, an even greater resurgence of National Bolshevist ideas came with the hammer-blows of the Great Inflation of 1923 and the occupation of the Ruhr, both of which seemed to threaten the very existence of the Weimar Republic. This provided such National Bolshevist tendencies as Karl Radek, the most powerful functionary on the executive committee of the Communist International and a close confidante of Stalin, with the opportunity to push through the Nazi-Communist tactical alliance known as the so-called "Schlageter course" and the tactic of National Bolshevism itself.

Ruth Fischer, who since May 1923 had been a "leftist" on the Central Committee, told a meeting of *volkisch* students:

> The German Reich . . . can only be saved if you, gentlemen of the German-*volkisch* side, realize that you must fight together with the Russians who are organized with the KPD. Whoever raises the cry against Jewish capital . . . is already a fighter in the class struggle, whether he knows it or not. . . . Stamp out the Jew capitalists, hang them from the lamp posts, trample them to death!

The broadest-based upsurge of National Bolshevism, however, took place in 1930. The world economic crisis was reaching a climax, the soup lines were growing in length, and, in the form of the Young and Dawes plans, the victorious powers were again attempting to unload a large part of the burden onto Germany. The National Bolshevist Strasser wing of the NSDAP, hoping to make the ideas of Moeller van den Bruck, Friedrich Naumann, and Mazaryk into reality, competed with Hitler for leadership of the party. Gregor Strasser coined the catchphrase, "anti-capitalist yearning" (*antikapitalistische Sehnsucht*), which captured the fancy of the entire German people.

In the tradition of Radek, the KPD attempted to assume leadership of this anti-Western current, and decreed such initiatives as the "Programmatic Declaration of the KPD for the National and Social Liberation of the German People" on Aug. 24, 1930, and the "Farmers Aid Program" in the spring of 1931. Within the KPD itself, the group around Heinz Naumann sought out active contact with National Bolshevist forces on the right. This tendency was later called the "Scheringer Course," referring to the infamous Lieutenant Scheringer, who in 1930 had been arrested for his National Bolshevist activities within the Reichswehr and who had gone over to the KPD while still in prison. The German information service DID reported in a special Jan. 30, 1983 issue that:

> after his arrest, Scheringer joined up with the KPD and attempted to bring right- and left-wing radical opponents of the Weimar Republic together into a "rebels' circle." Following the outbreak of war in 1939, through the mediation of the later Field Marshal von Rei-

chenau, Scheringer formally requested that Hitler recall him into military service as a volunteer with his old rank. As the "division's most courageous officer," Artillery Captain Scheringer now successfully turned his guns against his Communist comrades. After World War II, Scheringer's silence about his Nazi past enabled him to become a state secretary, and he dedicated himself to the task of gathering together former functionaries from the "Imperial Food Trades" in the Communist-influenced "Association for Forestry and Agriculture." Scheringer was also influential in the "Leadership Ring of Former Soldiers," whose primary task was to follow Moscow's plan to mobilize ex-Nazis and former German officers against the so-called "remilitarization of the Federal Republic." Since the "reconstitution" of the Communist Party of Germany (DKP) in September 1968, Scheringer has been an "agricultural expert" on the DKP's executive committee. The activities of this Nazi-Communist not only undermined the Weimar Republic, as they do now the Federal Republic, but the personnel of this network has remained intact down to the present day.

On Aug. 9, 1931, under Moscow's strict instructions, the KPD supported the *Stahlhelm*'s plebiscite against the Prussian administration, and on election day, in accordance with this order, in front of every voting place there was posted a red flag with hammer and sickle, side by side with a red swastika flag. (They lost the plebiscite just the same.) One year later the NSDAP and KPD jointly supported the strike of the Berlin Transportation

Union. Under the leadership of Walter Ulbricht they followed the motto that anything which weakened the West would help them, putting faith in Stalin's slogan: "Through Hitler we will take power!"

This time the National Bolshevist tendency acquired more influence over the population than before. Strasser's wing in the NSDAP, however, still could not win out over Hitler's Munich clique, and formally subordinated itself on June 30, 1930, with Gregor Strasser knuckling under and his brother Otto leaving the NSDAP entirely. In 1932, it finally came to an open break between Gregor Strasser and Hitler, and on June 30, 1934, the "Night of the Long Knives," Hitler used his own methods to end the faction fighting within the NSDAP, shooting down Gregor Strasser along with all his followers in the SA.

Once again, as in the period before World War I, the so-called theoreticians of the Conservative Revolution had a much greater long-range influence than the pragmatic Gregor Strasser, or those who thought they could accomplish something by forming a new "popular conservative" party. In the wake of the power struggle, the so-called authors of the Conservative Revolution—the National Revolutionaries and National Bolsheviks of the Weimar Republic—had been partially wiped out by the Nazis, partially put into concentration camps, and partially driven abroad, where they were able to surround themselves with an absurd aura of resistance. Nevertheless, today they once again represent a serious threat.

Such current "leftist" publications as the right-leaning *taz* or the journal *Wir Selbst* are quite frank about their admiration for Libyan madman Qaddafi, and they are building up positive images for Otto Strasser, the Jünger brothers, Karl Radek, Walter Stennes, Claus Heim, August Winnig, Hanno Schultze-Boysen, Ruland Scheringer, Hans Zehrer with his *Tat* circle, Ernst and Bruno von Salomon, Eberhard Köbel, and so forth. Ernst Niekisch, the most famous National Bolshevist of all, is worshipped as a veritable cult figure.

In the book *Preussische Profile,* jointly published by Sebastian Haffner and the Conservative Revolutionary Wolfgang Venohr, Haffner presents a thesis which, despite its strangeness, contains a dangerous quantum of truth:

> There are two questions to which 99 out of 100 Germans today would only respond to with an embarrassed wince or a shrug of the shoulders. The first one is: who was actually the last great Prussian? The second: who in Germany was actually Hitler's real opponent? One can search long and hard for an answer. One can try out various names, only to reject them later. In the end, the final answer to both questions has to be: Ernst Niekisch.

Armin Mohler was unfortunately right when in 1979 he spoke of a Niekisch renaissance among the youth, who had withdrawn in disappointment from the flood of neo-Marxist literature, and were passing around photocopies of Niekisch's writings. Large parts of the Social Democratic Party (SPD) were also not immune to this new-found admiration for Niekisch.

What is the essence of Niekisch's views? Only a revolutionary, socialist Germany, he says, in alliance with revolutionary Russia, would be able to defy the bourgeois (i.e. industrialized) West. So, a Germany allied with Russia against the decadent West! The prophets of the Conservative Revolution gave symbolic meaning to the four points of the compass: against the civilized capitalistic West, against the Roman-Catholic South; and for and with the rustic-Germanic North and the Bolshevist East.

But the Conservative Revolutionaries are by no means talking about a Communist Russia. Schumacher always spoke of "Bolshevik" Russia, and the writers in *Tat* have described Bolshevism as a "re-Asiatization" of Russia with a thin Western European veneer. For such people as Ernst von Salomon, it was clear that "vague expectations from the East" were the correct perspective for all those who could not reconcile themselves to the defeat of Germany. It also meant the establishment of a new empire without any ties to the West or reliance on its traditional values.

After the experiences of World War I, the twentieth-century authors merely reformulated the vision already outlined by the two most important nineteenth-century theorists of the Conservative Revolution—one in the West, the other in the East. Nietzsche, in his posthumously published works, sketched out a four-point program containing his call for a "greater German policy":

> We need an unconditional partnership with Russia, along with a new common program which will prevent Russia from coming under the influence of any English stereotypes. No American future! . . . A purely European policy is intolerable, and any confinement to Christian perspectives is a great malady.

On the other side, Nietzsche's Russian counterpart Dostoevsky, who also promulgated the idea of a holy Russian race and a coming Russian world empire, wrote that "Germany does not need us for a temporary political alliance, but for an alliance lasting into eternity. . . . Two great peoples, we and they, are destined to change the face of the world!"

But what was to be changed? What was the synonym for the "West," and what was Nietzsche's "American future," which had to be halted at all costs?

The Battle Against the 'American Future'

Because of today's renewed, this time global, offensive of the Conservative Revolution, we must once again review the epistemological basis defining both sides. The aim of Nietzsche, Dostoevsky, Niekisch, and the other National Bolshevists was to destroy the republican model we have described earlier, while they themselves were nothing but aggressive spokesmen for the oligarchical model. Their hatred was directed against the dictatorship of reason; they worshipped the power and unlimited domination of the irrational will.

The "West" against which their attack was directed—the "American future," whose seeds had been planted during the American Revolution—embodied the noblest ideas produced by the humanism of Christian European culture over the past 2,500 years. This culture is founded upon a conception of man which emphasizes the mental capacities of man, who, according to Nicolaus of Cusa, can make himself into a second God.

Such human beings are capable of thinking three successive levels, as defined by Socrates. On the lowest level, that of sensuous desire, man lives only for the satisfaction of his material needs. On the second level, that of the Understanding, he accepts a certain ordering of things, but is incapable of actual creativity. On the highest level, the stage of Reason, human thought is in agreement with the lawfulness of the physical universe, into whose development he intervenes freely but lawfully.

Such a person, guided by the humanist ideal, has the duty to pursue his own self-development, and to do his utmost to develop all his latent capacities for the benefit of all mankind. That also includes the development of his emotions away from infantile egocentricism and toward a true intercourse with human reason. Such a person must no longer, along with Kant, force himself to do what reason decrees, but his actions must come into harmony with his own sense of joy; indeed, he could not tolerate anything else. The individual who passionately accomplishes that which is necessary has, as Schiller says, a beautiful soul.

It is the specific merit of European humanism that, unlike any other culture or civilization, it emphasizes the significance of the individual human being. In no other cultural milieu, whatever other advantages it might have, does the formation of the individual's character and personalality assume such a central role. "Free through Reason, strong through law," is how Schiller's poem "Die Künstler" ("The Artists") describes this ideal of humanity, to which we owe human history's most momentous qualitative advances. Perfected freedom and beauty in the perfection of form—this is the principle which applies as much to every individual as it does to science and works of art.

What, on the other hand, is the world of the Conservative Revolution, of National Bolshevism, of National Revolution, and of National Socialism?

The individual here is cipher in a mass, playing no role within the collective—including members of the elite and the master race. Identity is based not individually, but emanates from blood and soil, i.e. from the specific race and "homeland." Human reason is not the crowning flower of creation; man is but a lowly creature in the eternal cycle of nature. The dead must form the humus from which the young can grow—such was Colorado Governor Richard Lamm's brutal, rage-provoking characterization of this idea.

Eternal Cycle versus Renaissance

The Conservative Revolution consciously counterposes the "rebirths" of the cyclical world-view to the "Renaissance." According to Mohler, "sunken worlds" well up from below, revealing ancient regional mythologies—the principle of the Great Mother Earth, which transmits the collective's identity with blood and soil. Accordingly, men can come in closest contact with their "souls" when they are in the throes of a dionysian frenzy.

Nietzsche elevated the "dionysian" into a program to defeat Socratic reason. The essence of the dionysian could be most easily captured while in a state of intoxication, e.g., while under the influence of narcotic beverages, or in the ecstatic abandon with which the dionysian masses dance through the streets—be they the dancers of St. Vitus in the Middle Ages, the marching columns of the SA or SS, or behind the prayer-wheels of the Islamic fundamentalists. "When millions fall trembling in the dust, we are close to the dionysian," wrote Nietzsche. It is all too clear that the individual—this greatest treasure of European culture—played a role here as a mere part of a collective mass. Contempt for the individual in favor of the collectivity is one of the touchstones of the Nazi-Communist alliance.

In contrast with classical art, what passes for art in the camp of the Conservative Revolution was never intended to ennoble the public, "playfully and merrily" bringing them up to the poet's level, as Schiller put it. Esthetic refinement of the emotions; joy in differentiated content within the perfected shape and form which art has as its aim; the ability to address the potentially finer side of popular impulses—no, the Conservative Revolution will have none of this. Their art is intended to allow the public to "go outside themselves," to drain themselves, to participate in a collective frenzy. Whatever one's inner beast might be, it should be let out in existentialist exhibitionism; the so-called lyrics of Gottfried Benn or the prose of Hermann Hesse invites us to do so. Dostoevsky's "Russian soul" is only completely genuine when the hero, a drunkard and a brute, maniacally smashes everything to bits, including his tubercular wife.

The Conservative Revolution's art is an assault against reason, as is perhaps best demonstrated by the music of Richard Wagner. The public is lulled into entering the cultist world of mythology. The opera is visited not in order to experience joy over human creativity as exemplified by music, but to observe and participate in a cult ritual.

An integral component of this tendency's belief structure is the perverse pleasure it takes in collapse and destruction, in all its various shadings. With Nietzsche it takes the following form:

Is pessimism necessarily a sign of decline? . . . of collapse, of aborted efforts, of exhausted and weakened instincts? . . . is there such a thing as a pessimism of strength? An intellectual obeisance to what is hard, terrifying, evil, problematic, stemming from well-being, of ebullient health, of fullness of existence? Is there perhaps a suffering from surfeit itself—a sharp-eyed, tempting boldness which longs for the dreadful as it would for the enemy, the honorable enemy upon whom it can test its power?

But this is not merely someone's sick fascination with pessimism, or a kind of ideological depression; this addiction to destruction is typical of the cyclical world outlook. Thus Nietzsche writes in *Thus Spake Zarathustra*:

Everything goes, everything returns again; the wheel of existence rolls on forever. Everything dies, everthing blossoms again; the year of existence runs on forever. Everything breaks, everything is put together again; the same house of existence is built forever. Everything parts, everything is reunited; the ring of existence remains true forever. Existence begins at every Now; at every Here the sphere is rolling there. The middle is everywhere. Narrow is the path of eternity.

It follows that the adherents of the Conservative Revolution consider Charles Darwin's theories to be the most important "scientific" idea of the nineteenth century. For if the eternal cycle is to be remain unbroken, then according to Darwin the strong must eliminate the weak and destroy those who "do not deserve to live," just as the race theoreticians Jahn and Hans Grimm, and finally the Nazis themselves, imagined themselves to be members of a master race, possessing the right to exterminate inferior races.

For the Conservative Revolution, revolution itself (including war) is a kind of blood-letting, a "trimming off of excessive and damaging growth." Its proponents are not amazed that birth must be paid for with destruction. Murder, especially political murder, finds its brutal justification here. It is therefore hardly accidental that all those regimes we group under the term "state terrorism," e.g., Khomeini's Iran or Qaddafi's Libya, not only practice systematic political murder against their opponents, but also exhibit all the other characteristics of the Conservative Revolution.

Its proponents believe that Nietzsche's arrival represents the great turning point, and that the following period has only been an interregnum during which the world of progress must first be entirely destroyed before the new one can take shape. Whoever reads these works of a hundred years ago, cannot help recognizing that their authors knew they were engaged in a conspiracy spanning generations.

In the Preface to his *Will to Power,* which is celebrated as the "most significant challenge of the interregnum," Nietzsche writes:

What I am going to relate is the history of the next two centuries. I will describe what will occur, and what can occur in no other way: the rise of nihilism. This story can already be told now, for necessity is already at work here. This future is already speaking to us with a thousand signs; this fate is announced everywhere. All ears are straining to hear this music

of the future. Our entire European culture
has long been moving with agonizing tension,
increasing from decade to decade, and is now
tumbling loosely, restlessly, violently into catastrophe: like a river which wants to reach
its end, which no longer thinks, which is afraid
to think.

This "tension" has already been unleashed once
in the catastrophe of the Third Reich and World
War II—a direct consequence of the philosophy
cited above. But just as the Conservative Revolution
disdainfully claimed that the National Socialists had
"watered down" their theory, so they regarded Hitler as merely an "episode on Germany's political
stage," as a "drum beater" for national revolt, as
the "catalyst sent by fate." Löwith sees this as a
development whose beginning is the death of God
(Nietzsche's God is dead), whose middle is the re-
sulting nihilism, and whose end is nihilism's conquest of itself and the eternal return.

This transition to a new age has cosmic dimen-
sions—an idea which has weathered well. Under
the pseudonym Kurt von Ensen, a certain Dr. Karl
Strünkmann wrote in his 1932 book *Adolf Hitler und
die Kommenden* (*Adolf Hitler and the Age to Come*):

Today we are living through the catastrophic
transition from the Age of Pisces to the Age
of Aquarius. We are at a change of æons, as
at the time of the birth of Christ, when humanity left the Age of Aries and entered the
new Christian Æon of Pisces. An old world
collapsed, a new one rose up: the Christian
Occident. And now, 2,000 years later, a new,
powerful "die and become again" is begin-

ning: destruction of the Occident and rise of
the new atlantic world. The Third Reich's mission is to demolish the dying Occident. The
shaping of the new Atlantic cultural empire
in the Æon of Aquarius will be the task of the
Fourth Reich.

In good National Bolshevist style, Herr von Ensen alias Strünkmann knew precisely what the hub
of this Fourth Reich would be: the intimate alliance
between Prussia and Russia.

The previous æon, the Age of Pisces, was under the joint leadership of Roman and Germanic intellectual and cultural forces. *The new
Æon of Aquarius will be directed not toward the
South, but toward the East.* The Prussian-Aus-
trian, Deutsch-Germanic will, on the one side,
and Russian-Siberian elemental forces on the
other side, shall shape a new type of man and
a new humankind on earth.

Preparation of all these things was to be the task
for a future intellectual general staff.

It is quite surprising and highly fruitful to read
the writings of the Conservative Revolutionaries
and National Bolshevists of the 1920s and 1930s,
and then to compare them with the modern trends
toward a so-called neutralized, independent central
Europe and a decoupling with the United States.
One finds the same hatred against the "West" and
against rationality and reason. The negotiating
partner is never Communist Russia; it is always the
Bolshevist East.

If we regard the transformations cited by
Nietzsche, Jünger, or von Ense not merely as ab-

surd astrological hokum, but rather as a program for the oligarchical faction, then we must unfortunately conclude that this paradigm shift, the destruction of Western values, has been largely successful.

With the arrogance of someone who has already won the battle, Marilyn Ferguson, a fellow at the futuristic Stanford Research Institute, has given us a popular account of current experimentation in this shift. Without even covering her mouth, in her book *The Age of Aquarius* she describes the process of mass brainwashing which has led an increasing number of people around the world, especially the youth, into joining up with this Age of Aquarius—this cosmic touching and feeling which unites everyone in a great dynamic family.

Even if it is perhaps not evident at first glance, the members of the alternative movement, with their dream of a post-industrial Age of Aquarius, share their epistemological groundwork with the so-called peace movement. When this latter group finds not the slightest problem in unilateral disarmament; when Horst Ehmke sees "America's confrontation policies" as a greater problem than the threat of becoming subjugated under "Soviet domination"—is this not identical to Kurt von Ensen's earlier dictum: "the new Æon of Aquarius will be directed not toward the South, but toward the East"?

The dictatorship of the irrational, a combination of sentimental, romantic wallowing in the boundlessness of emotion, and the corresponding hatred of all lawfulness of reason, is the common denominator where Nazism and Bolshevism coincide. This is the basis of the convergences of the 1920s and 1930s, and it provides an epistemological explanation for the Hitler-Stalin pact.

The Hitler-Stalin Pact

In spite of its weakness, the Social Democratic Party (SPD) of the late Weimar Republic still was the gathering point for most of Germany's republican elements. After the Sixth World Congress of the Comintern, the Communist International declared its main enemy to be the SPD, and not, as one might otherwise expect, the NSDAP. The Communists' decision can only be understood with reference to the affinity between Nazism and Bolshevism described above. If this affinity did not exist, Stalin would never have thought of Hitler as his tool, just as the East would not be supporting the Greens today to suit their own purposes.

The Nazis were not important to Stalin because of their ideology, but because he saw them as the best lever for breaking Germany out of the Western camp. As is usually the case with such Hobbesian alliances, Stalin secretly planned to incorporate Germany into the Soviet sphere of influence at the earliest opportunity; in the meantime, however, he proceeded according to the old principle, "anything which hurts our enemy, helps us," the enemy in this case being the capitalist system in the West.

At the close of 1931 Stalin formulated his thinking as follows: "Don't you also believe, Neumann, that, if the National Socialists were to take power in Germany, they would be so exclusivly occupied with the West that we could build socialism here in peace?"

Moreover, at the Dec. 15, 1931 meeting of the executive committee of the Communist International in Moscow, Comintern executive secretary Dmitrii Manuilskii stated:

The main enemy is not Hitler; the main enemy is the system of Severing-Brüning-Hindenburg. We will make no treaties with Hitler or enter into secret negotiations with him. We will let Hitler go his own way, but will make use of everything his victory over the state machine will bring. With his aid we will first smash the Social Democratic police machine and the Brüning state machine. . . . In the present phase of development of the German revolution, Hitler is our most steadfast ally. . . . Our future tactics, and the tactics of the German Communist Party, depend upon a correct evaluation of this fact.

The content of these arguments are completely consistent with the peasant wisdom which later formed the basis for the Hitler-Stalin Pact of August 1939 to 1941. In Hitler, Stalin thought he had a useful instrument for realizing his dream of a world socialist empire. Hitler is known to have thought the same of Stalin, namely that Stalin was a stepping-stone to his future seizure of world power. If we consider that Neville Chamberlain, French Premier Edouard Daladier, and powerful Wall Street financiers were also supporting Hitler in hopes that Hitler would go to war against the Soviet Union, then the Second World War begins to look like a classic case of miscalculation on the part of all involved.

The Nazi regime's economic policy had, in the meantime, done precisely what oligarchical forms of extreme domestic austerity always do. As soon as the domestic economy's industrial capacity and labor force is exhausted—and the Nazis took this to the extreme with their labor and concentration camps—there remains only one way out for such an economy: wars of conquest, so as to bring new resources within reach. Hitler, speaking to his generals on Aug. 22, 1939, argued for the invasion of Poland in the following terms: "This is an easy decision. We have nothing to lose. Our economic situation is such that we can go on for a couple of years at best. Göring can back this up. We have no choice. We must act."

On Aug. 23 the world was taken by surprise with the announcement of a non-aggression pact between the Third Reich and the Soviet Union, signed in the Kremlin by Stalin, Molotov, and Nazi Foreign Minister Joachim von Ribbentrop. Poland was to be the booty, divided up between the two empires. At the conclusion of the Polish campaign, on the evening of Sept. 27 von Ribbentrop traveled to Moscow in order to conclude a German-Soviet border and friendship treaty. This was the only friendship treaty Hitler ever made with any state outside the Axis.

If we call to mind the Soviet reaction to France's and Great Britain's declaration of war against Hitler, we are struck with the parallels to Soviet argumentation following their recent shooting down of a Korean commercial jet liner. After Hitler had decided to set into motion a "peace offensive" in October 1939, Stalin ran the following statement in the Nov. 29 issue of *Pravda*:

> It was not Germany which attacked France and England, but France and England have attacked Germany, and thus they bear responsibility for the present war. . . . The ruling class of France and England has presumptuously rejected the German peace proposals and the Soviet Union's efforts for

a rapid conclusion to the war. These are the facts.

As hard as the Soviets might have subsequently tried to give themselves the aura of anti-fascist struggle, no one can ever erase the these lines in the Oct. 9, 1939 *Izvestia*: "To start a war to destroy Hitler, is a criminally stupid policy." And on Oct. 31, Molotov stressed in a public statement:

> There is no possible justification for a war of this kind. One can accept the ideology of Hitlerism, or one can reject it. . . that is a question of political attitude. . . but it is not only senseless but also criminal to wage a war to wipe out Hitlerism and disguise this as a fight for democracy.

The Hitler-Stalin Pact, particularly the concomitant expansion in East-West trade, kept the Hitler regime alive for the duration. In accordance with the German-Soviet trade agreement signed just before the pact, the Nazis received from the Soviets one-third of their oil, two-thirds of their phosphate, one-third of their cobalt, tungsten, molybdenum and tin, many other raw materials, and ten percent of their animal fodder. During the period between August 1939 and August 1940, trade between the two states rose by 3,000 percent. If it had not been for Russia, the British naval blockade would have done serious damage to the Nazis; but instead the Russian bought goods from the Far East, and even from the British, in order to sell it more cheaply to the Nazis.

The myth of the Soviet anti-fascist struggle becomes even less credible when we take into account the fact that when the U.S.S.R. had the best opportunity to stop the Nazis, Moscow let it go by. In 1940 the Nazis deployed 139 divisions on the Western front, and a mere four divisions and six territorial regiments remained on the Eastern front to face Stalin's more than 100 divisions. If Stalin had really intended to move against the Nazis, this would have been the ideal moment.

Only when the Third Reich and the Soviet Union started getting in each other's way, for instance, around raw materials supplies in Romania or Finland, did the tide begin to turn. It is certainly true that, in the course of the bloody warfare which followed, the Soviets lost 20 million of their citizens at the hands of the Nazis. But it helps neither themselves nor the West when they hold up anti-fascist resistance as a holy cow.

It is also undeniably true that the Soviet Union bitterly resisted the Nazis after they opened up the Eastern front. But the fact remains that the rise of the Nazis in Germany had fit perfectly into their concept; this gives them a large degree of co-responsibility for the course of events. The greatest tragedy, however, lies in the fact that no one today—in East or West—is willing to learn the lesson of this story. Immediately after the end of the war, the Soviet Union did not hesitate to make use of the old Nazi intelligence networks. Today the Soviet Union continues to provide us with daily proof of its unabashed support for Nazi organizations in the West, be these old formations or newcomers such as the alternative movements of the so-called Age of Aquarius. Has the Soviet Union still failed to learn that it never pays to support Nazi movements in the West?

The oligarchy in the West is equally determined

to repeat the same mistakes. The political friends of Lord Carrington, the Kissingers, Genschers and Andreottis, evidently believe that by isolating America and concluding a new Yalta Agreement with the Soviet Union, they can re-divide and plunder the world. An "independent Central Europe accord," no matter how it were formulated, would surely have an even shorter life-span than the Hitler-Stalin Pact. Today there are certain European oligarchs who would like to control their own arsenal of nuclear weapons—a proposal currently being negotiated under the shameful trademark of the "two-pillar theory of NATO." If their dreams ever become reality, the result is pre-programmed: whoever refuses to learn from history is condemned to repeat it.

Bibliography

Augustine, Saint, Bishop of Hippo, *Confessions*, New York, 1961.

———, *City of God*, New York, 1972.

———, *Later Works*, New York, 1950.

Carey, Henry Charles, *Commerce, Christianity, and Civilization, Versus British Free Trade; letters in reply to the London Times*, Philadelphia, 1876.

———, *Principles of Social Science*, Philadelphia, 1883.

———, *Principles of Political Economy*, Philadelphia, 1840.

———, "Review of the Decade" [preface to an edition of a German translation of his work on social science], Philadelphia, 1867. Also in *Miscellaneous Papers on the National Finances*, Philadelphia, 1875.

Chaitkin, Anton, *Treason in America*, New York, 1984.

Ferguson, Marilyn, *The Aquarian Conspiracy*, New York, 1980.

Hegel, Georg Wilhelm Friedrich, *Gesammelte Werke*, Hamburg, 1968.

Haffner, Sebastian and Venohr, Wolfgang, *Preussische Profile*, Königstein/Ts., 1980.

de Lagarde, Paul, *Deutscher Glaube, deutsches Vaterland, deutsche Bildung*, Jena, 1913.

Langbehn, Julius, *Rembrandt als Erzieher, von einem Deutschen*, Leipzig, 1890.

LaRouche, Lyndon H., *The Case of Walter Lippmann*, New York, 1977.

———, *There Are No Limits to Growth*, New York, 1983.

———and Goldman, David P., *The Ugly Truth about Milton Friedman*, New York, 1980

Ledeen, Michael, *Universal Fascism*, New York, 1973.

Malthus, Thomas Robert, *An Essay on the Principle of Population, as it affects the future improvement of society*, London, 1798. Also published as *An Essay on the Principle of Population; or, a view of its past and present effects on human happiness*, London, 1826.

Moeller van den Bruck, Arthur, *Germany's Third Empire*, London, 1934.

Mohler, Armin, *Die Konservative Revolution in Deutschland 1918–1932*, Darmstadt, 1972.

Mosse, George, *International Fascism*, London/Beverly Hills, 1979.

Niebuhr, Bartold Georg, *The History of Rome*, London, 1855–60.

———, *Geschichte des Zeitalters der Revolution; Vorlesungen an der Universität Bonn im Sommer 1829*, Hamburg, 1845.

Niekisch, Ernst, *Politische Schriften*, Cologne/Berlin, 1965.

———, *Erinnerungen eines deutschen Revolutionärs*, Cologne, 1974.

———, *Gewagtes Leben*, Cologne/Berlin, 1958.

———, *Die Legende von der Weimarer Republik*, Cologne, 1968.

———, *Ost, West; Unsystematische Betrachtungen*, Berlin, 1947.

Nietzsche, Friedrich, *Kritische Gesamtausgabe*, Berlin/New York, 1967.

Nikolaus von Kues (Nicolaus of Cusa), *Schriften des Nikolaus von Kues*, Hamburg, 1936.

Plato, *Collected Works*, New York, 1921–62.

von Raumer, Kurt, *Die Autobiographie des Freiherrn vom Stein*, Münster, 1954.

von Salomon, Ernst, *The Answers of Ernst von Salomon to the 131 Questions in the Allied Military Government "Fragebogen"*, London, 1954.

von Savigny, Friedrich Karl, *Geschichte des Römischen Rechts im Mittelalter*, Bad Homburg, 1961.

———, *Vermischte Schriften*, Berlin, 1850.

———, *System des heutigen Römischen Rechts*, Darmstadt, 1956.

Schiller, Friedrich, *Werke, Nationalausgabe*, Vols. 1–42, Weimar, 1943–77.

Shirer, William, *The Rise and Fall of the Third Reich*, New York, 1960.

Spannaus, Nancy and White, Christopher, *The Political Economy of the American Revolution*, New York, 1977.

vom Stein, Karl Freiherr, *Briefwechsel, Denkschriften und Aufzeichnungen*, Berlin, 1931–1937.

Zepp-LaRouche, Helga, "Kulturpessimismus, eine Geisteskrankheit," in *Ibykus: Zeitschrift für Poesie, Wissenschaft und Staatskunst*, Wiesbaden, June 1982.

2

The National Socialist World-View: Racial Darwinism, Gnosticism, and Mysticism

The sheer quantity of scholarly—and non-scholarly—literature about Hitler and National Socialism has reached massive proportions. But a quick perusal of the bookstores in New York, West Berlin, or Frankfurt reveals that most of these works have little to do with historical truth.

As both the distance from the Nazi phenomenon and the amount written on the subject have increased, two basic myths about Nazism seem to have established themselves. The first myth is the sharp distinction between Hitler's National Socialism on the one hand and fascism on the other, with the result that fascism appears in an increasingly differentiated and even sympathetic light. The second myth reflects a fundamental consensus that has crystalized about Nazism, resting on the axiomatic equation   Nazism = Germany + anti-Semitism + industrial capitalism. Both myths contain partial truths, were not "made up out of the clear blue sky," and hence appear plausible and easy to grasp.

Nonetheless, both myths are irreconcilable with historical truth, and miss the essence of fascism and Nazism. More importantly, they obstruct insight into new fascist tendencies, in the present and the future.

In the present, second world crisis of the twentieth century, it is absolutely necessary to grasp the essentials of fascism and Nazism. We must avoid being blinded to the essential by a fixation on the form and predicates. For it may very well happen that a new Nazism and fascism will rear its head under the guise of "anti-fascism." There are already very clear tendencies in this direction in both East and West.

The following presentation is closely related to an essay by Helga Zepp-LaRouche which was published in 1982 under the title, "The Historical Roots of Green Fascism," in which the ideological roots of Green fascism were presented, primarily as they appear in Armin Mohler's work, *The Conservative Revolution.* Here, we wish to sketch out, on the one hand how the Nazi elite came into being and what ideological factors determined it; and on the other, how this Nazi elite was able to build a Nazi mass movement.

According to Hitler himself, National Socialism was started as follows: "In July 1919 I joined the German Workers Party (DAP), which then consisted of seven members, in which I finally found an organization in the political arena which reflected my ideals." This statement fits nicely into the conception that the "Führer" built the Nazi mass movement out of nothing. In reality, the German Workers Party (DAP), which shortly afterwards became the National Socialist German Workers Party (NSDAP), was in no way a minuscule political splinter group. Founded by Anton Drexler, a railway worker, and run by Karl Harrer, a sports writer, the DAP set itself the task of spreading anti-Semitic racism throughout the working class. The anti-capitalist rhetoric used for this was carried over into the NSDAP, especially in Gottfried Feder's slogan of "breaking from the servitude of [Jewish] interest rates."

Harrer, Drexler, Feder, and Hitler were not only members of the DAP, they were at the same time members or at least sympathizers of the Thule Society. The German Workers Party was actually founded on orders from the Thule Society and functioned as its front organization. Alongside the DAP, the Thule Society created dozens of splinter groups, parliamentary organizations, and terrorist associations. Of all of these organizations the DAP-NSDAP proved to be the most promising, and the Thule Society decided to focus its energies on this project. This, no doubt, had a lot to do with Hitler's quickly emerging talent as a political organizer and demagogic orator.

The Thule Society and Haushofer

The Thule Society functioned as a secret mystic-political organization modeled on Freemasonry. The existence of this organization first became known when members of the Thule Society were taken hostage and murdered during the final stage of the so-called Munich Soviet Republic. On April 29, 1919, ten Thule members were killed, among them Prince Maria von Thurn und Taxis, Countess Westarp, Baron Teikert, and Baron Seydlitz. About two months earlier, another member of the Thule organization, Count Arco-Valley, had shot the "revolutionary" Bavarian Prime Minister Kurt Eisner. The Thule organization later continued to exert substantial control over political terrorism, especially through the so-called Consul Organization. In connection with these terrorist activities, it became evident that the Thule Society, unlike the DAP-NSDAP, was no band of muddleheaded mystics who happened to get together; to a significant extent, its members were recruited from ruling oligarchical families. The Thurn und Taxis were, after all, one of the richest and most influential noble houses in Germany, and remain so to this day.

The official head of the Thule Society was one Baron Rudolf von Sebottendorf, a.k.a. Glauer. Born in 1875 in Thuringia, he had lived in the Middle East at the beginning of the century, where he was adopted by a von Sebottendorf. He became an expert in Islamic Sufism and maintained very close ties to Sufi networks in the Ottoman Empire. Through these ties he was soon able to get his hands on political influence and substantial financial means. Already in the Balkan War of 1912–1913 he served as a leader of the "Turkish Crescent."

His career in Turkey has certain parallels with Alexander Helphand-Parvus, who also, "from nothing," rose from being a revolutionary in 1905 to enormous wealth and influence in Turkey, and worked in the First World War for the German imperial secret police (and probably others as well).

Sebottendorf, a wealthy man by 1917, returned to Germany and settled down in Munich. There he worked on reorganizing the populist-mystic groupings, especially the "Vril Society."

As has already been indicated, Sebottendorf's organizing abilities enabled him to turn the Thule Society into an organization which recruited from noble families, academics, literati, and officialdom. Major-General and Professor Karl Haushofer was a particularly important member of the Society. Along with Halford Mackinder of the London School of Economics, Haushofer is known as the founder of "geopolitics," the theory that the fate of a people and nation depends on their racial characteristics of "blood and soil." The very life and survival of nations, so the theory goes, rests on securing and expanding its *Lebensraum* (living space). Since the population increases, whereas the size of the earth's surface remains unchanged, a dynamic, ambitious people must continually conquer new areas at the expense of weaker peoples. Not industry, but agriculture must form the primary base of subsistance. Haushofer proclaimed that Germany's *Lebensraum* lay in continental expansion into the Eurasian land mass. The Anglo-Saxons had taken the sea route and conducted their colonial and imperialist expansion overseas. Since the British Empire and the United States had developed unchallengable naval power, Germany must therefore concentrate on expansion into southern Europe, Russia, the northern Orient and central Asia. As we shall see, these ideas were directly taken over by Hitler. Indeed, it has been established that the key geopolitical section of Hitler's *Mein Kampf* was dictated by Haushofer through Rudolf Hess during Hitler's imprisonment at the Landsberg fortress, when *Mein Kampf* was written. Hitler, Hess, and Hermann Goering had all attended Army indoctrination sessions just after World War I at the University of Munich, where Haushofer taught.

But geopolitics was only one side of Haushofer's activities. Haushofer was one of the most important mystic ideologues of the Thule Society. Members of this society bore little resemblance to the typical image of the xenophobic, beer-guzzling, narrow

German chauvinist. Many members of the inner circle of the Thule Society lived abroad for many years or had been born there, such as Sebottendorf, Rudolf Hess, Alfred Rosenberg, and Erwin Scheubner-Richter.

Haushofer spent many years as a military attaché in Japan and traveled extensively in Asia; his trips to India and Tibet are important in connection with the origins of his ideology and Nazism. Haushofer made two acquaintances there which were to have important future consequences: the British Viceroy Lord Kitchener and the Russian expert on Tibetan mysticism Georg Ivanovich Gurdjieff, who lived in Tibet. Through Kitchener and Gurdjieff, Haushofer was introduced into the inner circle of racist-gnostic mysticism. This circle also included the Swedish-born Asian scholar Sven Hedin.

Through the beginning of World War II, Haushofer continued to cultivate contacts with his Anglo-Saxon mystic friends, such as the "Order of the Golden Dawn." Houston Stewart Chamberlain, nephew of the British Colonial Minister Joseph Chamberlain and Richard Wagner's son-in-law, was another of the Thule Society's important ties with Anglo-Saxon mystic ideology. Chamberlain's book, "The Foundations of the 19th Century," became one of the most important source documents for National Socialist ideology.

The Thule Myth and Tibet

The special significance of India and Tibet for the ideology of the Thule Society and the Nazis centers around the term *Thule*. In northern European mythology, Thule signifies a prehistoric "golden age" which ended in a sudden catastrophe. With the mysticism of the Thule Society and the Nazis, but also in circles in Russia, England, Scandinavia, and in other European locations, the Thule mythos became the alpha and omega of all human history. But only in Tibet had this secret knowledge of this ancient Thule been preserved along with the way to a "new Thule," a "thousand-year Reich" of the Aryans.

Without resorting to primary sources, the Thule myth can be approximately reconstructed as follows: In prehistoric times there existed a flourishing culture in the North Sea region. This empire of blond, blue-eyed, racially pure Aryans was led by an aristocracy with "superhuman," cosmic powers and abilities. Without relying on technology, they could exert these "cosmic" powers to determine and change the course of Nature.

But then there came a natural catastrophe of cosmic proportions. The planets' orbits were altered. Continents and oceans shifted, and the flora and fauna in the North Sea region were destroyed. The Aryan Thule empire sank into the sea. Only a few of the Aryans and their supermen managed to escape, finally finding refuge in the Tibetan Himalayas. There the supermen preserved the secrets and powers of the collapsed Thule empire. Still during the prehistoric period, a few supermen wandered back northward. Scandinavia and the area around the Baltic as far as Germany became the new Aryan settlement. In the course of their wanderings they also settled in India and Persia, the Caucasus, and parts of Russia. Along the way, however, the Aryans relinquished some of their racial purity and so lost access to the higher knowledge and supernatural capacities of the old Aryan superman aristocracy. Only a very few, selected Aryans remained capable of gaining access to the inner secrets of the Aryan supermen, and these supreme secrets survived only in the secret cult centers of Tibet.

The Thule Society, and later the leading Nazi circles, thought of themselves as an exclusive secret cult which had re-established its connection to the Aryan supermen's knowledge. This knowledge and concomitant power, however, was reserved for only the select few who submitted to racist-gnostic rituals and cult practices. The mission of these chosen few of the Thule Society and the Nazi leadership, was to lead the Aryan people into a new Thule empire, with themselves as a new superman aristocracy.

This Thule-Nazi mysticism was, of course, not espoused publicly; it remained the knowledge of a select few. The writings of Haushofer, Rosenberg, and Hitler contain only vague hints. But a monologue given by Hitler in 1942 to his closest associates, and later written down by Martin Bormann's assistant Heinrich Heim (in *Hitler's Table Talk*), contains explicit discussions of the Thule myth. Hitler said that

> It is amazing how small a period of time man is capable of grasping. . . . Where do we get the right to believe that man was *not* originally what he is today?. . . We would do well to assume that what is reported by the mythology of the deities is in fact a memory of a previous *reality*. At the same time, within every body of legends we always find the story of the collapse of the heavens. . . . My only explanation for this is that an immense natural catastrophe destroyed a race of human beings who possessed the *highest* level of culture. *What we find on earth today must be a small remainder which,*

living for that memory, will gradually find its way
back to culture [emphasis added].

Hitler felt that his mission was to resurrect the
Thule empire of the Aryans along with its superman aristocracy and their superhuman faculties,
and so to create an Aryan "thousand-year Reich."
But despite his repeated attempts to portray himself as such, Hitler was not the originator of these
ideas. Hitler was *initiated* into this mystical ideology
by the Thule Society.

Haushofer played a crucial role in the Thule
Society's inner circles because he was the only member to have been personally initiated into the Tibetan secret cult. A similar role was played by the
poet and minor nobleman Dietrich Eckart, who
served as the Thule Society's chief ideologue and
who was also Hitler's own mentor.

Dietrich Eckart

Eckart was a prominent figure in the "Schwabing
Bohemians" circle before World War I. He wrote
several dramas, including "Henry IV" and "Lor-
enzaccio," which were frequently performed at the
time. His best-known work is his German version
of Ibsen's *Peer Gynt*. Eckart loved to drink, consumed narcotics, and was a proponent of "racial
mysticism." He personified the culture of Nietzsche
and Wagner, which was becoming increasingly rad-
icalized into an activist, racist-gnostic mysticism. It
is not surprising that Eckart was on the best of terms
with influential oligarchical families. Eckart was one
of the founders of the Thule Society, and edited
its literary-political journal *Auf gut Deutsch* (*In Proper
German*).

Eckart was probably the first member of the

Thule Society to recognize Hitler's talent as a demagogue and an organizer. He saw in Hitler someone who could translate racist-gnostic mysticism into action. It was under Eckart's guidance that Hitler was first made into a political Führer, and Eckart's August, 1921 article was the first to describe Hitler as the Führer of the German People. He put his library at Hitler's disposal, educated him in mysticism, and taught him to express himself more articulately. At the same time, he introduced Hitler to influential families and businessmen. On his deathbed in 1923, Eckart left the following political testament:

> Follow Hitler. He will dance, but I am the one who composed the music. Do not regret my death. . . . My idea will not die with me. The Germans, once they have become a nation of biologically perfected human beings, will lead their people toward those great goals already known by the initiates of Aryan antiquity living in Tibet. Follow Hitler, for through him I will speak to you.

As we have already seen, in his public statements Hitler deliberately attempted to conceal his political origins in the Thule Society. After Eckart's death, Hitler made himself "independent." After years of inculcation by the Thule Society and apprenticeship under Haushofer and Eckart, the "Führer" could now rely on his own dynamism. From the mid-1920s onward, Hitler began to outgrow his fellow conspirators in the Thule circle. Hitler's mystic-ideological sources of inspiration had developed to such an extent that he could henceforth publicly call upon "Providence" to guide his actions. For

Hitler, rationality and logical calculation were nothing compared to the mystical "intuition" which determined his thought and actions through "Providence."

It is therefore all the more noteworthy that Dietrich Eckart was the only member of the Thule elite for whom Hitler felt respect and gratitude up to his death in 1945. Hitler not only dedicated the second volume of *Mein Kampf* to the deceased Eckart; in Heinrich Heim's above-cited transcript of Hitler's monologues, there is no name mentioned more frequently than his. In the warmest tones, Hitler was always ready with new stories and anecdotes about his old mentor.

In addition to promoting Hitler, Eckart was also the mentor of the future official ideologue of National Socialism, Alfred Rosenberg. Rosenberg's career likewise highlights the international connections of the Thule Society and the Nazi inner core. We have already mentioned Haushofer's close relations with the Russian mystic and Tibet expert G. I. Gurdjieff; Rosenberg's connections were even more explicit. He grew up as a "Balkan German" in Reval (Tallinn) and spoke perfect German and Russian. He studied architecture at Moscow University and graduated there in 1917. After the Bolshevik Revolution he left Russia for Germany.

Perhaps one of the least-acknowledged facts is the influence exerted by Russian racist mysticism on the formation of corresponding ideologies in Germany. The political writings of Fyodor Dostoevsky, along with the ideological content of his fictional works, played the crucial role. With the exception of a few British imperialists, before Hitler only Dostoevsky advocated world racial hegemony so radically, so brutally and with such frankness.

Dostoevsky proclaims, without restraint, Russia's mission was to become the third and final Rome. In order to free the world from the yoke of Western rationalism, Russia must, in the spirit of gnostic Christianity, achieve world hegemony. Russia was the only nation with an instinctive national "divine" soul.

Dostoevsky vehemently advocated a war of conquest against decadent, rationalist Western Europe. "War refreshes people," he exclaimed. "War is indispensable in our time; without war the world could collapse, or at the very least would change into filthy slime." Dostoevsky took it for granted that this war of conquest would put all of Western Europe under Russian domination, "and perhaps not we, but our children will witness England's demise."

It is wrong to assume that this is merely an extreme form of Russian chauvinism, having nothing to do with the Nazis. Dostoevsky envisioned Russia as the leader of the entire Aryan race, declaring that Russia "is just as concerned about the fate of the great Aryan race as it is about Russia itself." Dostoevsky was also, of course, a raving anti-Semite: "The Jews and the banks control everything: Europe and the Enlightenment, all civilization and Socialism. . . . And when nothing remains but anarchy, then the Jew will be sitting on top of it all."

Dostoevsky's political ideology exerted an enormous influence on German intellectual currents. Dostoevsky inspired the ideologue of the "Conservative Revolution," Moeller van den Bruck, to write his book *Das Dritte Reich* (*The Third Reich*). His influence is also evident in Alfred Rosenberg's book, *The Mythos of the Twentieth Century*. By the time Rosenberg had joined up with Dietrich Eckart and the Thule Society, his experience in Russia had already predisposed him to adopting this racist-gnostic mysticism in Germany.

Rosenberg was not transformed into a racist and an anti-Semite by the Thule Society; he brought it with him from Russia. Moreover, in contrast with the German anti-Semites, Rosenberg had already become familiar with the so-called Protocols of Zion during his Moscow days. This forgery, concocted by the czarist secret police, the Okhrana, was first published outside Russia by Eckart and Rosenberg as part of a campaign launched by the Thule Society in 1918.

Hatred of Christianity

In 1930, Alfred Rosenberg proceeded to make a grand attempt at an ideological synthesis of the Thule Society's mysticism, racism, and gnosticism: his book *The Mythos of the Twentieth Century*. The enemy of Rosenberg (and of the Nazis in general) was the Judeo-Christian tradition. By Judeo-Christian tradition, we do not primarily mean theological-dogmatic statements of belief, but rather the essence of Western European culture and its constantly self-renewing force of progress. Hatred of this conception continues to be a distinguishing characteristic of all neo-fascist tendencies.

Rosenberg and the Nazis dealt with the Jewish intellectual and spiritual tradition, which of course had strongly influenced Christianity, by simply turning it into the expression of an inferior race. The creations of an inferior race must thus axiomatically be inferior and evil, unworthy of serious intellectual discussion.

Their attack on Christianity took a different tack. After all, the overwhelming majority of the "Aryan" populations adhered to the Christian faith or were

rooted in Judeo-Christian culture. It was therefore
impossible to make an open frontal assault against
Christianity. Hence Rosenberg's solution was to
promote gnostic distortions of Christianity. Mon-
istic Christian doctrine was transformed into a Man-
ichean ideology of "the blood-soul." Christ became
Lucifer, a prophet for the master race. Christ himself, of course, had to belong to the "Aryan race,"
and his earthly parents were not Jewish, but rather
Roman legionnaires, or else of Persian descent. This
northern Christ-hero became the scourge of all racially inferior and rationalist elements. Christ would
counter the "poisoning" of the race and "aberra-
tions" in world-outlook—Lucifer-Christ against the
Satan of racial inferiority and rationality.

According to Rosenberg, the Nordics must
therefore possess a "violent Luciferian power which
overcomes space and time," and must produce a
harmony of blood and soul. This "blood-soul,"
manifested through the convergence of the Luciferian and the mystical side of the Aryans, is pre-
determined among Nordics: "On the level of the
unconscious, in cult and in life the individual fulfills
the commands of the blood, as in a dream."

Rosenberg's Nazi world-view explicitly draws
upon the gnostic tradition. Starting with the Thule
mysticism of Tibet, Rosenberg extols the religion
and philosophy of Aryan India, which achieved
"unparalleled metaphysical depths." He likewise
praises the Zarathustra and Mani cults of Aryan
Persia—which are still active today. The allegedly
Germanic-influenced religions of Greece and the
Roman Empire drew his highest admiration.

Rosenberg, like Hitler, harbored the greatest
hatred for the Catholic Church, for quite obvious
reasons. According to Rosenberg, the Nordic race

never completely and unreservedly embraced the Roman Catholic faith, and indeed engaged in a gigantic struggle with the Church. Rosenberg therefore glorifies all Christian heresies and schisms: Albigensians, Cathars, Waldensians, Calvinists, and Lutherans. Aside from Luther, he has great sympathy for the heroic battle of the Cathars in southwestern France.

The Grail

This attitude toward the gnostic Cathars is related to a further aspect of the Thule Society and the Nazis, namely, the myth of the Holy Grail. The Grail is an ancient heathen-gnostic symbol of wisdom and power. In England, France, and Germany, the poets of the early Middle Ages transformed it into a Christian symbol, principally in the form of a cup holding the blood of Christ. In the nineteenth century, the Grail was de-Christianized and became again a heathen-gnostic myth-object, as expressed most influentially in Richard Wagner's opera *Parsifal*.

The Thule Society and the Nazis took up this myth of the Grail and interpreted it so that the Grail was understood as an inscribed stone or tablet. This tablet was a crucial document of Aryan gnosticism, preserved and passed on from Aryan prehistory. According to the myth of the Grail, the tablet was finally hidden in a Grail fortress in southern France; according to Nazi lore, it originally came from Aryan Persia, then reached Jerusalem, and was brought to Rome after Jerusalem was destroyed. During the sack of Rome, the tablet fell into the hands of the Goths, and when they were forced out of Spain by the Arabs, it found its way to southern France, where it supposedly constituted the gnostic center for the Cathars. Finally, when the French monarchy bloodily routed the Cathars and ravaged the Aquitaine region, a few surviving Cathars smuggled the Grail from the fortress and hid it somewhere. The Nazis in the inner mystic circle thought they were now able to understand the contents of the tablet, which the Cathars had never deciphered, and to penetrate further secrets of Aryan gnosticism. SS experts in Aryan esoterica actually conducted a search for the Grail, with the support of Heinrich Himmler. And Hitler was not being ironical when he spoke to his intimate friends about his Berchtesgaden Berghof as "my Grail fortress."

Rosenberg's racialist-gnostic distortion of Christianity and the Nazi regime's publicly stated posture vis-à-vis the church in no way coincides with the views of Christianity and the churches actually held by the Nazi elite, let alone that of Hitler personally. Hitler's attitude toward Christianity is characterized by hate-filled, radical rejection.

As previously mentioned, Bormann's assistant Heim had kept notes of the content of Hitler's nocturnal monologues. Between 1941 and 1944, these show an almost daily repetition of tirades of hate against Judaism *and* Christianity, and there is virtually no difference in the number and frequency of his attacks on Judaism and those on Christianity. Here are some examples:

> Christianity is the greatest setback in the history of mankind.
> The most severe blow that mankind has ever endured is Christianity; Bolshevism is the bastard son of Christianity.
> Christianity was an all-destroying Bolshe-

vism. [Christ was] the son of a whore and a Roman soldier.

Nero didn't set fire to Rome; that was done by the Christian Bolsheviks.

If some little peasant woman or proletarian believes it, fine, then I have nothing to say about it. But for people who are intelligent to embrace such satanic superstition. . .!

These priests! Whenever I so much as see such a black-robed inferior being coming my way. . . . Whoever wants to think, gets burned by one of those black bugs.

The worst cancer is our priests of both confessions. I can't deal with them now, but it's all going into my notebook. The moment will come when I will settle accounts without further ado.

It is interesting to see how, during these tirades, Hitler referred to Dietrich Eckart and to the Thule Society, which had shown him how "priests" and Christianity were to be dealt with. Nietzsche's philosophical slogan "God is dead" was the main trumpet-call of the Thule Society and the inner Nazi circles. They were determined not only to battle Christianity intellectually and spiritually, but to liquidate it physically. They clearly recognized that the destruction of Christianity was the indispensable precondition for the destruction of Western European culture. Hitler deeply regretted that he was still forced for political reasons to compromise with the Christian churches, which contradicted his deepest convictions. He ridiculed the Nazi collaborators in the churches, especially the Protestants, saying that they could not prevent him from settling accounts with Christianity.

Hitler's Gnosticism and Racism

Hitler's "deepest conviction," his conception of God, was based on a racialist gnosticism. For him and his inner leadership circle, God is a cold, Darwinian "law of Nature," of struggle against and elimination of all "inferiors." The other side of this God of pitiless destruction is the cold "beauty" beyond all good and evil.

> We can do nothing more than take joy in what we find beautiful. I strive for a condition in which each individual knows that he lives and dies for the preservation of his species.

Hitler was sharply critical of the metaphysics of the race theorist Houston Stewart Chamberlain, whose gnosticism was too "intellectual," a criticism which implicitly extends to Nietzsche. Hitler's gnosticism is strictly biological and Darwinian; therefore "divine" beauty for Hitler is something physical. Hitler characterized Wagner's music in this way, saying that this music with its "divine beauty" transported him into a state of physical and emotional excitement.

> But when I imagine that bland Christian heaven! We have had Richard Wagner here on earth, and all you can do up there is listen to hallelujas and look at palm fronds.

In this connection, investigators usually overlook the influence of French nineteenth-century intellectual life on Hitler's racialist gnosticism. The influence of Gobineau on Hitler's racialism is usually mentioned, but not the strong influence of Joseph

Ernest Renan, whom Hitler studied carefully. In Renan's *Life of Jesus* (1863), Renan wrote:

> The broad application of the science of physiology and the principle of selection could make possible the creation of a higher race, which would have the right to rule over others, not because of its knowledge but because of the superiority of its blood, intelligence, and determination. We would then have a species of gods or "divas.". . . And we can imagine that we could set up something like a factory for cultivating aces [pure Aryans], an "Aceburg.". . . I repeat, intellectual superiority means religious superiority. We should think of these future beings as the incarnation of the Good and the True, and all must totally subordinate themselves to them.

Hitler had already adopted this racialist gnosticism in his early Vienna days. It is therefore hardly a world-historical accident that Hitler came into contact with the Thule Society in Munich in 1919. The Thule Society became aware of Hitler because of his talent as a political demagogue and organizer; this is the actual surprise or accident, since up to that time Hitler had been a notorious loner, with no demonstrable talents in that direction, whereas his racialism, gnosticism, and mysticism were fully developed before that time. It would have been extraordinary indeed if, given Hitler's views when he arrived in Munich, he had not bumped into the Thule Society.

This is especially true of Hitler's racialism and anti-Semitism. While still in Vienna, i.e. before 1913, Hitler joined an "Anti-Semitic Union." Hitler's turn toward anti-Semitism goes even further back. There are indications that Hitler's father had anti-Semitic ideas, though this has not been definitively established.

Certain conclusions can be drawn from Hitler's school days. Between 1896 and 1898 Hitler attended the Benedictine cloister school in Lambach, which decades before Hitler's school days had been directed by an abbot named Peter Hagen, an expert in oriental mysticism who spent the years 1856–68 in the Middle East and Persia. Abbot Hagen's personal coat of arms was the swastika, a wooden carving of which stands above the abbey door. Furthermore, Hagen left behind an extensive library of mystical works. This library was intensively used by another Benedictine monk in the 1890s named Peter Adolf Josef Lanz, whom we will meet later under a different name. All this, of course, only had a general influence on Hitler's childhood, but such things must be taken into account.

The influences on Hitler during his high school days in Linz from 1900–1905 were probably more direct. Hitler's history teacher, Dr. Leopold Poetsch, played an important role. Poetsch was an active member of the Austrian All-German Party, and served as the party's town council representative. Hitler himself said in *Mein Kampf* that his historical and political conceptions had been strongly influenced by Poetsch. The All-German Party of Austria had been founded by Georg Ritter von Schönerer, who rejected the royal poly-racial state of the Danube monarchy, and demanded the separation of non-German areas from Austria and the annexation of German Austria to the German Reich. Schönerer was also the inventor of the slogan "Away from Rome!" and was an active anti-Semite. His party was represented in the Vienna Reichstag. When Hitler left Linz, he became a follower of Schönerer's party and was already anti-Semitically inclined.

In Vienna, Hitler's political sympathies shifted toward Viennese Mayor Karl Lueger and Lueger's Christian Social Party. Like Schönerer, Lueger was anti-Semitic, perhaps more so. In 1895, he and his party had already won a majority on the Viennese City Council on the basis of an anti-Semitic program, and from that time until his death, the anti-Semite Lueger served as the virtually autocratic mayor of Vienna.

Though Hitler did not become a member of Schönerer's or Lueger's party, they were his political models. His viewpoint as a political anti-Semite was firmly fixed. His criticism of Schönerer and Lueger was simply that he rejected their political compromises and thought that their anti-Semitism and their stance agains the Hapsburg regime and the Catholic Church was not sufficiently principled.

Hitler himself repeatedly emphasized that, in addition to general political considerations, his own experiences in the "racial Babylon" of Vienna had crystalized his attitude. He relates how emotional encounters with orthodox Eastern Jews and their hairstyle and clothing, finally fixed his anti-Semitism. We can see that in pre-World War I Vienna, anti-Semitism was by no means a fringe phenomenon, but was a broad current which had not only gripped the petite bourgeoisie but was also "fit for polite society" (*salonfähig*).

Lanz von Liebenfels

Now we must return to the Benedictine father already mentioned above, Peter Lanz. In 1900 Lanz left the Catholic Church, went to Vienna, and founded the "Order of the New Temple." He called himself Jörg Lanz von Liebenfels and published a journal *Ostara*. This journal, which appeared irregularly but was always available at the kiosks, was characterized by its publisher as follows:

> *Ostara* is the only journal dedicated to the creation and cultivation of the heroic racialism and male justice that actually seeks to apply the results of race science, in order to keep the heroic noble race on its path of organized pure breeding and of male justice, and to protect it from socialistic and feminist revolutionaries.

In 1905, Liebenfels published his "major work": *Theozoologie oder die Kunde von den Sodoms-Äfflingen und dem Götter-Elektron* (*Theo-zoology or the Knowledge of Sodom's Monkeys and the Electron of the Gods*). In it he relates how the Ario-heroes, or aces, lived like gods in prehistoric times. When their Aryan women fell from grace, they mixed with dark, ape-like beings, which resulted in the inferior "Chandala" race. This race reproduced rapidly, while the Ario-heroes steadily lost their racial purity and, with it, their "electro-magnetic-radiological" powers.

The New Temple Order saw itself as a human breeding society whose aim was to bring produce new Ario-heroes. This may seem incredible, until we recall the racial mysticism of the Thule Society and compare it to the Lebensborn Program of the SS, in which selected women were impregnated by SS members to help engender the "master race." Liebenfels claimed that Lord Kitchener was a member of the New Temple Order, a claim which should be taken seriously. It is also documented that the Swedish dramatist August Strindberg was a member of this organization and stayed for some time in Lower Austria at a castle which served as Liebenfels' "Fortress of the Order."

Liebenfels demanded the most extensive extermination of the darker-skinned races, referring to Thomas Malthus and the British colonial regime as examples to follow. The Jews, he maintained, were the most intelligent of the ape-races, and therefore the most dangerous.

Hitler studied the *Ostara* newspapers during his years in Vienna, and there is no doubt that he was deeply influenced by them. This same insanity, though in a more moderate form, was advocated by the Vienna-based "Guido von List Society," which published a book-series of "research results" which do not differ in content from *Ostara*.

As Hitler testified later at his trial in 1924, he "left Vienna an absolute anti-Semite, a deadly enemy of the collective Marxist world-view, and as an pan-German in my orientation." In his Vienna student days he had come to understand that "if the power to struggle . . . is no longer there, then our right to life in this world of struggle has ended."

Hitler's Racial Genocide

With his deep-seated ideological fixation on a racist-Darwinist struggle for life and death, Hitler's desire to exterminate the Jews and other inferior races had existed implicitly since his Vienna days. The idea that Hitler escalated his endless, hate-filled tirades against the Jews step by step until they ended with the mass exterminations of the Second World War, is misleading. Hitler had already drawn the consequences of his racialist-ideological postulates during the Vienna and Thule Society days, and the early days of the NSDAP. His convictions only became firmer over time.

Hitler could not immediately carry out his racialist-Darwinist world-view because he lacked power; when he had it, he had to maintain restraint because of political considerations. As in the case of Christianity, mass extermination had long before been written down in the "great notebook" of his *Weltanschauung*. For the Thule Society, Hitler, and the inner leadership of the Nazis, gnosticism, mysticism, and racial Darwinism were not mere external appendages or crazy eccentricities; they were the ultimate driving force.

In the inner circles of the Nazi and SS leadership, Hitler spoke often and matter-of-factly about the mass extermination of the Jews and other "inferiors": "I say only that [the Jew] must go. . . . I see only one way: mass extermination. . . ."

Since the Jews had corrupted the Aryan race, extermination was a completely natural process. Animals could not be blamed if they ate other animals. He, Hitler, saw himself as a Pasteur or a Koch in questions of race. The bacillus of the Jews must simply be killed. In the world-view of the Nazi elite, mass murder of the Jews and other "inferior races" followed with virtual necessity from racial Darwinism.

The Role of the SS

Hitler was only being consistent when he commissioned Heinrich Himmler as Reichsführer of the SS, with orders to carry out the mass murder of Jews and other "inferior races." Hitler was reluctant to issue this as a signed order; he gave it verbally to Himmler himself. Hitler designated Himmler as an "Ignatius Loyola, in a good sense," and Hitler told one-time Nazi Hermann Rauschning (who later fled Germany) that he would let him in on a big secret: he had founded an order. And indeed, the SS must be seen as the continuation of the Thule Society as a state institution. In the tradition of the gnostic knightly orders, the SS was not merely a military and police organization, but rather the principal carrier of the world-view of Hitler and his closest associates. The SS was created by a strict selection process, and was conceived as a "blood brotherhood" for breeding. Among the highest echelons of the SS hierarchy, racial Darwinism, gnosticism, and mysticism predominated, increasing with each rung. The SS elite around Heinrich Himmler can be seen as the continuation of the inner circle of the Thule Society and their racialist-gnostic mysticism. In the SS, Hitler saw the ideological and racial incarnation of this world-view; the SS was to be the cell formation of the Aryan Greater Reich toward which he was striving; the SS was to produce the racial and philosophical elite of "Ario-heroes" and supermen.

This is why Hitler ordered Himmler and the SS to carry out the mass extermination of the Jews and other inferior races. The SS, as the incarnation of racial Darwinism, was entrusted with conducting the "racial war" in Europe all the way to its "final solution." Himmler explained:

I urgently request that no regulations be made concerning the "Jew.". . . The occupied Eastern areas will be Jew-free. The Führer has shouldered me with the execution of this very difficult order. . . . It is therefore not discussable.

Hitler was completely unrestrained in his endless, raging public tirades against the Jews and other "inferior" races. At the same time, he knew that he could *not* put his extermination plans before the German public. His most explicit public statement came a speech on Jan. 30, 1942, in which he said that "the the war can only end when either the Aryans are exterminated or Jewry disappears from Europe." Hitler knew that he must keep the mass exterminations secret from the German people, who would find it unthinkable that Jews and other inferior races could be exterminated in "assembly-line" death camps.

Nazi Ideological Propaganda

Hitler had a finely developed sense of how far he could go, not only on the question of Jewish extermination but generally, with public proclamations of his actual ideas and goals. He knew that it was impossible to confront the population with the full force of his world-view.

Two things played a role here. In accordance with the Nazis' hierarchical mentality, the "need to know" principle was applied. With respect to racial Darwinism, the population was constantly barraged with anti-Semitic propaganda, while they were also subject to the Nuremberg Race Laws, under which marriages were made contingent on certification of Aryan racial purity. The anti-Semitic propaganda was comprehensive and often cleverly done, but it did not have immediate implications for the non-Jewish population. Anti-Semitic activities were carried out by Nazi organizations; the anti-Jewish boycott and the "Kristallnacht" were done by the SA or party members. For the general population, the mysticism of the Nazis was boiled down to symbols such as the swastika, mass marches or "solstice celebrations." Other mystical ceremonies were reserved for the various Nazi organizations. Similarly, the population was only exposed to Nazi anti-religious gnosticism cautiously and in measured doses. This, as we mentioned earlier, was not merely a question of "need to know," but was necessary in order not to shock the population. Even though Germany had been a perfect police state since 1933, the system still depended upon keeping the population calm and passive.

What we have outlined here for the post-1933 period is also true for Hitler in his early period. In 1919 the leaders of the Thule Society had already recognized Hitler's talents as a speaker and political organizer. But Hitler at that point was anything but a lone politician. Hitler utilized the political questions of Germany's chaotic situation immediately after World War I in order to propagandize for racialism and irrationalism. The method he used later remained unchanged.

There exists no speech or written document by Hitler in which he said he acted according to the secret Aryan teachings of Tibet, or that he wanted to destroy Christianity and exterminate the Jews in Europe. Instead he incessantly talked about the "Weimar system," Marxism, the ignominy of Versailles, ending unemployment, the rearmament of Germany, and so forth. But whatever the political theme of his statements was at the time, his racist-mystical world-view would always shine through; this "real" message was always there, sometimes only in vague, dark hints, but other times more explicitly.

Thus, Hitler applied the principle of ideological "need to know"—the careful dosage and clever packaging of his ideological convictions. His world-view is continually evident in connection with political questions. At the same time, he knew how to give the impression that *all* his utterances were ultimately and solely based on his world-view, without ever explicitly saying what that world-view was.

Hitler often said that National Socialism was first and foremost a world-view—and this was not just a passing mood of his. "I have become a politician against my will. For me, politics is merely a means to an end. . . . If there had been somebody else, I would have never gotten into politics. . . ."

Economics, technology, natural sciences, or administration did not interest Hitler in the least. His sole interest was his own of racialist mysticism, along with its corresponding "art." In keeping with this, Hitler continued his bohemian style of living and working through the beginning of the war.

Hitler quickly realized that his almost autistic fixation on his own and the Thule Society's world-view could only work to his advantage. His audiences and supporters did not expect well-considered, elaborated ideas from him. As Hitler himself said, the "mass" to which he turned was "inclined to the feminine," and was only capable of "emotional responses." He went so far as to avoid holding rallies in the morning and afternoon, since the "masses" could only be reached while in a certain state of mental exhaustion, at night.

World War I and the Weimar Republic

This state of mental exhaustion has a more comprehensive significance for the period when Hitler and his leadership group were building the Nazi movement. The German masses whom Hitler and the Nazis were addressing were indeed deeply shaken, uncertain and mentally exhausted.

In spite of a cultural crisis and social tensions, the German population, including the labor movement, had experienced the period before World War I as a time when "the world was still in order." Patriotism prevailed at the outset of the war. Germans entered a war which they expected to end in swift victory. But instead the war lasted for years and degenerated into unbelievable butchery. The Allied food blockade drew the German civilian population directly into the events of the war, to an extent unseen since the Thirty Years' War of the seventeenth century.

Then, with unprecedented speed, the military collapse came in 1918, so fast that the ill-prepared population could literally "not comprehend" it. Overnight, the state monarchical institutions disappeared. In their place came political chaos which was to last for a decade. Shortly thereafter came the next blow, the dictate of Versailles with its monstrous conditions. Europe's map was crumpled up; the three empires of Germany, Austria, and Russia no longer existed, and dozens of new states suddenly sprang up. Along with hyperinflation came the economic ruin of large sectors of the population, and after a certain amount of minimal stability had been achieved during the second half of the 1920s, this too collapsed into nothing with the world economic depression.

Within a dozen years the German population had been subjected to an unbroken chain of blows and collective shocks. For the majority of the population this was "incomprehensible," and could no longer be grasped rationally.

The fact is, that under the conditions of constant

stress, one can observe in both individuals and groups a reduction in rationality. In the group, a kind of "multiplier effect" also comes into play. There is no doubt that during the Weimar period at least, large numbers of Germans were in danger of losing their trust in rationality.

Now it is hardly the case that this worked quickly and directly to the Nazis' advantage. Only under the traumatic conditions of the 1932 world economic crisis were the Nazis able to gain a mass of followers and voters, and even then, at the last free election in November 1932, the Nazis received no more than 34 percent of the vote.

There was, however, a kind of basic intellectual attitude which the Nazis were able to utilize in Weimar Germany. The population's disposition towards a lowering of consciousness was systematically exploited and strengthened by Hitler and the Nazis. Precisely because it was irrational, the Nazi worldview had a chance of striking a responsive chord under the conditions of Weimar Germany. The tendency to doubt rationality enabled the Nazis to win a following not in spite of, but because of, their views. To be sure, the Nazis knew that there was no chance that the full spectrum of racial Darwinism, gnosticism, and esotericism would be accepted, except by a few fringe groups. But in the appropriate dosages and packaging, this world-view could indeed be "sold."

Ultimately, the Nazi world-view is merely a specific form of a pre-cultural mythos. A "leader" who claims to be guided by "providence" fanatically promulgates a world-view of "blood and soil." The "leader" and his "providence" derive from supernatural sources, inaccessible to reason. From out of this supernatural-supersensuous region now comes the message of "blood and soil."

It should be briefly mentioned that "blood and soil" are the predicates of the "Magna Mater" mythos, which has been around since the prehistory of human culture. More precisely, this myth always emerges when a culture undergoes a fundamental crisis. In periods when intellectual and religious values collapse, accompanied by economic slumps and depressions, the "Magna Mater" emerges with great regularity.

To be sure, the Nazis did not propound an explicit "Magna Mater" cult like the cults of Astarte, Cybele, Isis, Madonna Maria, etc. But the Nazis did have a "Magna Mater" world-view: "blood and soil." "Blood" was symbolically associated with death, birth and feminine sexuality, while "soil" symbolized "Mother Earth," the "earth goddess," and so forth.

These references should make it sufficiently clear that the Nazi world-view, as it is summed up in the slogan "blood and soil," was *one* causal element in the rise of the Nazi movement. In times of crisis, this ideology enabled the Nazis to exploit latent despair in rationality and to massively strengthen this emotion. The Nazi world-view was therefore no add-on, but was rather the Nazi movement's vital attracting and motivating force.

The cult of irrationality will forever remain the primary distinguishing characteristic of every fascist movement, regardless of which predicates it might otherwise employ.

Bibliography

Angebert, Jean Michel, *The Occult and the Third Reich,* New York, 1974.

Baignet, Michael; Leigh, Richard; and Lincoln, Henry, *Holy Blood, Holy Grail,* New York, 1982.

Daim, Wilfried, *Der Mann, der Hitler die Ideen gab,* Munich, 1958.

Doucet, Friedrich W., *Im Banne des Mythos,* Esslingen, 1979.

Haushofer, Karl, *Der Kontinentalblock,* Munich, 1941.

Heiber, Helmut, *Reichsführer—Briefe an und von Himmler,* Munich, 1970.

Hitler, Adolf, *Adolf Hitler—Monologe 1941–1944. Die Aufzeichnungen Heinrich Heims,* Munich, 1982.

Kohn, Hans, *Prophets and Peoples, Studies in 19th Century Nationalism,* New York, 1946.

Maser, Werner, *Der Sturm auf die Republik,* Frankfurt/Berlin, 1981.

Pool, J. S., *Who Financed Hitler?,* New York, 1978.

Semyonov, Julian, *Die Alternative,* Berlin (DDR), 1978.

White, Carol, *The New Dark Ages Conspiracy,* New York, 1980.

Zepp-LaRouche, Helga, "Die historischen Wurzeln des grünen Faschismus," in *Stoppt die grüne Gefahr,* Wiesbaden, 1982.

3

The 1930-45 Collaboration Between Switzerland and the Nazis

When SS Obergruppenführer Walter Schellenberg, who in 1939–44 was the deputy chief and then chief of the foreign department of the Sicherheitsdienst (SD) secret security service, betook himself to his superior, SS Reichsführer Heinrich Himmler, to ask him to obstruct "the wish expressed over and over again by Hitler for a preventive occupation of Switzerland," he found a receptive hearing. The SS leadership was determined to leave Switzerland in its status as a financial pivot. Far too much was at stake for the SS and the Allgemeine SS. Switzerland was the channel between leading bankers and aristocrats and the top of the Nazi regime. In his memoirs, Schellenberg recalled his "efforts to enter into negotiations with the chief of the Swiss secret service at that time, Col. Roger Masson, and the chief of staff of the armed forces, Gen. Henri Guisan." He wrote further: "It was clear to me that this was the only way to protect the country's neutrality. . . . After I had secured the necessary contacts to Masson and

Guisan, I proposed that Himmler use his influence in the Führer's headquarters to block the plans for a military invasion of Switzerland. Himmler assured me, however, in unmistakeable fashion, that my head would roll if the other side failed to maintain its neutrality."

Since Schellenberg died a natural death—he lived out his last months in Switzerland, for that matter—one can assume that the Swiss held to Hitler's and Himmler's demands. There exists in fact adequate proof that the Swiss fully and completely fulfilled the Nazis' expectations. According to Schellenberg: "In my efforts to keep Switzerland out of the war, I received the help of the Reich's Economics Minister, Walther Funk, who was able to convincingly set before the senior military command the reasons why Switzerland should remain our financial lever." With Walter Funk's intervention, a new dimension was achieved in the military and secret-intelligence relations between Switzerland and the Nazi apparatus: the appearance of one of the most powerful men inside the Nazi war machine leads us to the realm of international high finance, for which Switzerland is indeed the recognized channel.

Let us look back to the period of the First World War and examine the founding of the Swiss Gesellschaft für Metallwerte, a front group for the Deutsche Metallgesellschaft. This company was not only a multinational raw-materials entity, but also served as a lever for a giant international intelligence and espionage network, built up by the Frankfurt financier Richard Merton together with the chief of the Third Reich's general staff, General Gröner, and General von Schleicher, who reorganized the Abwehr military intelligence service in 1918. To facilitate this operation, Merton turned to the scion of one of the oldest patrician families of Basel, Felix Iselin, whose family tree in Basel can be traced back to the year 1346 A.D. Iselin & Cie. was (and is) one of the most powerful private banks in Switzerland, which has dominant holdings in the giant Swiss Bankverein, the La Baloise insurance group and the pharmaceuticals multinational Hoffman-LaRoche. It also plays a key role in the Church Council of the Evangelical-Reformed Church and the "charitable" trust, the Gesellschaft für das Gute und das Gemeinnützige. In short, the Imperial General Staff and the most senior Swiss patricians were setting up a major joint intelligence venture.

In 1929, shortly before the explosion of the financial crisis, whose origins were in the insane Versailles Treaty's German Reparations clauses, and whose ultimate result was the Second World War, F. Iselin became the deputy head of another, similar venture: the I.G. Farben chemical giant—formed in 1925 at the behest of Germany's financial dictator, Hjalmar Schacht, head of the Reichsbank and the Allied Reparations Commission Commander-in-Chief in Germany—was setting up a Swiss front, the I.G. Chemie, a holding corporation for all assets of the immense international empire of the future manufacturer of the Zyklon B gas, of concentration camp fame.

The co-chairman of I.G. Farben, Hermann Schmitz, the burly fifty-year-old who presided over the company's fate until 1945, had deputized his own nephew, Hamburg's Max Ilgner, a board member of I.G. Farben too, to develop the company's gigantic international espionage and intelligence apparatus, the NW7, which was closely allied, even before Hitler's seizure of power, with the

NSDAP/AO, the "Foreign Organization," which performed parallel functions. The Swiss front was designed to centralize international operations from neutral territory, thus acquiring precious immunity from any investigative intruders. By 1939, F. Iselin had become the chairman of I.G. Chemie, which he remained until retirement in 1958, yielding only then to the super-star of Swiss banking, Union Bank of Switzerland chairman Dr. Alfred Schaefer—a name that will appear again in this tale of Switzerland and Nazism.

I.G. Farben was one of the industrial-financial linchpins of the Swiss-Nazi apparatus. Schmitz himself, for one, was a board member of the Bank for International Settlements (BIS), the central bank of the central banks, also located in Basel, the powerful institution that had been created in 1930 to oversee the financial collapse of Europe and its reorganization in a "new order."

The Treaty of Versailles had prescribed that the vanquished Germany, made into the war's sole culprit, should pay billions of gold marks in "war reparations" to the victors. The motto of the victors was "squeeze [the Germans] until the pips squeak," which had even the cynical aesthete J.M. Keynes write in disagreement that the agreement would test "the reactions of a people of the White Race under conditions of slavery." Among the artisans of the agreement, on the German side, was Hjalmar Schacht, who was later, in 1923, imposed by the Reparations Commission as head of the Reichsbank, with powers that induced a majority of the Reichstag parties to protest "the dictatorial powers and policy of the Reichsbank under Dr. Schacht." At the Versailles conference itself, lifelong friendships were established between Schacht and two brothers from New England, John Foster Dulles, who acted as a proxy for Bernard Baruch in the Reparations Committee of the Conference, and Allen Dulles, himself on the Boundary Commission that gave the Sudetenland to the newborn "Czechoslovakia."

The Banking Collapse

The 1920s staggered from one financial crisis to the other, with the reparations at the center. The House of Morgan-dominated Reparations Commission, which virtually dictated Germany's monetary policy, issued in succession the "Dawes Plan" and the "Young Plan," aimed at making an "orderly" process of the looting of the German economy. History relates that the Wall Street Crash of 1929 and first the Austrian, then the German banking crises of 1931 destroyed the system as a whole. But in 1930, the same group of international financiers had established the BIS, as "the foster child of the Versailles Treaty," wrote Eleanor Dulles, sister of the aforementioned John Foster and Allen, who added that "Dr. Schacht was in a sense the originator of the plan." It was a supranational institution of central bankers who were independent of their respective governments, or of any elected body, to run world finances. Inevitably, the seat of the bank was established in Basel.

The BIS, nominally set up after the breakdown of "normal" international financial relations in order to prevent a downward spiraling of international payments, and ensure the feasibility of German reparations payments, in fact finished off the hapless Weimar Republic by its stern refusal to come to the help of a virtually bankrupt Germany in the crucial summer of 1931, after the Danat-

Bank collapse had brought the whole nation to its knees. Schacht, who had been a member of the original BIS team and was to return to its board from 1933 through 1938, had been campaigning since his 1930 resignation as head of the Reichsbank, for Anglo-American support for a takeover by the NSDAP and its leader, Herr Hitler. He had resigned on March 7, 1930 and the BIS was formally established in June. In September, Schacht was off to London and the United States, to "sell" the Nazi option to the Anglo-American leadership, notably Bank of England Governor and BIS director Montagu Norman, and the already influential Dulles brothers, of the Sullivan & Cromwell law firm, one of America's most influential—and the attorneys for I.G. Farben, and many other large German companies and provincial governments. Schacht's Hamburg friend and colleague, patrician Nazi Gerhardt Westrick, ran the correspondent law firm to the Dulles's in Germany. By December, Schacht—who by then acted with the full support of the BIS establishment—was dining with Goering, Goebbels, Fritz Thyssen, and Hitler himself, and urging "Hungerkanzler" Brüning, a friend of the Dulleses, to "let the Nazis in." For them, he and Wilhelm Keppler were organizing the so-called Keppler Circle of top bankers and industry tycoons—which included Baron Kurt von Schröder of the J.H. Stein Bank of Cologne, a business partner of the Dulleses.

When destiny knocked at the door in the form of the bank crisis, the BIS decided to let Germany remain without external financial help. One of the bank's directors said, "The Germans need Dr. Schacht there," and the crisis should be allowed to wreck Germany first before Schacht could come in as a savior in time of need. The Danat-Bank panic itself was immediately caused by a Swiss newspaper, the *Baseler Nationalzeitung,* which on July 7, 1931, wrote under the big headline "Troubles of a Major German Bank," that "representatives of major German banks in Switzerland expressly demanded of the newspaper that it publish the name of the Danat-Bank in the next morning's edition." On July 9, Reichsbank president Luther, in desperation, rushed to Basel to get help—to no avail. On July 13, the BIS board decided to do nothing to help Germany. The way to World War II was open, and the BIS had chosen—at Schacht's behest—Hitler and the Nazis as the pathfinders.

The BIS bankers wanted "an [international financial and monetary] scheme of which the controls and the funds are truly international" according to Montagu Norman. A new order was required. Nation-states were a hindrance. Schacht's seed-crystal idea, that of the BIS, had been gradually elaborated in the 1920s debates of the "Central European Economic Union," the Pan-Europa Union of Count Richard Coudenhove-Kalergi, of which Schacht, I.G. Farben's Carl Duisberg, and Carl Bosch were prominent members. Their geopolitical conception of "The Idea of Economic Space" was highly coherent with that of the left radical-revolutionary wing of the Nazi party, that of the Strasser brothers. Otto Strasser took shelter in Zürich from 1931 through 1936 after he split from Hitler. The Strasser program called for a decentralized Federalist Europe unified by a customs union of Germany, Switzerland, Austria, Hungary, Denmark, Holland, and Luxembourg.

The financiers' deliberate death sentence against the Weimar Republic lifted Hitler to power. By

November 1932, it was Kurt von Schröder who mediated Franz von Papen's willing surrender to Hitler. On Jan. 4, 1933, the threesome met at Schröder's Cologne villa to seal the pact. On Jan. 30, 1933, Hitler was Reichskanzler. On Mar. 16, 1933, BIS agent Hjalmar Schacht returned in triumph to his Reichsbank. In 1934, Hitler had called upon Schacht to take over the economics ministry. Now, the BIS was going to help the Third Reich—by 1939, it had no less than several hundred million Swiss gold francs invested in Germany. On the BIS board of directors were Baron Kurt von Schröder, by now a general in the SS Death's Head Brigade; Dr. Hermann Schmitz, of I.G. Farben—whom Schacht had trained at the imperial economics ministry from 1915 on—and later, Hitler's two personal appointees, Walter Funk and Emil Puhl, of the Reichsbank. Schmitz also happened to be very close to the fast-rising whiz-kid of Nazi intelligence, Walter Schellenberg. In the words of British historian Charles Higham, "the BIS was to be a money funnel for . . . funds to flow into Hitler's coffers and to help Hitler build his war machine. The BIS was completely under Hitler's control by the outbreak of World War II."

Switzerland indeed was, through the Swiss National Bank, which shared directors and staff with BIS, the "financial pivot" Schellenberg was to refer to later. Now, Hermann Schmitz's I.G. Farben intelligence, NW7, was coordinated under Walter Schellenberg's Amt VI of the SS Security Service, the SD, and worked very closely with the Foreign Organization of the NSDAP, whose head was SS leader Ernst Bohle. Should a military occupation of Switzerland have been implemented, Bohle was slated to become the Nazi Gauleiter of—Switzerland! Schmitz's own appreciation of Schellenberg was such that, in plans developed later in the war for a putsch aimed at replacing Hitler by a monarchist regency, Schmitz intended to include him in the "Council of 12" that would administer the regency.

The German side of the Swiss-Nazi deal was complete. It is time we looked at the other side of the border, into Swiss fascism in its two elements, the fascist movements proper, the Fronts, and the archfascist Swiss oligarchy of financiers.

Adolf Hitler was no unknown quantity to Swiss oligarchs and their fascist operatives. In March 1921, A National League for the Independence of Switzerland (VUS) had been established by General Wille, a high-ranking Army official, the war-time Commander-in-Chief Theophil von Sprecher and others. The secretary of the VUS, Dr. Hektor Amman, archivist of the Aargau canton, had met Adolf Hitler in 1920 in Munich and led long discussions, "until late at night" with him. Amman had also made the acquaintance of the hysterical anti-Semite Julius Streicher, editor of *Der Stürmer*, and, reportedly, through such channels, "had exerted some inflence in the shaping of the Nazi Party's program."

In 1923, German Ambassador Müller reported to the Auswärtiges Amt (Foreign Office), "the anti-Semitic leader Adolf Hitler went to Zürich at the end of August (and later to Bern too) and took up contact with the leaders of the [right-wing paramilitary] Kreuzwehr as well as pan-Germanist circles. The publisher of the *Schweizericher Monatshefte für Politik und Kultur*, journal of the VUS, Dr. Hans Oehler, paid a visit to Hitler at the Gotthard Hotel, supposedly for mere journalistic reasons." In fact, a dozen-odd persons paid a visit to Hitler, who was later wined and dined at Villa Wiesendonck by Dr. Fritz Rieter, with forty persons in attendance, who listened to Hitler's presentation of the NSDAP program and supplied him with funds. The extreme right-wing "Swiss establishment" league, the Schweizerische Vaterländische Verband (Swiss Patriotic Union) chairman, Dr. Emil Soinderegger, asked to see Hitler in person. Before that, Hitler's fundraising envoy, Dr. Emil Gansser, had also visited SVV founder, Col. Eugen Bircher. In the 1920s, Hitler more than once traveled to Switzerland and back with a false-bottomed trunk. On the return trip to Munich, the false bottom was filled—with American dollars, British pounds, and Swiss francs. Freikorps founder and SA leader Ernst Röhm maintained extensive Swiss contact networks for illegal gun-running to Germany in the 1920s.

Native Swiss Fascism

In the spring of 1933, a blossoming of fascist and Nazi organizations swept the streets of Switzerland. The "Springtime of the Fronts" brought thousands into the streets of the big cities. A newly created Nazi party swept elections in the border town of Schaffhausen with 30 percent of the popular vote. Ultimately, there were to be up to 60,000 Swiss Nazis during World War II. Four thousand Swiss citizens joined the Waffen SS, which was part of the Germany military. Switzerland, A.G., was merging some of its subsidiaries with the Third Reich. The chief of the NSDAP/AO, Ernst Bohle, and his subordinate, SS officer Dr. Klaus Huegel, who ran operations in Switzerland from his Alemanic Workers Circle in Stuttgart, had a maze of pro-Nazi organizations throughout Switzerland at his beck and call, notably through his German-Swiss Movement. One Dr. Franz Riedweg, a Swiss citizen from Lucerne, became in 1934 an adviser to Hitler personally, and was a member of the Secretariat of the Swiss Action Against Communism of the ex-president of the Swiss Confederation, Jean-Marie Musy, who had turned pro-Nazi outright.

Unlike Austria, no Anschluss was necessary; unlike Poland, no invasion was called for. Switzerland *was* the Nazi Reich—with a different regime. The contents, rather than the letter, of "Action Plan Switzerland," were fulfilled: Switzerland was going to be the workshop of the Axis powers, and, in keeping with the Himmler-Schellenberg demands, there would be freedom of action for the local Nazis, and freedom of action to develop, as the head of the SD demanded, contacts with the Special Assistant at the U.S. Legation in Berne, Allen Dulles.

For such a situation to have developed, which made a direct Anschluss counterproductive, the job done by the Swiss Nazis had to have been of consequence. It was.

Nazi organizations in Switzerland, were the baker's dozen: Kreuzwehr, Eidgenossiche Froht, Kampfbund Neue und Nationale Front, National-Sozialistische Eidgenossen, Neue Schweiz, Ordre et Tradition, Union Nationale, Schweizerische Heimatwehr, Schweizerische Fascismus, Volksbund, Volksfront, this myriad of organizations being broadly decentralized at the grassroots, in faithful Swiss cantonal-federalist tradition, while being closely unified at the top, also in tradition. Their war-cry, the old Swiss Confederates' "Haaruss" (Get Out!) was not to be aimed equally in all directions.

In French-speaking Switzerland, Swiss fascism was mainly represented by Georges Oltramare's

National Political Order (OPN) and its successor organization, the National Union, and the Swiss Fascist Federation of retired Col. Arthur Fonjallaz. Oltramare, who rose to prominence in Geneva during the 1920s, was the scion of an old Ligurian family that had come from Genoa to Geneva around 1550, and enjoyed a prominent position on the patrician city's rostrum. The weekly he founded in 1923, *Le Pilori,* quickly sold 20,000 copies per issue, and became the success story of weekly anti-Semitism. Oltramare was the mouthpiece for a small intellectual elite of French-speaking Swiss who, under the leadership of Gonzague de Reynold, had adopted a Pan-European outlook based on the traditional "Four Antis," anti-Semitism, anti-capitalism, anti-Marxism and anti-liberalism. Their "Federalist Circle" had been created in 1924 "to combat the error of democracy," and, as de Reynold put it in his *Doctrinal Theses,* to combat "the [democratic] ideas about freedom, the individual, science and mind," which had to be subordinated, in his words, to "knowledge of the natural and supernatural world."

This Pan-European fascism, which worked in organic connection with Coudenhove-Kalergi and the Catholic, South-German and Austrian advocates of Hapsburg restoration and Clerical Black Fascism as implemented by Austrian Chancellor Dollfuss, produced, within the narrower confines of French-speaking Switzerland, a genuine fascist mass movement. In 1924, Theodore Aubert, scion of a major Geneva banking family, founded the Entente Internationale Anti-Communiste (EIA), which worked in close connection with the Nazi Weltdienst (World Service) of Col. Ulrich Fleischauer, a Goebbels-supervised operation also supported by Ribbentrop, and with Mussolini's international intelligence operations. For the more inside-the-border operation, it was Georges Oltramare who reigned (the two operations were ultimately merged in 1932). When he ran in the cantonal elections in Geneva in 1930, Oltramare scored an upset near-win, which allowed his National Political Order to become a major political factor.

Theodore Aubert wrote a letter to the NSDAP Foreign Policy Office in 1934, proposing to "create an anti-Marxist intelligence service," a very valuable point for the historian which shows that Swiss Nazi-fascism had at least as much of an intelligence function as a "political" one. The "successes" or failures of the Fronts cannot therefore be gauged from the sole standpoint of electoral gains or mass audiences, but also, and primarily, from this secret intelligence standpoint. Aubert and the EIA worked closely with the United Alliance of German Anti-Communist Associations of Dr. Adolf Ehrt, known as the "Anticomintern." Ehrt, an Evangelical Church official, was in fact running a covert operation of Joseph Goebbels' Ministry of Propaganda. In January 1934, Ehrt was in Geneva with Aubert for the conference of the Pro Deo Commission, an outfit created in 1933 to run Nazi intelligence operations through religious networks, with the immediate objective being running relief operations for Russian Christians and organizing the fight against the godless.

In September 1932, Oltramare was in Munich to meet leaders of the NSDAP. In October 1933, Joseph Goebbels, in Geneva for a visit at the Völkerbund, held a secret dinner with Oltramare and the German consul, to set up conditions for funding the National Union, which Theodore Aubert had warmly recommended to his German Nazi friends.

In 1934, Mussolini's Committee of Action for the Universality of Rome, led by Gen. Eugenio Coselchi, and advised by Gonzague de Reynold, held a major international conference in Montreux, on Lake Geneva, which was to ratify the notion of universal fascism, a fascism not bound by any national constraints, but in line with de Rougemont's imperial criteria. Alongside Georges Oltramare, in attendance to represent Swiss fascism, was Colonel Fonjallaz. Oltramare also tied up with Christian-fascist leader Leon Degrelle, of the Rex organization of Belgium. In February 1936, Mussolini invited Oltramare to Rome and received him most cordially, bringing him to a session of the Gran Consilio Fascista. This was to be the first of eleven (recorded) personal meetings from 1936 through 1940. Said Mussolini, in a message to Italian officials at the League of Nations: "Our comrade Oltramare leads a difficult fight in Switzerland. He must be able to reckon with the sympathy and moral support of Fascism. When he has something to communicate [to me], I am adamant that no obstacle be made."

In 1937, Oltramare proposed to Mussolini to establish a "counter-League of Nations," also in Geneva, under the name of "Alliance des Patries" (Alliance of the Fatherlands) with Italy, Germany, Hungary, Bulgaria, Spain, Portugal, Brazil, Venezuela, and Japan. Who was going to be the secretary general of this organization . . . ? Gonzague de Reynold, Mussolini's mentor! By then, Mussolini had bemedaled Oltramare and made him an officer in the Very Venerable Order of Saint Maurice and

Saint Lazarus. Returning the compliment, as it were, the University of Lausanne, on the proposal of its School of social and political science—the old abode of Swiss fascist ideologue and Mussolini inspirer Wilfredo Pareto—had made Benito Mussolini a Doctor Honoris Causa with the comment: "This school . . . has devoted attention to the enterprise of social renovation thanks to which you have . . . given back to the Italian people the vital sentiment of its spiritual, economic and social cohesiveness."

The Pan-Europeans

There was, of course, some differentiation between the "Mediterranean Catholic" brand of fascism, and the "Northern Protestant" Nazi movement. Tensions ebbed and flowed between the two, with the Pan-European movement trying to carve its own empire in between. This reflected itself, predictably, in Oltramare's movement, where the "Pan-European" wing and the outright pro-Nazi wing went through several phases of polemics, until all divergences melted away, as early as 1936: "The genuine menace against European peace has not arisen from the fact that German soldiers took the right of keeping the guard on Germany's border," the National Union stated after Hitler's remilitarization of the Rhineland. And Oltramare himself: "We know that Germany has a large appetite and that we must be vigilant, but we also know that ten or twenty years of German hegemony—Empires collapse quite fast—would be less fatal to mankind than the hegemony of the bankers from the synagogues has been." And when Austria was subjected to the Anschluss on Oct. 8, 1938: "Either we shall participate in the New Order, or the New Order will trample us underfoot."

Pan-Europa had finally tied up with *Mitteleuropa*. All were agreed that nation-states would be broken up into small ethnic-religious, perhaps tribal, entities, or satrapies, based on the Hapsburg Empire model. Coudenhove's (and de Rougemont's, and de Gonzague's) doctrine, which violently opposed industrialization out of devotion to Mother Earth, opposed science for the sake of the primacy of irrational emotions, opposed to "artificial" urban life the love for the "natural" pastoral life. The industrialists so-called and financiers involved in this, such as Schacht, von Schröder, Carl Duisberg of I.G. Farben, etc., fully shared in that conception. De Rougemont himself had spent the late 1920s and the 1930s in Paris as a propagandist and educator for such Pan-European "non-conformist revolution," very close to today's "Conservative Revolution" of former SS volunteer, Swiss citizen Armin Mohler. De Rougemont worked with Third Rome herald Nikolai Berdiaev, and thus defined the historical mission at hand: "The Royal [French] State, the future nation-state, defines itself expressly with respect to the Holy Roman Empire and against it, as one part opposes itself to the whole, and claims self-sufficiency. The state opposes itself to the Empire in its very form. The Empire is spherical and global, and its ruler holds a symbolic globe in his left-hand. State and Empire are no less opposed in terms of the type of human relations they imply and enhance. . . ."

Nation-states were evil and ephemeral, de Rougemont argued. An "apocalypse" would come in the form of the universal catastrophe which would cause the fall of Babylon—the United States especially, the citadel of industrialism and the republican nation-state. What was to be wiped out was "the European virus," as he wrote as recently as 1974 in his book *The Future Is in Our Hands,* "Europe as a colonizer spread throughout the world the formula of the nation-state, the belief in 2,500 calories a day for all and the morbid desire to have nuclear power plants."

De Rougemont's most explicit comment to the Hitler question was an outrageously frank confession: "I have heard Hitler pronounce one of his great speeches. Where do the superhuman powers he shows on such occasions come from? It is quite obvious that a force of his kind does not belong to the individual, and indeed could not even manifest itself unless the individual were of no importance except as the vehicle for a force for which our psychology has no explanation . . . what has been accomplished by this man—or rather through the forces working through him—is a reality that is one of the wonders of the century."

Swiss 'Neutrality'

In the wake of the 1938 Kristallnacht which saw new levels of barbaric anti-Semitic pogrom rage in the Reich, the Swiss government signed with the Gestapo and the Foreign Office an agreement whereby passports of German and Austrian Jews would be marked with a "J" letter which allowed Swiss border forces to prevent the latter from escaping! Federal Council member Motta, the former president of Switzerland, told the German Ambassador that "he did by no means wants to criticize the treatment of the Jews in Germany. . . ." In fact, the Swiss-German "J" ensured that most countries in the world would refuse to let the persecuted emigrants come in at all! Official Swiss complicity with Nazi anti-Semitism was total. In the words of

Swiss historial Daniel Bourgeois, today the Keeper of the National Archives in Berne, "the pitiless attitude of the Swiss government in the question of Jewish refugees" was based on the fact that "the presence of Jews in Switzerland was not liked at all," and "various foreign policy considerations" had "played a role in the attitude of the Federal authorities towards the Jewish refugees."

The SS and SD (Sicherheitsdienst) apparatus working on Swiss affairs, which played no little role in these events, was based in Stuttgart, with a string of interrelated institutions: the SD Leitabschnitt Stuttgart Amt VI, led first by SS Hauptstürmführer Ernst Peter and later by SS Unterstürmführer Klaus Huegel, working under NSDAP/AO chief Gauleiter Bohle, Amt VI chiefs SS Brigade Leader Heinz Jost and his successor Walter Schellenberg. In 1939, it spawned a new outfit, the Alemanic Workers Circle, which handled Nazi agitprop in Switzerland, intelligence operations and subversion, in liaison with the Foreign Division of the Propaganda Ministry. The SD's job in foreign countries, in particular, was "the preparation and pursuit of operations that the Reich's diplomatic representations abroad cannot order nor execute nor assume responsibility for."

The Embassy's staff in Berne was augmented with Councillor of Legation Hans Sigismund Baron van Bibra, who functioned as the SD liaison. At the Zürich General Consulate, there was Hans Georg Ashton, who coordinated with the Nazi Foreign Organization (AO), while an envoy of the Party Division of the Wilhelmstrasse—he was an old SD agent. Switzerland also had its own NSDAP, with Wilhelm Gustloff as State Group Leader, who kept close contacts with the National Front and the other

Swiss Nazi organizations. General coordination was in the hands of the SD Amt VI, and, also in Stuttgart, the National League for German Identity Abroad, whose chairman was Prof. Dr. General Karl Haushofer, the founder of modern geopolitics and Rudolf Hess's mentor. The Stuttgart-based organization, German Foreign Institute, also played a role for the "Volksdeutsche"—ethnic German— Swiss.

From 1934 through 1936, the Reich's Ambassador in Berne had been the influential Ernst von Weizsäcker, later to become the head of the political section of the Wilhelmstrasse foreign ministry under Ribbentrop. His links with Swiss Nazis had been if anything strengthened when his son, nuclear physicist Carl-Friedrich von Weizsäcker, today a leader of the nuclear freeze movement, after having led Hitler's team to try and build a nuclear bomb, married Gundalona Wille, daughter of the Nazis' chief asset in the Swiss military, Corps Commander Col. Ulrich Wille. His successor Köcher went out of his way to support the native Swiss Nazis.

In 1936, Nazi chieftain Gustloff was assassinated. The Federal Council, as a result of the anti-Nazi outcry that backed an acquittal of the murderer, banned the NSDAP State Group Command and the Local Commands of the Party, but "the toleration of the AO locals in Switzerland, even without their central leadership, still was a privilege," a historian recounts. "It must be said in addition that the ban on the party's official central direction was a lesser evil. It did not significantly hinder the activities of the AO in Switzerland. Köcher said that it hit the party's prestige in Switzerland, but did not hamper its work." In fact, Embassy Councillor von Bibra took over the job, without the external trappings. When the murderer was tried, Federal Council member Motta officially approached the Reich's government to "express the [Swiss] government's regrets to the Reich for the attitude of the defendant's attorney" and explain that he had tried to "intervene to orient the trial in a pro-Reich way"!

Pursuing the track of Swiss appeasement and incipient collaboration with the Third Reich, parliamentarian Edmund Schulthess, a scion of a wealthy and powerful patrician family, got his friend Hjalmar Schacht to facilitate an interview with Chancellor Adolf Hitler, which took place in February 1937. The upshot of the very friendly conversation was a communiqué authorized by the Führer and issued by Schulthess, where Hitler stated that "at all times and whatever may happen, we shall respect the integrity and neutrality of Switzerland."

Another crucial liaison with the Nazi establishment was Basel patrician Carl J. Burckhardt, chairman of the International Red Cross whom "Hitler received on Aug. 11, 1939 in the Obersalzberg to discuss the Danzig question." At the occasion, narrates historian D. Bourgeois, Hitler "reiterated his pledge to respect Swiss neutrality: "Switzerland runs no risk, since it protects my left flank. I shall respect its neutrality. . . ." Switzerland, grateful once more, pulled out of the League of Nations system of "collective security."

Quasi-official historian Bourgeois analyzes thus the 1940 situation: "It is in the military area that the German failure is the clearest. . . . The pro-German elements in the military only had second-rank positions. Corps Commander Colonel Wille did not manage to be appointed General [in chief] and at the end of 1939, the chief of the General Staff, Corps Commander Colonel Labhart and the chief of the Operations section Rudolf D'Erlach, were pushed out of the general staff by the Commander in Chief, Gen. Henri Guisan." Guisan even took informal and secret contacts with the French General Staff to coordinate a French intervention in case of a Wehrmacht invasion of the Confederation. This "resistant" attitude, however, must be put in perspective: "It so happened that Hitler had no intention to attack Switzerland." The reasons for that "happenstance" are increasingly clear! In fact, Weizsäcker had told Ulrich Wille during summer 1940 that "if he learned that Hitler was manifestly committed to invading Switzerland, he would warn him of this. He did not have to do that."

On Sept. 4, 1940, Ambassador Köcher visited Swiss President Pilet-Golaz after the British Royal Air Force had multiplied overflights over Swiss air space, to vehement Swiss protest. Neutrality carries obligations. Pilet, reported Köcher, had "extraordinarily harsh words toward the British." Further: "Toward the end of the interview, Pilet stressed Switzerland's spontaneous desire to collaborate with Germany. . . . Switzerland was on the path of Renewal and wanted to align with the New European order. She wanted, for her part, to provide a contribution in the economic field and accepted that Swiss industry receive tasks useful within the framework of European collaboration. . . . The president of the Confederation spoke in great praise of . . . the social achievements of National Socialism. I drew from the interview the impression that the Swiss government is prepared, to a large extent, to collaborate with us not only in the economic field but also in the political field."

Collaboration with the Third Reich

Swiss leaders lent themselves to much of Berlin's scabrous diplomatic maneuvering during the war. In June 1940, International Red Cross chairman Carl J. Burkhardt, of the prominent Basel patrician family, transmitted to London some "German approaches." In 1941, London was abuzz with "peace feelers" supposedly sent from Germany through Switzerland, with Burkhardt once more in the middle of the game. The president of the Swiss confederation, Marcel Pilet-Golaz, was also deeply involved.

Switzerland's constitutional system calls for half a dozen Federal Council members (Bundesrat) to rotate the post of President. Pilet-Golaz had been in charge of the Posts and Railways Department from 1930 to 1940, and then became head (Minister) of the Political Department, which he remained until 1944. In the words of the so-called *Bonjour-Bericht*, the official Swiss government report concerning Switzerland's "neutrality during the war," published in 1970 by Prof. Edgar Bonjour (from which much of the foregoing is excerpted), "these combinations led to place Pilet under the suspicion that he had put himself in the service of the German Peace offensive. On Nov. 5, 1941, he was reported to have told the French Ambassador, who immediately reported to Vichy, that Germany would use the lull in the fighting with Russia to set up an organized European order . . . the interpretation given to such imprudent statements of such broad scope, was that Pilet wanted to encourage France to join a European Community, and wanted to initiate a mediation between London and Berlin . . . there were indeed Swiss political leaders who mained hopeful that there would be a conciliation between England and Germany . . . former Federal Council member Schulthess [from another leading family—ed.] thought it possible to tackle the peace question in talks with the German envoy. . . ." Schulthess himself had led the Confederate National Economic Department from 1912 through 1935, and had been president in 1933.

The argument of Pilet-Golaz was very cogent, within the Imperial framework we outlined above: "A complete victory of the Allies would threaten the independence of the small nations no less than a total triumph of the Axis powers, for the Allies would not fail to exert their economic hegemony over Western Europe. France too has an interest that Germany does not dominate the continent, but remains however strong enough to protect her from both the economic imperialism of the Anglo-Saxons and the penetration of Russian Communism. But alone a compromise peace would give Germany the possibility of exerting this beneficial function for Europe. . . . In England too [continued Pilet] part of the Conservatives, who were worried at the strength of Bolshevism and the economic might of the United States, would be attentive to peace offers." That was "Pilet's pacifist campaign."

The campaign reached an extraordinary level on Sept. 23, 1940, with the "Wülflingen Conference." The Nazi Alemanic Workers Circle convened a conference there with the National League for the Independence of Switzerland, the VUS, "at the initiative of various Swiss circles, from the military, the press and industry," Jost wrote in a report. Contacts had started much earlier, in November 1939, when the SS officer Hegel and a few collaborators had been received in Zürich by Colonel

Hasler, an important Swiss military official. A second meeting had taken place in December in Lausanne, and a third in January 1940—which the Swiss government, in internal documents, construed as "mere exchanges of views."

By 1943, Pilet had become so bold as to openly advocate "to let the Russians finish the war on their own," in other words, to let the Nazis off the hook of the Second Front. "The diplomats of the Allied countries apparently discussed with each other the question of the action reportedly conducted by Pilet in order to drive a wedge in the bloc of the Allies and the Russians . . . careless as he often was . . . [with] a facile tongue," the Report has to admit. So outrageous, and public, was Pilet's activity on behalf of the Nazis that one Swiss parliamentarian filed a question to the Federal Council asserting that "there are even diplomats who say that Mr. Pilet's efforts aim at having the Allies help the Germans beat the Russians. . . ." According to the then-British trade attaché in Berne, Sir John Lomax, "Pilet-Golaz was pro-German and pro-Vichy . . . that coterie of a half a dozen chaps—they took advantage and kept the Swiss public in ignorance of what was going on. . . . The Swiss made the most unnatural arrangements [with the Nazis]. The Swiss should not have accepted the pressure—and kept the balance equal. . . . We should have blockaded them. The officials wanted Hitler to win the war. They thought he would win. By 1942–43, they became easier to deal with."

To say that the Swiss did not keep the balance equal is a vast diplomatic understatement. As the facts released by Bonjour alone testify—and this is an official Swiss government report, not one to be trusted overly for its impartiality and ability to face unpleasant truths—Switzerland, throughout the war, worked as the high-technology military factory for the Nazi war machine.

On Sept. 4, 1939, a German trade delegation arrived in Switzerland to negotiate economic exchanges between the two countries. On Sept. 8, Switzerland called off its regulation that banned the export of arms and ammunition. At the beginning of the negotiation, Germany had an 80 million Swiss francs deficit (debt) on the trade account of the clearing system (there was no convertibility as a result of the depression). The Nazi delegation demanded that Switzerland fund the clearing, as an advance to the Reich, in order to settle claims of Swiss exporters. Which is indeed what happened—Switzerland was opening credits for the Reich to buy weapons from her. The Caisse des Prêts of the Confederation funded the German clearing. In the negotiations, "the Swiss delegation untiringly tried to find, in the question of war materials, a solution coming closer to the German thesis." One could hardly be clearer! Further, "to relax the atmosphere, Switzerland temporarily suspended the issuance of permits needed to export to the Western powers." Pilet-Golaz, inescapably, added his two bits: "Germany can now set to us draconian conditions. It will not be a military invasion, but they have the noose around our necks. They can tighten it even more and take what we need for a living. We must seek practical solutions."

On Aug. 9, 1940, an agreement was signed in Berlin which settled for one year, until the end of 1941, the trade relations between the Confederation and the Greater Germany. It is likely that the return to favor of Hjalmar Schacht, who spent much time during the war shuttling between Germany,

Basel and Geneva, and the fact that he was "newly persona grata again, and put in charge of elaborating an economic plan for the New Europe, based on a Monetary Union," helped smooth over the rough edges. In return for German raw materials, coal, etc., Berne agreed to open a credit of 124 million Swiss francs to the Reich, plus the right to purchase an additional 133 million worth of goods. The agreement settled on 150 million worth of additional purchases, 100 million in arms and ammunition, 15-20 million in machinery and aluminum for the Nazi war machine.

Cynically, Bonjour comments, "to the advocates of a Renewal who vehemently proclaimed that the Confederation could only continue to live by closely aligning itself with Germany, the outcome of the clearing agreement proved that it was still possible to accomplish in Switzerland what was necessary to keep the economy afloat while safeguarding the independence of the state and the vital interests of the country."

A provisional protocol was signed on Feb. 2, 1941, whereby it extended a supplementary credit to the Reich of 165 million and additionally allowed it to purchase 317 million worth of military goods. Later that month, the German trade negotiator proposed to lift the ceiling of the Swiss credit to 600 million and, later, in April, to 850 million—without any interest, which must be a unique case of Swiss bankers lending interest-free! The Swiss, after some ritual protest, agreed in May 1941 to do that. One Swiss official even went so far as to state, "Once more, credit has proved its efficacy as a defensive weapon for the neutral Confederation"!

A member of the Swiss Permanent Council, the upper house, E. Loepfe-Benz, was so outraged by that situation that on Sept. 1, 1941, he stated: "We only supply arms, against raw materials, to Germany. We only supply textiles to Germany alone. We supply Swiss wood, which has become so scarce, to Germany alone. We open an 850 million credit to Germany alone, and another, 150 million, to Italy. We place our productive power, to its very exhaustion, at the service of the military interests of Germany. Financial relations between the Confederation and the Reich are settled totally to the advantage of Germany. Switzerland bans [Hermann] Rauschning's book because it is so terribly truthful ... she renounces banning tendentious German publications. She lets foreigners organize themselves nearly militarily. . . . Switzerland wants to avoid any unpleasant confrontation with the neighbor state."

'A Very Convenient Arsenal'

By mid-1942, while deliveries from the Reich were unilaterally lowered, new, massive demands came from Berlin: new advances of credit and the demand that "Switzerland bring to an immediate end the interferences of the Anglo-Americans in the framework of economic warfare. The Swiss delegates replied that their country was fighting as much as possible against the interferences of the Anglo-Americans." In the first half of 1942, Switzerland exported no less than 250 million Swiss francs of war-related goods to the Reich—and 1.7 million to the Allies! These machine-tools, clockworks, precision tools, and optical instruments were among the most decisive technologies for the conduct of the war. As was officially stated, "given the situation created by the war, Switzerland remains available to work in a preponderant way with the Axis powers, which assuredly represents a very important contribution, given the value of the items supplied." Indeed! In the last nine months of 1942, 360 million of war goods were supplied, of which more than 200 million was for weapons. The Allies received 4.7 percent of that in exports! Worse, the Reich had overstepped the clearing ceiling for its purchases by the enormous margin of 300 million— Switzerland had extended a credit of 1.15 billion Swiss francs to the German war machine. "Should the response to this action that contravened the laws be a denunciation of the clearing agreement? Given the circumstances, it appeared wiser not to do anything of the sort. . . ."

The July 1943 negotiations saw the Swiss obtain a quota, restricting German purchases to 80 percent of the 1942 shipments. But the Reich's demands continued. At the joint commission meeting in December 1943, a Swiss memo complained that "it is unpleasant to discern in the [German] memo the threat of the damages Germany could inflict upon Switzerland. And it is also unpleasant to see that this country is suspected of taking the side of the powers which are the enemy of Germany." After 15 years of pro-Nazi efforts, it was indeed somewhat impudent to harbor such suspicions. A comparison of shifts in trade balances is instructive: in 1937, Swiss exports to Germany had been, in commodities, 47 million, and 425 million in 1943. To the Allies, 80 million in 1937 and 19 million in 1943. 1944 and 1945 especially saw first a decline and then, of course, a debacle of Swiss-German trade. But not before a wave of committed anti-Nazi fervor led the Swiss government—on Feb. 16, 1945— to freeze German assets in Switzerland—at least officially, for if the Allied blockade of Switzerland included that demand, the Swiss agreement was systematically violated to the benefit of the Nazis.

Early in the war, on July 19, 1941, the Swiss Minister in London, Thurnneer, had cabled to Pilet-Golaz that "the British are watching closely the Swiss-German negotiations which might seriously affect policy towards Switzerland; we cannot take lightly further Swiss credits to Germany [they say]. It is unfortunate that Switzerland became a very convenient arsenal for the Germans and that factories are working full speed for Germany." The Swiss, with imperturbable aplomb, responded that "the [German] clearing debt is not a loan granted to the Germans. It is advances to the Swiss exporters so that they do not have to wait, to settle their claims, for the German commodity imports to allow payments to be made." Unmoved, the British installed a blockade on the sea for most goods to Switzerland. Of course, the truth of the matter was that "Switzerland is supplying Germany with war goods she pays herself with the money advanced," reported even Hans Sulzer, who added "the Axis powers are exploiting to the hilt the economic potential of Switzerland . . . these unfortunate deliveries of goods that are typically military goods . . . represent a serious danger to the country's neutrality."

The Briton Sir John Lomax became very angry from his Berne office. Talking to industrialist Bührle, head of a major arms company on Aug. 27, 1942, he exploded: "Britain cannot tolerate that Switzerland play a double game. He who will not declare himself for the democracies is against them; in the long run, the Confederation will not be able to maintain its so-called neutrality!" Bührle answered with astounding audacity: "Switzerland is not stupid enough to sacrifice itself for Britain as did Poland, Yugoslavia, Greece, Holland, Belgium, Norway, and finally France, and to get, like these countries, the installation of a government-in-exile in London as a reward for such heroic follies."

Most of the detonators used by the Nazi army were manufactured in Switzerland. For the Office of Economic Armament, in Berlin, the Swiss engineering industry was crucial: machine-tools, automatic metal-cutting machines, precision lathes, micro-gauges, miniaturized roll bearings "could not be manufactured in Germany in required quantities nor with equal quality." Precision tools, measurement tools, chronometers as well as machine-guns, aircraft engines, anti-tank and anti-aircraft guns and their ammunition, small arms, shells with clockworks, optical instruments were similarly indispensible, to be drawn from the Swiss workshop. The Swiss arms industry delivered 60 percent of its products to the Reich, the foundries 50 percent, the optics industry 50 percent too. Of the high-technology machine-tools, 80 percent went to the Reich, and 30 percent of the clockwork industry.

The Nazi dependency on Swiss military goods became so pronounced that an anxious Weizsäcker even allowed himself to ask the Swiss government, in June 1942, to reinforce the Gotthard anti-aircraft defenses and emplace anti-aircraft defenses around those manufacturers that worked for the Reich. One month later, Pilet-Golaz had made sure that the request had been implemented! Pilet, commenting on the Americans, described them to Weizsäcker as "totally devoid of scruples, especially brutal and reckless concerning their means"—how can this tirade delivered to a top Nazi official be further underscored in terms of its implications for the Swiss leadership? Seven percent of the Swiss GNP of 1942 went to the Nazi Reich in the form of military goods!

In July 1942, U.S. Secretary of State Cordell Hull stated, with his finger pointed in the direction of Berne, that "Any neutrality in the present conflict is absurd and suicidal." Homilectics were not enough to convince the Swiss, who declined the November-December Allied proposals. The pragmatic British understood this well, and, in the spring of 1943, purely and simply bombed the city of Oerlikon, near Zürich, where the Bührle factories were located. "This was seen in Switzerland as a firm invitation to bring to an end the military production for Germany." Marvels of intelligence! In early 1945, U.S. Secretary of State Stettinius announced a complete review of U.S.-Swiss economic relations, which took effect promptly. "One of the major victors had inflicted on Switzerland an affront unparalleled in the annals of Swiss diplomacy," Bonjour bitterly commented.

In 1945, negotiations were started between the Allies and Berne. "The activities of the Swiss banks had for long aroused the mistrust and violent criticism of the Anglo-Saxons. They blame the Swiss National Bank for accepting German and Italian gold, even though its origin be suspicious and it came in part from occupied countries. They also hit at the brokering and credit activities of Swiss private banks with the Axis powers or strawmen . . . in 1942, the United States decreed a 'freeze' on all Swiss assets on U.S. territory." On Feb. 23, 1944, His Majesty's Government announced that it would not recognize any transfer of property concerning "stolen goods" put in circulation by the Reichsbank. "On Aug. 23, 1944, an Allied Memo demanded that the Federal Council prohibit any purchase and deposit of gold from an Axis country. Since Switzerland did not respond to this approach, they insisted anew on Feb. 1, 1945. Reasons of principle as well as juridical considerations went counter to the Confederation's agreeing with the Allies' demand," Bonjour writes. Eleven days later, the chief U.S. negotiator told his Swiss counterparts that "the Allies hope that the Swiss Government will show itself ready to stop all help to the Axis powers . . . and that, in keeping with the Resolution VI of the Bretton Woods conference, it will take active measures against the enemies of the Allies, to prevent them from disposing of their booty, from funding their war effort, from dissimulating their assets in order for their chiefs to use after the [end of the] hostilities, in short, from having a use of the advantages offered by the Swiss financial organizations."

Helping the Nazis Monetize the Loot

The billion Swiss francs at play in these trade relations in Nazi-overwhelmed Europe did not come out of the Reichsbank itself. Just as in the 1930s, the Bank for International Settlements and the Swiss National Bank had funneled massive amounts of money into the Nazi Reich, so during the war. As told by British historian Charles Higham, there were "the $378 million in gold that had been sent to the BIS by the Nazi government after Pearl Harbor for use by its leaders after the war. [That was] gold that had been looted from the National Banks of Austria, Holland, Belgium, and Czechoslovakia, or melted down from the Reichsbank holdings of teeth fillings, spectacle frames, cigarette cases and wedding rings of the murdered Jews." In February 1942, the BIS pushed the criminality to extend a

loan of several million Swiss gold francs to the "protectorate" of Poland, the Nazi-administered genocide operation conducted under Dr. Frank.

The war went on, and, in spite of all lying claims
to the contrary, board meetings of the BIS went on
too—no matter whether the countries of residence
of the central bankers were at war. On March 23,
1943, U.S. Congressman Jerry Voorhis of Califor-
nia entered a resolution in the House calling for
an investigation of the BIS, "this bank being used
to further the designs and purposes of the Axis
powers." Less than one year later, Congressman
John M. Coffee also filed a resolution to that effect:
"The Nazi government has 85 million Swiss gold
francs on deposit in the BIS. The majority of the
Board is made up of Nazi officials. . . ." The result
was that the Bretton-Woods conference resolved
for the BIS "to be dissolved at the earliest possible
moment," and also resolved to investigate the books
and records of the Bank during the war. That this
never came to pass is an eloquent testimony to the
power of Swiss Nazi finance over the nation-states.

In "defense" of his institution, the BIS chairman
stated: "In order to understand [it] one must first
understand the strength of the confidence and trust
that the central bankers had had in each other and
the strength of their determination to play the game
squarely. Secondly, one must realize that in the
complicated German financial setup, certain men
who have their central banker's point of view, are
in very strategic positions and can influence the
conduct of the German government with respect
to these matters." In normal language, that meant
that the Nazi Reichsbank was to be entrusted with
the future of Germany, with the benediction of the
Allies!

As far as the Swiss themselves were concerned, the Nazi-looted gold was sent not directly to the BIS, but from the Reichsbank to the BIS account at the Swiss National Bank. The SNB has demanded that a "trustworthy" Reichsbank official "certify" that the gold sent was not the proceeds of loot. The official in question was Hitler's own appointee on the BIS board, the Reichsbank's Emil Puhl! "Funk [at the Nuremberg trial in 1946] said that Puhl had informed him in 1942 that the Gestapo had deposited gold coins and other gold, from the concentration camps, in the Reichsbank. Puhl had been in charge of this. Jewels, monocles, spectacle frames, watches, cigarette cases and gold dentures had flowed into the Reichsbank, supplied by Puhl from Himmler's resources. They were melted down in gold bars. . . . Funk had made arrangements with Himmler to receive the gold." The gold coming into the Reichsbank came in bags marked "Auschwitz," etc. Under interrogation, Puhl admitted that these gold transfers to the BIS/SNB were "subordinated to the broader question of assisting the SS, all the more—and this must be emphasized—because these things were for the account of the Reich."

In 1942, in one year, the Nazi state had laundered 500 million Swiss francs worth of gold into Switzerland. "At the beginning," writes Bourgeois, "the Germans only passed on small quantities of gold whose origins made no problem. And when the sales became substantial, the Swiss did not dare stop a practice that had always existed for fear of giving offense to the Reich."

By March 1945, the situation became somewhat hot for the Swiss. After the salvo from Bretton Woods, the BIS tried to avert any direct receipt of the looted gold. "Instead," reports Higham, "the SNB, as a shareholder of the BIS, would take it in its vaults. But in order to camouflage the receipt of it, the SNB had disguised it as payments to the American Red Cross and the German Legations in Switzerland." In short, the Swiss National Bank and the BIS were aiding and abetting the flight of Nazi capital in contravention to the formal commitments they had themselves taken under international agreement.

Their behavior was so impudent that on Nov. 15, 1945, the U.S. Senate's Kilgore Committee reported that "the Swiss banks led by the BIS and its member bank the SNB (which shares directors and staff members) had violated agreements made at the end of the war not to permit financial transactions that would help the Nazis dispose of their loot." Sen. Harley Kilgore stated: "Despite the assurances of the Swiss government that German accounts would be blocked, the Germans maneuvered themselves back into a position where they could utilize their assets in Switzerland, could acquire desperately needed foreign exchange by the sale of looted gold, and could conceal economic reserves for another war. These moves were made possible by the willingness of the Swiss government and banking officials, in violation of their agreements with the Allied Powers, to make a secret deal with the Nazis."

Ironically, the key to most of that monstrous affair came to Switzerland from the United States, in 1942, in the form of OSS master-spy Allen Dulles, whose family psychoanalyst was Swiss Nazi Carl G. Jung, the ideologue of man's inherent, archetypal submission to irrationality. Dulles was no newcomer to Nazism. In 1930, while visiting his law firm Sullivan & Cromwell's client Fritz Thyssen (one of the early financiers of Hitler, who had just contributed 50 million Reichsmarks to the NSDAP), and also in his capacity of a member of the board of the New York subsidiary of the Schroeder Bank, Dulles met with Adolf Hitler. His brother John Foster Dulles, not to be outdone, had met Hitler in the late 1920s already, having received the invitation, with his wife, while negotiating debt with Schacht.

In the 1930s the Dulles brothers openly propagandized for the Nazi regime. John Foster insisted in a 1936 Princeton University addresss that "what is happening in Germany and Italy is part of the inevitable struggle between dynamic and static nations. America must adjust to the changes. If [we] all yielded gracefully [to Hitler and Mussolini], Hitler will just be a passing phase." Friend John J. McCloy remarked "I rather gathered that he was not particularly concerned about it." From his powerful position at the Federal Council of Churches (the predecessor organization of the World Council of Churches), Foster was collaborating with the pro-Nazi elements in the Protestant Churches.

Allen Dulles, from his prewar contacts with Sullivan & Cromwell correspondent, Hamburg attorney G. Westrick—an Abwehr spymaster—was "in the picture." He was to land right in the middle of the cauldron of intrigue that Switzerland was for the networks of Admiral Canaris and Colonel Schellenberg. "In Switzerland," writes historian Anthony Cave Brown, "a powerful Abwehr force existed as the harbinger of occupation," save that the said occupation was never to occur. In fact, the collaboration between the Abwehr and Swiss military intelligence was so deep that 40 years later, when the author asked a ranking official of Swiss

Military Intelligence for an explanation, the latter launched into a spirited tirade in defense of the Abwehr!

The Abwehr network in question was run in particular through aristocrats, bankers and other upper-crust individuals. Swiss citizen, freshly naturalized Baron von der Heydt, of the family running the Delbrück Bank of Cologne where von Schröder, Thyssen and Schacht had opened the business community's "Hitler Fund" in 1932, and a representative of top levels of Dutch high finance, ran the Thyssenbank in Locarno with the help of the Schweizerische Bankgesellschaft. He worked closely with maverick entrepreneur Gottlieb Duttweiler, who was tried by the Swiss after the war as a Nazi collaborator. He also worked with Abwehr Hans Bernd Gisevius, Canaris's special envoy—who was also on Dulles's payroll! Fritz Thyssen himself, while his Berlin bank was being renamed Von der Heydt Bank, had emigrated from Germany in 1938, to settle in Switzerland. Von der Heydt managed large family portfolios, including that of the Stinneses, the Haniels—and that of former Kaiser Wilhelm, who died in exile in Holland in 1941, and that of the Kaiser's sons. One of his missions, from Canaris, was to fund Nazi intelligence activities in Latin America, probably seeding for the postwar future.

Schellenberg, Guisan, and Dulles

Schellenberg's network was of a more simple make: he collaborated directly with Col. Roger Masson, the head of Swiss military intelligence. There also, the business side was not forgotten. Schellenberg was a director of the German branch of International Telegraph & Telephone, ITT, whose chairman was Dulles friend and colleague Gerhardt Westrick. ITT boss Col. Sosthenes Benn was a close friend of Hermann Goering, whose Luftwaffe he continued to supply throughout the war, as well as the Sicherheitsdienst (SD) run by his employee Schellenberg. Benn was also closely working with the Foreign Ministry Undersecretary Wilhelm Keppler, founder in the early 1930s of the Keppler Circle that contributed so much to Hitler's rise to power. And to close the circle, Schellenberg worked hand in glove with I.G. Farben chief Hermann Schmitz of the BIS—while John Foster Dulles was the attorney for I.G. Chemie (the Swiss front's) U.S. subsidiary, American I.G.—which Sosthenes Benn bought up during the war in order to avoid expropriation of the Nazi asset by the U.S. government. Directly running I.G. Farben/Chemie's large network of 5,000 spies in the Western hemisphere was Ernst Bohle, the SS officer also in charge of some operations in Switzerland.

The Schellenberg-Masson collaboration led to one of the most extraordinary events of the World War II, the series of conferences between Schellenberg, Masson, and the "pro-Resistance" general Henri Guisan.

On June 25, 1940, Guisan, addressing all the senior Swiss military officers at the historic site of the Rütli Meadows, outlined what, on the face of it, was a "Resistance" strategy. "The Army must remain prepared . . . we are still the masters of our destiny. . . . Believe not only in the right of our cause but also in our strength and, if each of us wants it, in the efficacy of our resistance." Nazi Ambassador Köcher was duly flabbergasted, and visited forthwith President Pilet-Golaz. In his report, "the president of the Confederation concluded [the discussion] with the wish that this incident would be settled with his explanation and added, confidentially, 'I hope now that the General will not talk any more'." A few days later, however, Guisan was requesting from the Nazi authorities a trip of a Swiss military mission to Berlin—a proposal immediately endorsed by the VUS and the Industrial Association!

Shortly thereafter, the German Abwehr discovered, abandoned in a small French town, La Charité-sur-Loire, a series of documents of the French General Staff documenting the informal deal passed by Guisan with the French for cooperation in case of a German invasion of Switzerland. This golden opportunity to get rid of Guisan by creating a scandal of unheard of magnitude—Guisan had not consulted the Federal Council, nor even informed it of the deal!—was not seized. Weizsäcker, who was not fully in on the real affair, wrote in his memoirs that this "weakened the standpoint of those who, like me, had always tried to keep Switzerland out of the game under any circumstances." Did that mean that the Schellenberg faction was going to lose their precious financial pivot? Not in the least— to the contrary! A few days after that, Guisan, still surrounded by echo of his Rütli speech, proposed that Carl J. Burckhardt be sent to Berlin for purposes of appeasement—an idea that originated from his intelligence chief Masson.

One of Dulles's main informants was Prince Max-Egon von Hohenlohe, who had run German Intelligence in Vienna during World War One—when Dulles had first met him. The prince's former wife, Princess Stefanie von Hohenlohe, was close to Schellenberg and to Otto Abetz, the Paris ambassador. She was interned in the United States during

World War Two as a Nazi spy—Hermann Schmitz had lavished gifts on her for her services, and Hitler called her "my princess." She was part of the Foreign Organization of the NSDAP. With such collaborators, was Dulles fighting against the Nazis? No more than his earlier profile indicates! He was working with one wing of the Nazi establishment against the other, gaining factional advantage for the future. As A. C. Brown reports, "Schellenberg did not trust the British. His main channels of communication were with Dulles at Berne. . . . Schellenberg's go-between was Prince Max-Egon von Hohenlohe-Langenburg. . . ." Yet another Dulles collaborator, his closest, was Gero von Schulze Gävernitz, the son of a prominent Berlin liberal economist whom Dulles had met 20 years before in Berlin. After he had married into the Stinnes family, Canaris had helped him relocate in Switzerland.

One fine morning of February 1945, Major Max Waibel of Swiss Military Intelligence knocked at Dulles's door to say that he could put him in touch with representatives of SS Obergruppenführer Karl Wolff, at present the top SS officer and police chief in Northern Italy, who "wanted to talk about surrender." Wolff had been Himmler's chief of staff, Himmler's personal liaison with Hitler, and with Ribbentrop. In the SS, he was second only to Himmler. And now, according to fairy tales retailed by Dulles in his book *Secret Surrender*, Wolff kindly wanted to surrender the troops under his command to avoid a bloodbath, and so on and so forth.

Coming to the rescue of Swiss agent Allen Dulles, the *Bonjour Bericht* naively writes: "Wolff's interlocutors naturally did not know that this man was one of Hitler's associates at Headquarters, and that he had been involved in mass executions of Jews.

That became known only long after the war." The negotiation process, code-named "Operation Sunrise," indeed led to a surrender that averted a considerable bloodbath. It also led to the major operation to evacuate Nazi and SS war criminals, with their funds and dossiers, out of Europe, an operation which Dulles supervised, along with his cronies at Swiss intelligence. Dulles admits in his cited book that "it was obvious, and we realized it, that the Swiss intelligence service had contacts with the Allied and German intelligence services. As Swiss, it was possible for them to maintain relations with each group of belligerents, and, in their own interest, they had an absolute right to do so. Misunderstandings were reduced by the fact that one group of intelligence officers was mainly working with the Germans, and another with the Allies. Col. Roger Masson of the Swiss General Staff, was in contact with Walter Schellenberg, and Max Waibel . . . with us. What occurred between Masson and Waibel, who both reported to General Guisan, to this day I do not know." Masson, code-named "Senner One" (a *Senner* is a Swiss cowherd) in Schellenberg's files, whose Swiss contacts were code-named "Senner-People," was no less busy than Dulles reconstructing the Nazi networks for the postwar period. The Dulles part of the operation was code-named "Land on fire," perhaps as a preview of the Nazi International's postwar terrorism.

One of the major aspects of the operation to save the Nazi infrastructure went through the collaboration of Guisan with the old Geneva Nazi Theodore Aubert. On June 22, 1944, Aubert penned a memo to the general where he proposed to prepare for the post-war and make all "directly available forces" available for that. This included his own

league, the EIA: the old SVV; the National Reconstruction (Redressement National) and a maze of
other intelligence organizations. In his note of
transmittal to one of his subordinates, General Dollfuss, head of the powerful Haus und Heer division
of the Swiss General Staff, Guisan noted apprecia-
tively: "For 20 years Monsieur Aubert has dedicated himself to the struggle against subversive
movements and, based on past experiences, he is
presently seeking to find the means to spare our
country from a new period of unrest like that after
the last war." The post-war infrastructures were
being emplaced.

A front-organization was set up in hospitable
Lausanne under the name of Diethelm Brothers,
at the initiative of Hitler's personal chief of staff
and assistant Martin Bormann, with the help of
Hjalmar Schacht and his son-in-law, SS Col. Otto
Skorzeny, who worked with the Abwehr's number
two man, Count Erwin von Lahousen. The Credit
Suisse Bank and the Baseler Handelsbank—
founded by the Iselin family—were key conduits
for the transfer of funds. In the year 1944 alone,
Schellenberg succeeded in transferring no less than
$600 million to Switzerland! Several hundred Nazi-
controlled dummy companies were set up, of which
more than 200 were identified in Switzerland. While
Hitler may have entertained silly dreams of an "Alpine citadel," the Schellenberg-Schacht group, supported by the BIS and SNB, was investing long
term, for the future. In August 1944, a secret meeting took place in Strasbourg, then still occupied,
with the leaders of the SS financial and industrial
apparatus. The agenda was to prepare for after the
war. One principal method was once again to have
SS-controlled firms create or consolidate "inter-

faces" with foreign firms and thus escape de-Nazification scrutiny. Swiss companies massively bought such SS-controlled firms and thus gave them "respectable Swiss" covers. Another method was the laundering through the Swiss of hundreds of millions in faked dollars and pounds.

The individual whose personal role was perhaps the single most significant one in the financial transfers was Dr. Alfred Schaefer, a senior official at the Schweizerische Bankgesellschaft (Union Bank of Switzerland). An open, outright, ostentatious Nazi during the 1930s, and the lover of Adolf Hitler's "mistress" Eva Braun, Schaefer, also an officer in the Swiss military, "was not only part, but an essential part of every single major financial negotiation between the Swiss and the Germans throughout the 1930s and 1940s," according to a Swiss historian. Schaefer was to become the chairman of the bank, the "Great Man" of Swiss banking, and the personal financial advisor to the Shah of Iran. He also was the key partner, in business and other matters, of Madrid-based Otto Skorzeny and the latter's wife, Elsa, a Schacht relative.

Dulles, back in the United States, was receiving loads of SS and other Nazi war criminals, which he was recycling into his State Department-connected intelligence organization, until he managed to acquire a chunk of the CIA to place his darling Nazi legions. As early as 1945, a new Swiss military attaché in Washington worked closely with him in order to screen the Nazis-for-hire—Major Max Waibel, who ended with a general's stars.

Denis de Rougemont, a veteran from Swiss Military Intelligence, founded the Ecoropa umbrella-group for Europe's key environmentalist organizations, a control job he shares with the KGB and the Nazi International. The BIS's and the Swiss National Bank's economic and financial strategy is to inflict on the Third World—and at world scale this time—what they succeeded in inflicting on Germany first, and the whole European continent next.

Bibliography

Bank for International Settlements, *The Bank for International Settlements: 1930–1980,* Basel, 1980.

Bonjour, Edgar, *Histoire de la Neutralité Suisse,* Neuchâtel, 1970.

Borkin, Joseph, *The Crime and Punishment of I.G. Farben,* New York, 1978.

Bourgeois, Daniel, *Le Troisième Rich et la Suisse,* Paris, 1974.

Brown, Anthony Cave, *Bodyguard of Lies,* London, 1975.

Clarke, Stephen V. O., *Central Bank Cooperation, 1924–31,* New York, 1967.

Dulles, Allen W., *The Secret Surrender,* New York, 1966.

Freymond, Jean, *Le Troisième Reich et la Réorganisation Economique de l'Europe,* Geneva, 1974.

Frischknecht J., et al., *Die unheimlichen Patrioten,* Zürich, 1979.

Grimm, Bruno, *Gau Schweiz?,* Berne, 1939.

Higham, Charles, *Trading with the Enemy,* New York, 1983.

Joseph, Roger, *L'Union nationale 1932–39,* Lausanne, 1975.

Ledeen, Michael, *Universal Fascism,* New York, 1973.

Lomax, John, *Diplomatic Smuggler,* London, 1965.

Lueke, Rolf E., *Das Geheimnis der deutschen Bankenkrise,* Frankfurt, 1981.

Mosley, Leonard, *Dulles—A Biography,* New York, 1978.

Müller, Helmut, *Die Zentralbank, eine Nebenregierung,* Opladen, 1973.

de Reynold, Gonzague, *Mes Memoires,* Geneva, 1963

———, *La Democratie et la Suisse,* Berne, 1929.

de Rougemont, Denis, *The Devil's Share,* New York, 1944.

———, *The Heart of Europe,* New York, 1941.

Schellenberg, Walter, *Memoiren 125 de la Grande Loge Suisse Alpina*, Lausanne, 1973.

Simpson, Amos E., *Hjalmar Schacht in Perspective*, Paris/Den Haag, 1969.

Urner, Klaus, *Der Schweizer Hitler-Attentäter*, Stuttgart.

4

The Grand Mufti and Hitler: National Socialist Networks in the Mideast

In July 1982 a group of predominantly North African Muslims met in the foreign quarter of Paris. Officially, its purpose was to make up a plan for the pilgrimage to Mecca. That, at least, was what the French police were told when the group applied for the usual assembly permit. The signs posted at the meeting room, however, indicated a different purpose. There were the familiar Islamic portraits, including a gigantic poster of the Ayatollah Khomeini. Dominating the room, however, was a very strange portrait indeed: a likeness of the Grand Mufti of Jerusalem, Haj Amin el-Husseini, Hitler's closest ally in the Arab world!

The conference, chaired by the former Algerian president Ahmed Ben Bella, was keynoted by the Bern, Switzerland journalist Ahmed Huber, a convert to Islam and leading spokesman for the Nazi International. The aim of the conference was to prepare for the festivities commemorating the fiftieth anniversary of Hitler's seizure of power!

The year 1983, Huber told his audience, should

be dedicated to reviving the ideas of the Grand Mufti. Huber, like Ben Bella, had befriended the Grand Mufti during the 1950s while in exile in Cairo, and he described in detail the volume of propaganda which would be required to accomplish this revival. "During the coming year, genuine Muslims must take over the Islamic world. Corrupt infidels such as Arafat, Saddam Hussein, Mubarak, and hypocrites such as the Saudi royal family who claim they represent Islam, must be eliminated. Today the Iranian Islamic Revolution of the Ayatollah Khomeini is the true inheritor of the ideas of the Grand Mufti. We must strive for a universal community of believers."

Even as Huber was delivering his speech, printing presses in many parts of the Islamic world were already gearing up to flood the markets with editions of Hitler's *Mein Kampf* in Arabic, Turkish, and other languages. A few copies of these books were later found by the Israelis in various sections of the city of Beirut. The translations were not all identical, of course; an edition from the "Marxist" Popular Front for the Liberation of Palestine of George Habash differed, for example, from the edition of the Muslim Brotherhood in Lebanon or in Egypt, or the Turkish fundamentalists' translation.

Today, one year later, this revival of National Socialist thought in the Arab world is in full swing. Hitler's name is once again becoming a topic for polite conversation among the many adherents of Islam. First and foremost in this regard is the Libyan dictator Muammar Qaddafi, who in February 1983, in the French daily newspaper *Le Matin* said that "Hitler was right! He understood that the Jews were a deadly threat to the German nation. He was obliged to exterminate them!" Only a few years earlier such a declaration, even coming from someone as deranged as Qaddafi, would have unleashed a storm of indignation; now it was barely noticed. Interestingly, *Time* magazine's published version of the same interview suppressed this passage without comment.

The fact that Ahmed Huber is a friend of Qaddafi, whom he praises as a "wonderful, romantic Bedouin," cannot be unrelated to Qaddafi's ability make such monstrous public statements. Huber's July 1983 "prophecy" that Arafat would soon be out of the way, is also on the verge of becoming reality. We can trace Huber's footsteps back to certain Palestinian factions in Iran, as well as to the Lebanese rebels controlled by Assad in Syria. Hidden behind Syrian President Assad's most important security advisor, a certain George Fisher, is one of Huber's closest collaborators, Alois Brunner. Brunner was Adolf Eichmann's deputy during the Third Reich!

There are many other "Brunners" in the Arab world who train the Iranian "Revolutionary Guard" or certain elements within the Palestinians around the terrorist Abu Nidal. In Iran, for example, a certain Juan José Torres, a 35-year-old engineer and ardent admirer of Hitler who belongs to the second generation of neo-Nazis, is working as the chief designer of a new generation of anti-tank rockets. In Libya many of Qaddafi's advisors are European Nazis who have converted to Islam, just as many Islamic and Arab terrorist organizations such as the Muslim Brotherhood, are run by people who, though they are not old enough to have been in World War II, actively support the goals of the Third Reich. Most of these individuals can be traced back to the Swiss Nazi banker François Genoud, a

man who has been close friends with the Grand
Mufti of Jerusalem since at least 1935, and who at
the start of 1943 began to build up what was later
to be known as the "Odessa" network. It was this
network which laundered the Nazi war chest
through the Swiss banks, so that these funds, from
1950 on, could be used to rebuild the old networks
of the Third Reich in Latin America and the Middle
East. The Berne-based Huber was Genoud's contact man with Paris and to Ben Bella. In 1952 Genoud picked up Ben Bella in Cairo and built him up
as a "Führer" under his own control.

Few in the Middle East today want to discuss
these events and facts. Even the Israeli secret service
and government circles, who for years have been
using the cheap propagandistic equation "Arab =
Nazi," have never investigated François Genoud's
activities in detail; they have never looked into how
the Third Reich's secret service operated in the
Middle East during the war, or what happened to
these networks after the war. The Arab press has
behaved similarly, refusing to address this question
out of fear that the responsible editor's body might
be found in the gutter the next day.

Their fear is well-founded. Many thousands of
soldiers and officers from the Abwehr (German
Army Intelligence), the security services, and the
SS found secure refuge in every country in the
Middle East, Israel being no exception. Hardly had
the war ended when the British commander in Jor-
dan, Sir John Glubb Pasha, released thousands of
German prisoners of war from the prison camps
and enrolled them as members in his Arab Legion,
in order to march them against the newly founded
state of Israel. The latter state, on the other hand,
did not hesitate to employ a few specialists from

Nazi Germany in the building of its own secret service, the Mossad. For most of the newly independent Arab states these professional soldiers and secret service experts were more than welcome.

How the Nazis Infiltrated the Middle East

Paradoxically, the defeat of the Third Reich served to boost the reputation of "former" Nazis in many countries of the Arab world. During the war the Führer of the Third Reich had made all sorts of promises to the Arabs, none of which could be kept following the collapse of Nazi Germany. These Nazis gained an undeserved reputation as people who never broke those promises. As they settled down into positions as secret intelligence, security, or economic advisors, became converts to Islam, and adopted Arab names, former leaders of the Third Reich began to capitalize on more than one hundred years of German emigration into the Middle East.

This German influence began in 1835 when the young Colonel von Moltke, who later was to become the Kaiser's Chief of General Staff, was charged with the task of reorganizing and training the army of Sultan Mahmoud II. Those plans came to naught when the Sultan's forces were routed by Ibrahim, son of the Egyptian viceroy, and independence leader Mohammed Ali, whose troops had been trained by French officers of the École Polytechnique. However, despite this military defeat, and despite the fact that Bismarck was more preoccupied with England than with the Middle East and Turkey, Germany was able to expand its presence in Turkey and the entire region economically as well as militarily. This culminated later on in the construction of the Berlin-Baghdad Railway. The financial agreements for the project were signed by France and England in 1914.

This far-reaching economic project was only the leading edge of Germany's deep economic and political penetration of the area. Germany was not a colonial power in the region, and was therefore widely regarded as the "natural" protector of the Muslims against "European imperialism" or against Russia. This fact assumed great significance during the First World War, when von Moltke won the Turks over to his plan for a joint offensive against Great Britain in Egypt, while Germany's ambassadors von Hentig and von Niedermayer were negotiating with Afghanistan's Emir Habibullah to set off an Islamic rebellion against Great Britain on the Indian subcontinent, with the support of the Indian leader Mahandra Pratap. As outlined as early as 1911 by the Imperial staff, such a strategy was aimed at forming an alliance between pan-Germanism and pan-Islamicism, which would in turn bring about a Germanic Central European empire. This *Mitteleuropa* was to include the Balkan countries, Bulgaria and the Ukraine, which would join with Turkey in annexing the Caucasus region. Germany, Iran, and Afghanistan would proceed to carve up the Middle Eastern region among themselves.

With few significant differences, this was also the policy of the Third Reich. That was outlined in an April 1933 memorandum to Propaganda Minister Josef Goebbels written by Dr. Kurt Köhler of the University of Leipzig, Dr. Oluf Krückmann, director of the German School in Baghdad, and Dr. Wilhelm Eilers, director of the Archaeological School of Teheran. Titled "Raumpolitik—Kulturpolitik" ("Territorial Policy—Cultural Policy"), the memorandum begins:

Today we talk about geopolitics. Everyone in Germany agrees that the world is divided up into various large regions or will become so, whereby each of these regions is reserved for a master caste. . . . Whereas Great Britain, France, America, and even Japan possess their own *Lebensraum* [living space] . . . Italy as well as Germany still have not attained theirs. . . . For Germany, therefore, Eastern Europe, Southern Europe, the Middle East and Egypt are the obvious prospects. . . . The Balkan countries, on Germany's flank, are the bridge into the Middle East. . . . Anatolia in turn is itself a bridge into the Middle East and to Egypt. . . . Germany must demonstrate that it does not intend to repeat the European imperialism of the pre-1914 era, but is looking only for peaceful and friendly collaboration. . . . Economic propaganda and economic expansion alone, without the corresponding cultural propaganda and expansion, are an absurdity, and would only have the effect of undermining our goals. . . . By disseminating cultural propaganda we are working one hundred percent for Germany; if we only do economic propaganda, we will be working thirty percent to the advantage of our competitors.

Throughout the period between Imperial Germany's defeat and Hitler's accession to power in 1933, when this memorandum was drawn up, Germany was continuously present in the Middle East. By the mid-1920s, German economic and trade missions were operating throughout the Middle East, especially in Turkey, Afghanistan, and Iran, the only semi-independent states of the region. In the late 1920s, a German economic advisor by the name of Lindenblatt became the first director of the National Bank of Iran. Because under the Versailles Treaty Germany was forbidden to trade in weapons and certain other items, the Swiss also became involved, functioning as an intermediary between the countries of the Middle East and Germany.

Another country which continued to promote the German empire's economic and political activity in the region was the Soviet Union. Both countries were playing the anti-British card in the region. Taghi-Zade, an Iranian Communist who had found asylum in Germany, was for years a mediator between Imperial Germany and the Soviet Union on Iranian questions. Taghi-Zade was a founding member of the Baku "Congress of the Peoples of the East," which had been convened by the Comintern in 1920. A mutual German-Soviet collaboration was established in Iran, and evidently continues up through the present day!

But the policy of the Third Reich was not merely a continuation of the policy of the Imperial Germany of Bismarck and Kaiser Wilhelm II, even though the policies appear identical or coincide in some features. The principal difference lay in the ideology and the concept of universal fascism, or the "universal community of belief," as defined by Rudolf von Sebottendorf of the Munich-based cult group The Thule Society. Von Sebottendorf, a German with Turkish citizenship, was committed to promoting the erection of Islamic mosques in Germany, and had also struck up a friendship with the Pan-Turkish leader Enver Pasha, who would also turn up later at the Baku Conference. Pasha was an associate of the Bektashi dervish order which originated in Albania, and he maintained close contacts with Mazzini's P-1 (Propaganda Uno) Freemasonic lodge and the P-1's "Young Italy" movement. The latter movement spawned the "Young Turks," who overthrew Sultan Hamid II in 1908.

The programmatic content of such policies was laid out in a proposal put forward by Gregor Strasser during the first two years of the Hitler regime. Strasser advocated a "German-Soviet alliance" that would join up with the "league of oppressed nations like India, Arabia, China . . . against the European imperialists." Hitler and his Eastern "specialist" Alfred Rosenberg initially opposed such a policy, since they preferred a German-British alliance. It was later adopted, however, in the form of the 1939 Hitler-Stalin Pact. One of the most important advocates of this alliance was Hitler's personal secretary, Martin Bormann, who is often rumored to have been a Soviet agent. But the policy was also supported by von Sebottendorf and a key geopolitical strategist of the Third Reich, Prof. Karl Haushofer.

Under such influences, Hitler, who had written in *Mein Kampf* that he considered the Arabs an "inferior race," was induced to change his attitude, especially after his meeting with the blond and blue-eyed Grand Mufti of Jerusalem. Hitler decided to back the Grand Mufti, and after the meeting proclaimed that there were many similarities between Nazism and the Islam of the Mufti. No wonder that an Arab delegation sent to Hitler in the mid-1930s stated that if the Arabs not been defeated in 732 at Poitiers, then "Islam would have certainly taken over Europe. The German tribes would have been converted, and there is no doubt at all that the Muslim-Germanic tribe would have represented the spearhead of the Islamic movement. Islam is tailor-made for the Germans." Hitler took up these ideas in many of his musings on religion, declaring on one occasion that "We have the bad luck to have the wrong religion. Why don't we have the religion of the Japanese?. . . Even Islam would more suited for us than Christianity." Ahmed Huber, in his recent recollections of the meeting between Hitler and the Grand Mufti, explained briefly that the Grand Mufti had attempted to do everything conceivable to induce Hitler to convert to Islam, "in order to make him realize that his goals could be better served through a universal community of belief; but Hitler was not smart enough to understand this. . . ."

The Third Reich and the War

When war was declared, the Third Reich had at its disposal numerous organizations in the Middle East. The most important of these was the Party of the Arab Nation of the Grand Mufti of Jerusalem. This was a secret organization which had branches throughout the entire region and which worked for the unification of the Arab nation under the leadership of the Grand Mufti. The concept resembled that of the Baath Party founded in the early 1940s by Michel Aflaq, who is said to have been strongly influenced by the Grand Mufti and by Nazism. In Palestine itself, a key ally of the Mufti's party was the old Temple Society, which had been founded in Stuttgart in 1856 as a splinter group of the German Lutheran Church under the influence of the later Anthroposophs. The Temple Society was an association of German settlers in Palestine who believed they were the chosen people who could return Palestine to its ancient splendor. Although they were looked upon with suspicion during the days of the empire, the order was later instrumental in altering the Third Reich's initial idea of banishing all Jews to Palestine. Several delegations of the Society traveled to Berlin to strongly protest against the immigration of Jews into the region, and they shared the Mufti's opposition to the establishment of Jewish settlements.

In alliance with the British Protectorate of Palestine, the Temple Society and the Mufti saw to it that the numerous ships filled with Jewish refugees fleeing from the Nazis via Bulgarian and Romanian ports were all turned back. This was a replication of the racist policy of the Harriman's Eugenics Research Association, which oversaw the drastic curtailment of Jewish immigration into the United States, and who in one instance turned back a ship full of Jewish refugees, sending them to certain death.

Another fascist organization was the secret society of the "Golden Square" under Rashid Ali Geilani in Iraq. In Egypt, there were the Young Men's Muslim Association and the Workers' Syndicate led by King Farouk's uncle, Prince Abbas Hilmi; the Green Shirt movement of Ahmed Hussein and Mohammed Ali Alaba, the theoretician behind the idea of a Great Nile Kingdom; and the Young Egypt movement. In the Syrian-Lebanese region, the Arab Clubs had been established as early as the 1930s as a vehicle for Nazi propaganda. In 1937 these clubs invited the leader of the Hitler Youth, Baldur von Schirach, on a journey to the region.

A good indication of the atmosphere on the eve of the Second World War is a declaration of Sami al-Jundi, leader of the Syrian Baath Party and the League of Nationalist Action, a pan-Arabist pro-Nazi organization in Damascus:

> We are fascinated by Nazism, we study its writings and intellectual sources—especially Nietzsche, Fichte, and [Houston Stewart] Chamberlain. And we are the first to have seriously considered translating *Mein Kampf*. Anyone who lives in Damascus can appreciate the force of attraction Nazism exerts upon the Arabic people, and Nazism's ability to rouse the people to action. It is totally natural that the vanquished admires the vanquisher. . . .

How Nazi thought was transplanted into the Arabic movement is expressed in a declaration by Dr. Sami Shawkat, the mid-1930s Director General of Education in Baghdad:

> There is something more important than money and learning, which preserves the honor of a nation and prevents its debasement. This is strength. . . . Strength, as I use the word here, signifies the overcoming of death. . . . Sixty years ago Prussia dreamed of uniting the German people. What is there to prevent Iraq, which fulfilled its longing for independence ten years ago, from now realizing the dream of unifying all the Arab countries together?

With the exception of Hjalmar Schacht's visit to Iran in 1936, and von Schirach's trip to the region in 1937, very few Third Reich functionaries visited the region officially. Most Nazi visitors were secret service agents, who limited their activity there to using local organizations for collecting intelligence. It was not until 1941 that Berlin began to recognize the military importance of the Middle East; until then the Mediterranean and Middle East regions had largely been considered the sphere of influence of the Reich's major ally, Italy, even though Arabic organizations friendly to the Nazis had repeatedly stressed that Italy, with its colonialist past, could not be regarded as trustworthy. As early as October 1940, the Grand Mufti had dispatched his secretary Osman Kemal Haddad to Berlin in order to press for joint military operations against the British in the region. But it was only when Hitler realized that he could not carry out his plan for an alliance with Britain, and saw Italy's adventures in Greece and Libya end in failure, that he finally gave the green light for the deal.

On April 12, 1941, Rashid Ali Geilani seized power in a coup d'état in Baghdad, under the direction of the ambassador of the Third Reich, Dr. Grobba. The coup was preceded by a month of feverish activity and diplomatic exchanges. In the middle of January 1941, Al Husseini's secretary Haddad returned to Berlin for the purpose of discussing the regional situation. Otto von Hentig, the same Foreign Ministry official mentioned before with respect to World War I, was sent on a probing mission to Iraq by Nazi Foreign Minister Joachim von Ribbentrop; on his return the Nazi Supreme Command (OKW) decided to fully engage its forces in Iraq. Behind the coup was the plan to open a second, southern flank against the Soviet Union which was to be launched in June of the same year. Ironically, precisely because preparations for this offensive were fully under way, the Third Reich was not in a position to mobilize the necessary military forces when the British, moving from their bases on the Gulf of Basra, marched on Baghdad in order to crush the rebellion. By early May, Geilani's forces were only receiving limited military assistance from Vichy France-occupied Syria. The Vichy regime had only reluctantly and very tardily granted the Luftwaffe permission to fly over its territory in the direction of Baghdad. By May 30 Geilani was left with no choice but to flee to Teheran along with a few other leaders of the "Golden Square." The coup was foiled, and the Third Reich had missed its chance to establish a National Socialist regime in the Middle East.

The consequences of this failure were twofold. First, there was no other country where such an attempt could ever be repeated; the Nazis did not have sufficient military forces to redeploy out of the Eastern and Western fronts. Second, Berlin decided that, judging from their actions, the Arabs could not be relied upon. This motivated the establishment in July 1941 of the German-Arab Training Division (DAL) under the command of Special Staff F, which was to be associated with Italy's own Arab Legion. Complementing these new operations were the creation, in late 1942–early 1943, of two SS divisions within the Allgemeine SS, called the Kandabak and Sabre divisions, consisting of Balkan Muslims from Croatia, Bosnia, and Albania. In the Middle East the Abwehr Division II integrated its own Arab Legion into its Brandenburg Division.

It was not long before all these formations were put to the test. The creation of these special units as part of the Abwehr and of the SS clearly meant that from now on, the Arab allies of the Reich were to operate only under direct German command.

Redeployment of the Networks

In the summer of 1941, following the defeat in Iraq and in Palestine, the Mufti el-Husseini and Geilani fled into temporary exile in Berlin. Over the following six months, el-Husseini traveled back and forth between Rome and Berlin in order to obtain from the Axis nations a firm commitment that they would guarantee Arab independence in return for unconditional Arab support of the Third Reich. While Mussolini's Italy favored independence for the Middle Eastern countries, Hitler and his advisors dismissed these demands outright, doubtless on account of the Vichy regime's interest in Lebanon and Syria. An agreement could only be reached after the circulation of a secret letter in mid-1942, promising complete independence to the Middle Eastern countries and Iraq. The Mufti could boast of the existence of this secret agreement, and show the letter in case of need; the Axis powers, on the other hand, could deny their existence in the event that France became outraged.

The Mufti and Geilani were now deployed in their respective campaigns. The Mufti was put in charge of the command of the DAL in the Egyptian-Libyan theater of war which followed hard on the heels of Erwin Rommel's North African victory and the secret negotiations between King Farouk of Egypt and Berlin, negotiations which were mediated by Farouk's uncle Abbas Hilmi, who traveled to Berlin via Teheran. Geilani himself was meanwhile deployed to the Caucasus front against the Soviet Union, which only existed on paper. Berlin was well aware of the need for a division of labor between Geilani and the Mufti, both being involved in a bitter fight over who would lead the Arab world following the victory.

The next decisive battle for these forces was the Maghreb. In November 1942 the Italians demanded that the Third Reich and Vichy France release most of the Tunisian political leaders imprisoned before the war by the Popular Front government. Among these was Bourgiba, whom the Axis wanted to win over. The results of these secret negotiations have never been made public. In mid-December, the DAL, together with the Italian army under the command of Dr. R. Rahn—a German Foreign Ministry official and a veteran of the 1941 Syrian campaign—marched against Tunis and Algeria, where they could count on inside support from the Revolutionary Action Committee (CUAR) under J. Guilbaud. By mid-1943 this offensive was defeated.

This was the death blow to the Grand Mufti's dreams of a Grand Maghreb Unity. The Mufti turned his attention to the Balkan Muslims; but here, too, his dreams of a united Arab world in alliance with the Third Reich were dashed to pieces. The defeat of Rommel's army and of the fascists in Tunisia also put into jeopardy the biggest prize of all, Egypt.

In Egypt the Nazis not only had friends inside the Royal Court such as Prince Abbas Hilmi, but also friends within the secondary leadership of the Egyptian army such as Aziz Ali al-Masri, who had unsuccessfully attempted to escape to Rommel's forces in order to give a signal for a domestic uprising in Egypt. Anwar al-Sadat was associated with the rebellion, as was Prime Minister Ali Maher, who was subsequently kicked out by the British. When the Free Officers took over in 1952 and installed General Neguib as president, his prime minister was this same Maher.

Fortunately, most of these Nazi forces were defeated. What remained were chiefly secret-service and paramilitary groups with little strategic importance. These included the Khasghai tribesmen in Iran, who had been in contact with the Abwehr since 1940. Some of them could still be found in 1944 within the OKW's Arab Brigade, fighting alongside the special Kurdish Units on the Iraqi-Iranian border. On the Syrian-Lebanese front there remained dozens of pro-Nazi political parties which could be employed in operations such as sabotage. These included the Syrian Popular Party and the Syrian National Socialist Party, founded in 1935 by the Greek Orthodox Antun Sa'adeh and modeled on the NSDAP. There was also the National Youth and the previously mentioned National Action League; members of these parties had flocked into the Arab Brigades of the Brandenburg Division of the Abwehr. And, in Iraq, there was the underground Futuwwa, or youth movement, which was modeled on the Hitler Youth.

But the Arabs were not alone in seeking a special relationship with Berlin. In January of 1941 Otto von Hentig, while in Turkey with German ambassador Franz von Papen, met with a very strange delegation indeed. It consisted of members of the notorious Zionist Self-Defense League, Stern. They proposed an alliance with the Third Reich with the following terms: Germany would allow the German Jews to emigrate to Palestine; the Zionists, in exchange, would form an alliance with the Third Reich in order to fight against Great Britain! The answer to this proposition, dutifully communicated to Berlin, has never been made known publicly.

After the War

Following the destruction of the Third Reich, it took only two or three years for thousands of German military personnel to find secure refuge in the Middle East. Many of these had never fought in the region during the war. By the mid-1950s, one particular unit of the Egyptian secret services could count no less than six special advisors who were refugees from Germany, namely, B. Bender, former Gestapo commander in Poland; L. Gleim of the Gestapo in Warsaw; J. Daumling of the Gestapo in Düsseldorf; H. Sellmann of the Gestapo in Ulm; the former assistant to Col. Otto Skorzeny, F. Bünche; and a former Gestapo captain in France, W. Böckler. Closer to the seat of power there was Saleh Ga'afar, who served as Sadat's private secretary up until the latter's assassination. Saleh's half-brother was Johann Eppler, alias Hussein Ga'afar. Eppler, born of a German mother and an Egyptian father and educated in Germany, had operated during the war as a liaison between the group of officers around Sadat and General al-Masry, and Rommel's staff! Most of these appointments were not only well known, but were further consolidated in the beginning of 1954, when the Egyptian Interior Minister Zakharia Mohieddin, formerly of military intelligence, approached the chief of the West German federal intelligence service (BND), Reinhold Gehlen, who had served as chief of intelligence in the East during the war, for advice on reorganizing the Egyptian secret services. This created the ironic situation that the head of the Egyptian secret service, Marxist Ali Sabri, and his second-in-command, Colonel Salah Nasr (later arrested by Sadat as a KGB agent), were appointing scores of former Nazis as their advisors, on Gehlen's advice!

How such convergences were possible was the subject of Chapter 3. It should be mentioned here, however, that by 1947 the Swiss-based Nazi International leader François Genoud had reorganized the Maghreb and Middle East intelligence sections of the defeated Third Reich. The Grand Mufti el-Husseini, who had been placed under house arrest in Paris, succeeded in escaping and made his last trip to Cairo. In the early 1950s at the Cairo Windsor Hotel, one might regularly run into such people as Genoud, the Grand Mufti, SS General Wolff, SS Lieutenant Reichenberg, General Ramcke, and many lesser Nazi principals who were allowed to sneak in through the back door under the protection of Prince Abbas Hilmi. Old Nazis residing in Cairo reportedly still hold weekly meetings there today. Col. Otto Skorzeny arrived in Cairo in 1952, while his father-in-law, Hjalmar Schacht, was meanwhile traveling from one Arab country to another in his capacity as economic advisor to the Shah of Iran and the Saudi royal family.

These people easily gained control over the intelligence agencies of several countries, starting with Egypt itself. It was the Egypt-based Nazis who, in collaboration with East German and Soviet intelligence, set up the preconditions for the Suez Crisis, in order to prevent Egypt from striking too close a relationship with American President Eisenhower.

To ignite the crisis, they created new terrorist groups whose aim was to provoke Israel into a retaliatory strike. Palestinian gangs in the Gaza Strip, which for decades had been raiding Palestine in order to steal cattle, were suddenly transformed into the so-called Fedayeen. In agreement with Israeli hawks such as Ariel Sharon and Moshe Dayan, the Egyptian intelligence officers sent by Nasser into the Gaza Strip to bring these "Fedayeen" under control and to end the unrest, were all killed—with Israeli letter bombs! Later on, these Nazi networks attempted to sell Nasser a rocket system. Professor van Leers, brought to Egypt by Genoud, worked out a system whose only consequence was Egypt's further isolation from the international community and a tightening of the Soviet military and economic grip on the country's economy, pushing the United States into an increasingly isolated alliance with Israel.

Meanwhile, Genoud, Skorzeny, Reichenberg, and others were occupied with supporting the war of the Algerian FLN against de Gaulle's France. Here again, the sole aim was to create the conditions under which the Nazi International could take over a country in order to use it as a secure base of operations. The key person in this operation was Ahmed Ben Bella, an illiterate former soldier who fought against the French because of a personal vendetta, and who happened to be living as an exile in Cairo in 1952, where he met Genoud.

Over the years, the Nazi International apparatus reconstructed by François Genoud has grown in significance. Through Ben Bella's influence, it includes a significant part of the North African and Algerian Muslims in the Maghreb and in France. Through Libya and Teheran (a frequent stopover for Genoud's co-worker Ahmed Huber), these Muslims are also integrated into a broader-based international Islamic network. Huber and Genoud sponsor the Swiss-Arab Association, a grouping closely allied with the Swiss Communist Party, which, along with Huber, supports Assad's Palestinian rebels against Arafat. Another branch is Abu Nidal and his associates, who are the direct heirs of the "Fedayeen" former Gaza gangs. Underneath this umbrella, the Grand Mufti's networks are alive and well today in Iran and within the numerous radical Islamic fundamentalist parties like the Muslim Brotherhood in Egypt or the even more radical "Hizb al Tahrir al Islamiyya," the Islamic Liberation Party, which considers Qaddafi to be "too soft." It is no accident that Huber's sympathies nowadays lie precisely with these groups.

Above: Representatives of the German classical period: Schiller, Johann Wolfgang von Goethe, and Alexander von Humboldt in conversation.

Below: The American Revolution was the model for German republicans who in the Wars of Liberation did not wish merely to be rid of Napoleon but to create a republican constitution for Germany.

Spokesmen for the Conservative Revolution. Top: Houston Stewart Chamberlain (left), Ernst von Salomon. Center: Oswald Spengler (left), Karl Haushofer. Below: Armin Mohler.

Subverters of German classicism and the unity of the natural sciences and humanities. Above: G. W. F. Hegel (left), Friedrich Nietzsche; right, Fyodor Dostoevsky, whose blood-and-soil racism laid the basis for the Nazis' madness.

In 1940, as the Hitler-Stalin Pact was still in effect, shipments of Russian grain arrive at the demarcation point between the Soviets' wide-gauge rails and the German rails.

Before Hitler's seizure of power, it was the National Bolshevist-oriented Strasser wing of the NSDAP which did the most to organize the masses behind Hitler. Left, Gregor Strasser; right, Otto Strasser.

At right: On Oct. 16, 1933, Alfred Rosenberg, the racial theorist and head of the NSDAP's foreign-policy office, addressed a full audience of diplomats and international journalists in Berlin.

Below: Dietrich Eckart in 1921. The Munich counter-culturalist and Thule ideologue wielded decisive influence on Hitler and brought him into the Thule Society.

Below left: Colonel Schellenberg and Otto Skorzeny. Above right: General Guisan.

Above: The Grand Mufti of Jerusalem, an enthusiastic supporter of Hitler, on a visit to a Muslim Waffen SS unit. Below left: Eichmann's representative Alois Brunner was never captured. After he fled to Argentina, the Syrian secret service was built up with his assistance. He is now known as Georg Fischer. Below right: Hjalmar Schacht (left) as economic advisor to Egyptian Prime Minister Nagib (right).

Above: Otto Skorzeny (left) with Mussolini after Mussolini's rescue by Skorzeny in 1943. Below: From left to right: Sadegh Tabatabai, Iranian envoy for gun-running and drug trade; Ayatollah Khomeini; and Peter Scholl-Latour, formerly with Stern magazine.

Above: Wesel am Rhein, a city near Duisburg, was practically wiped from the face of the earth by Allied bombers.

Below: Applicants in front of the headquarters of the De-Nazification Commission in Berlin on Feb. 21, 1949.

Above: Re-education: An American officer observes a discussion between Social Democrats and centrists. Center: Daily food rations for Germans in the U.S. zone in 1947. Below: German workers demonstrate against the dismantling policy of the Allies.

Clockwise from above left: John Rawling Rees, Kurt Lewin, Theodor Adorno, and the editorial staff of the Allied newspaper Neue Zeitung. In the center is Hans Habe, alias Janos Bekessy.

Left: Otto John; behind him, Sefton Delmer.

Below left: Hans Globke, state secretary under Chancellor Adenauer, who worked closely with U.S. High Commissioner McCloy.

Below right: Reinhold Gehlen, first head of the federal intelligence service in Pullach.

Above: The staff officers of the Fremde Heere Ost. In the center of the first row is Reinhold Gehlen; next to him on the right is the first head of the Militärischen Abschirmdienstes (MAD), Gerhard Wessel.

Right: Gen. Hans Oster, chief of staff of the Abwehr under Canaris.

Top: From left to right, Rudel, Jodl, Keitel, Göring. At right: Colonel (ret.) Hans-Ulrich Rudel as candidate of the German Reich Party on Aug. 28, 1953 in Bielefeld. Above left: Future Chancellor Helmut Schmidt in 1954 as speaker at a meeting of the SS veterans' organization HIAG.

Above, Hitler and Schacht (above); below, corpses at Dachau, the result of Schacht's economic policies.

Chief U.S. Prosecutor Robert Jackson in his closing statement at Nuremberg. He wanted to see Schacht found guilty.

Bottom: Göring delivers his ten-minute final speech at Nuremberg.

Above: Neo-Nazi Michael Kühnen (standing) with comrades. Below: Major Otto-Ernst Remer (right) was promoted for his participation in smashing the July 20, 1944 assassination attempt on Hitler. At center is Joseph Goebbels.

Current representatives of the Nazi International, from right to left: Jacques Vergès, François Genoud, SS Gen. Karl Wolff, and Klaus Barbie.

5

Wilton Park and the Farce of German Re-Education

In America's Germany, whatever suits us happens. If it suits us that the Germans starve, then they will starve. If it suits us that they blow up aluminum factories, then they will blow up aluminum factories. If it suits us that they read Thomas Jefferson and watch Mickey Mouse, then they will also read Thomas Jefferson and watch Mickey Mouse.

The American journalist Julian Bach did not exaggerate in this 1945 characterization from the magazine *Army Talk*. The Germans did everything he said. But to what purpose did the Allied soldiers fight a war against Hitler's Germany, and what made so many Germans turn their backs on their own country? The best of them believed that a "zero hour" had arrived, which could bring with it a new, republican beginning for (self-)degraded Germany—a Germany whose history proved its willingness and readiness to do much good for humanity.

Zero hour never came. The powers which created the best weapons on both sides, lost the war on both sides; they discovered exciting new technological potentials, but they had forgotten that these potentials could only benefit humanity if the potential itself became the political goal.

The post-war period was politically shaped by others, by people who did not believe in technological development and progress. Their sole belief was that there exists no truth and reality, other than what the majority could be induced to believe. Technology for them was nothing—even military technology. Their actual conviction was expressed in 1945 by John Rawlings Rees in *The Shaping of Psychology by War*: "Wars are not won by killing the enemy, but rather by undercutting or completely destroying his fighting morale while maintaining one's own morale."

The British, having learned from the countless psychological breakdowns caused during World War I by intensive bombardment, assigned a psychiatrist to each British division during World War II. These psychiatrists were provided with their own staff, the Army Morale Division. Since the question of soldiers' morale and psychological warfare is closely connected with espionage and secret-service activities, the two divisions formed close ties. Army psychiatry thus became the birthplace for numerous organizations, working on a worldwide basis for "mental hygiene"—psychological control of the population—and at the same time became inseparable from secret intelligence operations and their publishing and media extensions. The policy-makers behind these operations was not only causally responsible for the Nazi movement, but now oversaw the new post-war political order, not only in Germany, but in all of Europe and especially in the United States.

One direct connection between this policy faction and the ideologues of the Nazi movement was the "exemplary" experimental work carried out by the Nazis. As Rees expressed it with typical British understatement: "Even if the final objective and the final goal of this [mind-control] work in Germany was ominous, there is no question that it was thorough and effective, even though they lacked some of the more imaginative and sensitive aspects of work in our countries."

Which aspects Rees meant are revealed by a co-worker of Rees, H. V. Dicks, in a retrospect on his own work at the London Tavistock Institute: "It is worth noting how our interest was unintentionally drawn from individual case histories to the larger problems of war and human relations, the nature of hostility, the condition of culture. . . . This problem had to be carefully considered in our philosophy, first in the military-psychiatric service and later in our post-war plans and policies."

Thus there had emerged a power bloc soon resolved to take the power which could be exerted over single individuals through psychological influence, and extend it to entire societies and nations. No public opinion could ever control this bloc, since it shaped public opinion itself. Post-war Germany looked like the ideal site for its experiments.

The Nazi movement was this group's original creation, which "unfortunately" got out of their control. The post-war period offered a unique possibility to examine mistakes and improve methods. The work was not limited to Germany; but here, in this conquered and humiliated country, were the best experimental conditions to be had.

Even if the measures used in post-war Germany seem to have been chaotic ones working at cross-purposes, this does not counter our thesis that Germany's post-war history sprang from a single unified psychiatric concept: the patient must remain unaware of the specific intentions and purposes of the doctor administering the treatment. Only from a "higher" standpoint, in historical retrospect, can we gain a coherent picture of all the apparently contradictory measures. As we shall see, numerous individuals who believed in noble goals were transformed unwitting into manipulated accomplices in the further moral destruction of their own country.

Since the beginning of the war, the plans worked out by the U.S.A. and Great Britain on how to treat Germany after the collapse were highly contradictory. T. N. Kaufman, in his *Germany Must Perish*, proposed that all women in Germany should be sterilized, and the men shipped to places "lacking in energy and vigour," so that the Germans' sperm could aid in the development of martial impulses. Other, hardly less Nazi-like plans, such as the Morgenthau Plan, which intended to completely eliminate Central Europe as an economic competitor and transform it into pasture land, were initially accepted policies, while certain German émigrés in the United States pressed for reconciliation with the German population, if certain conditions were fulfilled.

'Insane and Destructive'

All the diverse plans put forward share the premise that the cause of Nazi horrors somehow lay within the Germans themselves, in their thoughts, desires, and feelings. The radical planners were skeptical about the possibility of changing the Germans. The moderates, closer to American optimism, saw the last chance for the Germans in their conversion to democracy, which would transform the psychology that had supposedly made them into Nazis.

But what was typically "German"? There were books and pamphlets on this subject for every taste and level of education. President Roosevelt distributed copies of one such document to the members of his cabinet, and the later President Harry Truman wrote the following in the margin of his copy: "Every American should read it." General Eisenhower had it published in an edition of 100,000, and made it required reading for his officers, who had to write essays on it.

Some characteristic passages include:

The Germans destroyed Latin civilization in the Battle of Adrianople in 378. . . . They made war their mission. Wherever they went, culture died out. They plundered Paris, Arras, Reims, Amiens, Tours, Bordeaux, and dozens of other cities which in later generations were repeatedly plagued by their criminal descendents. Four hundred years after Adrianople, Charlemagne continued the German tradition. . . . He sought to conquer the world, a refrain that has echoed with insane and destructive persistence throughout Germany ever since. He fought a war every year. . . . The Germans followed him with the same savage devotion with which, in our own time, they have followed the Kaiser and Hitler.

In the twelfth century there was another leader, but the monotonous program was the same. Friedrich Barbarossa, who stabbed peace in the back. . . .

The Hanseatic League organized all Germans in every country on the basis of the teaching that their loyalty was to the German leaders. . . .

The Great Elector, the soldier-king, who was described as one of the most repulsive louts that had ever lived, Friedrich the Great, destroyed every freedom that existed among his followers. . . .

Yes, there are German world conspiracies against world peace and against every free man in every land. Nazism is no new theory, which arose out of the injustice of the Versailles Treaty or out of the economic crisis. It is the expression of German aspiration, which has expressed itself in every century.

Thus the enemy in the war became, not the reign of terror of National Socialism, but rather the "German aspiration" which arose out of the "typical German mind" or "German culture." National Socialism was thus simply an expression of this mind. With astonishing thoroughness, this distortion permeated the war propaganda of the Anglo-Americans. Its most visible expression can be found in the battle instructions given to Allied bomber squadrons. The target of these bombers were not armament factories crucial to the war, but rather the center of cities teeming with culture, the expression of the urban-industrial civilization of Germany dating back to the Middle Ages.

These terror-bombings become understandable only if they are seen in conjunction with the postwar re-education program, which continues today as the "educational reform" program introduced by West German Chancellor Willy Brandt in the 1970s. The key lies in the Psychological Warfare

Division of the Supreme Headquarters of the Allied Expeditionary Forces (SHAEF), which coordinated both bomber attacks and post-war re-education.

Two persons are particularly prominent in this connection: Sefton Delmer, the head of Britain's "black propaganda," i.e., secret operations outside democratic legitimacy; and Richard Crossman, head of Britain's "white propaganda," which encompassed all other forms of influence. Delmer was Lord Beaverbrook's correspondent in Germany before the war and practically the only journalist Hitler took with him on his election campaigns. He had been rather passionately pro-Hitler throughout the 1920s and 1930s. In post-war Germany he was put in charge of the reconstruction of the press and other media.

About Crossman, who had the ambition to "out-Goebbels Goebbels," his then-supervisor Bruce Lockhart wrote: "[he was] responsible for most if not all of what Americans learned on the psychological conduct of war." Crossman had written a book as a lecturer at Oxford entitled *Plato Today,* in which he put forward the thesis that the essence of fascism is found in Platonism, in opposition to British empiricism. His ideas were continued after the war by a man recruited from a re-education camp in Austria and later made famous by his book *The Spell of Plato*—Karl Popper.

"Fascism" served the psychological warriors as a pretext to attack every direction of thought which diametrically opposed fascism! In their attacks against the "German mind," their real target was the Judeo-Christian Platonism which has made Western civilization possible, and which had its last great blossoming with the German classics and the

Prussian reformers. The latter constituted the fruitful impulse for all fundamental scientific, economic, and technological advances in modern times.

With an astonishing display of empiricism and pseudo-empiricism, the psychiatrists attempted to prove that the so-called "authoritarian personality" tends toward prejudice. Such a person, they claimed, does not act according to his own immediate needs; powerful childhood anxieties cause him to suppress these impulses in himself and project them onto his environment. He thus guides his life according to strict principles and maxims, which constitute a kind of father image, from which he can no longer free himself. With this sick father image, the so-called "superego," the Freudian school explained away all the ideas and values to which men dedicate themselves. The following were cited as symptoms of this extremely dangerous character type: "Clinging to conventional values such as correct behavior, success, industry, competence, psychological cleanliness, health. . . ."

What was asserted negatively with regard to German attitudes by Theodor Adorno and the Frankfurt School, was presented in a "positive form" by Hans Habe (a pseudonym for Janos Bekessey), editor of the *Neue Zeitung* and responsible for the rebuilding and orientation of the press in the American zone. In a lead article entitled "On the Right to Happiness," Habe instructed the Germans about the fundamental values of the American Declaration of Independence of 1776 in the following terms:

Today, in destroyed, tormented, darkly brooding Germany, there is no goal which is worth living for if not the goal of the most highly individual, highly simple, highly human happiness. . . .

What remains for us to be happy about? There is . . . your mother who did your laundry without ever getting tired . . . there is your brother, who just returned from POW camp with an amputated leg . . . there is the snow on the mountains and the green of the valleys. . . .

Prevention of the German illness of continually thinking on a grand scale. Germans must stop waiting for plans for a new, larger, better mega-city to be established in 1966; instead, they must go and make a corrugated tin house for themselves, their father, and their mother until Christmas 1946. . . . [They will do so] once they grasp that not everything a man does, has to be done for his nation or for the world.

Max Horkheimer and Theodor Adorno of the Frankfurt School of Sociology had written earlier:

Our goal is not only to describe prejudice but to explain it in order to better exterminate it. Extermination means re-education, scientifically planned and resting on the foundation of understanding achieved through scientific investigation.

As a foundation for the re-education doctrine, it was assumed that the problem with the Germans and their culture was a serious mental illness and that the "mentally ill German people" would have to undergo the same treatment administered to mentally ill individuals. Archibald MacLeish, Undersecretary of State under James Byrnes, wrote in a working paper for the 1945 Potsdam conference: "A clear parallel can be drawn between the treatment of Germany and the treatment of individual criminals in a modern prison."

The Tavistock Controllers and Lewin's Democracy

Who really ran the German re-education program? The key person is the above-cited J. R. Rees, who envisioned "building a society in which it is possible for any member of any social group to be treated, without resort to legal means, and even if they do not desire such treatment."

Using ingenious tactics, in 1932 he had successfully driven his supervisor Crichton-Miller into a nervous breakdown, so that he could take control of the Tavistock Institute. He then worked toward taking over the Directorate of Army Psychiatry, where he put together his "invisible college," an informal association of all psychiatrists working in influential positions within the military. Following the war, these people were put in charge of re-education programs, whose aim was to foist a new value system onto an entire population—to "brainwash" it.

To this purpose, the Joint Committee of Postwar Planning was organized with the backing of of the most prestigious American psychiatric associations. Names turned up such as Margaret Mead, Richard Bricknew, Talcott Parsons, Kandel, W. Koschinigg, Frank Tannenbaum, Sigrid Unset, Erich Fromm, and, first and foremost, Kurt Lewin. Rees himself was the gray eminence behind the scenes who pulled the strings. Their ideas stemmed for the most part from the Berlin Central Institute for Education and

Instruction, where they had been worked up in the 1930s. Émigrés took them to the United States, where they became fundamental precepts of the Harvard Graduate School of Education.

In England, Rees's plans were soon taken up by the highest levels of government, as shown by a speech at the London Press Club on July 7, 1941, in which Anthony Eden said: "If we want to ensure peace in our time, the German people must learn to forget what has been inculcated in them, not merely by Hitler, but also, curing the last century, by his predecessors, by so many of their philosophers and teachers."

The "scientific" foundations for this task had been laid by Gestalt psychologist Kurt Lewin, a close co-worker of the one-time "Soviet socialist" Karl Korsch. It was through Korsch, who had been re-tooled from a Fabian into a pro-Bolshevik, that Lewin came in contact with Tavistock. After his emigration to the United States, he maintained contacts with Tavistock through Eric Trist, a close co-worker with Rees. Trist also opened many doors for Lewin in the United States, through which Lewin finally climbed to the pinnacle, the Research Center for Group Dynamics at MIT. Through an effective application of his methods of conditioning small children at Cornell University, Lewin attracted the attention of the Rockefeller Foundation, which sent him to the University of Iowa, where he worked out his position on group dynamics, of which he is considered the father.

Lewin's fundamental ideas are as follows: a man tends, under extreme stress, to revert to stages of early childhood. If this condition is induced within a "family-like" situation, then, through the group, the individual recovering from stress can be slowly reconstructed psychologically so that, in a brief period of time, he undergoes a new, more desirable development of consciouness. The result is dependent on the leadership of the small group, which functions in the process as a substitute family. Lewin developed a maximally effective leadership-style for this purpose.

The goal of the Joint Committee was to extend the successful re-education methods developed with over-stressed individuals in small groups and apply them to entire populations and nations. Here, too, Lewin's work in Gestalt psychology made the decisive contributions. He specified in his 1943 piece "The Special Case of Germany" that one could not merely doctor up a few isolated characteristics or features. An individual's consciousness corresponds in a nation to a "cultural atmosphere" determined by a very large number of components and attributes which stand in a recriprocal relationship to one another. Lewin applied systems-analysis field theory in his description: in order to be successful, the cultural atmosphere as a whole must be understood and transformed: "In order to be stable, a cultural shift must penetrate more or less all aspects of national life, since the dynamic interaction between the various aspects of a culture of a nation, such as education, morality, political behavior, religious views, lead to circumstances where every deviation from the existing culture soon will be bent back into the existing current."

As a consequence of this situation he demanded a "complete destruction of the equilibrium of forces which maintain social self-regulation." A nation to be re-educated must be driven back into an "early childhood situation"; Lewin called this situation the stage of "fluidity," his term for social chaos.

There were various conceptions of how such chaos was to be produced. For example, the American banker and author James Warburg, who later helped establish the pro-terrorist Institute for Policy Studies in Washington, D.C., proposed to put Germany into "containment," cutting it off completely from the outside world. Not only would this create a terrible crisis, but this crisis would break down all still existing institutions and moral ties, thus bringing about the condition of "fluidity." The Morgenthau Plan subsumed this sort of consideration.

Lewin warned that if the occupying powers forced any new content or "pattern" on the Germans, then a national resistance would be immediately triggered. It was necessary to create for the nation a new indigenous leadership elite which would establish these new values while giving the population the impression that the elite was actively working on the basis of popular support. As in his group-dynamics research, Lewin discovered that neither a radical-democratic leadership, which would be ready to give in to the greatest diversity of tendencies among the population, nor an authoritarian leadership, which would not allow the population to have a sense of active cooperation, could work: "In order to effect a change to democracy, a situation must be created for a time in which the leader uses sufficient control to eliminate the influences he does not desire."

The leader must "have power and apply it toward active re-education." But he must above all be able to act "as if" he were using the power in the majority's interest and with their consent. The essential thing is not that this actually occurs, but rather that such an impression is made credible.

Lewin therefore concludes: "It is easier to make autocratic leaders democratic than to do so with laissez-faire democrats and complacent half-democrats."

Thus, the die was cast concerning the active resistance fighters of Germany: they were not suitable as leaders of the re-education process. The decision was made to resort to a part of the Nazi elite which had not received too much public exposure. In preparation for this, former Social Democrat W. Koschnigg accordingly went into action in England and proposed in his 1943 book *Slaves Need No Leader* that suitable prisoners of war be sought out from the camps and trained as "opinion leaders" for appropriate re-education tasks in Germany.

The Joint Committee summarized its goals, formed on the basis of Lewin's proposals, in a resolution written in early 1945. The resolution said: "Psycho-cultural reinforcement, although new and untested, is promising because it is aimed at human beings, their ways of behaving and feeling as well as the traditions which control their individual and group life. It promises not only a new access to Germany but presents a new problem, in which the goal is the conscious transformation of a people through the alteration of their culture, their social practices, and their educational system."

Re-Education of the Resistance

If the goal had really been re-educating Germany in democracy and republican thought, the occupying powers in Germany could not have had a better opportunity. Immediately after the military surrender, the first trade-union meetings took place on a regional and industrial basis. In most cases, these were led by illegal labor groups which had conspired together during the Nazi period without coming into contact with the so-called resistance groups, which in most cases would have meant betrayal. It was due to the initiative of these groups that the arriving occupying powers found the workers in many locales already in their places, disciplined and ready to organize clean-up details or already at work on the conversion from wartime to peacetime production.

The groups grew out of the factories and were not trade unions in the narrow sense, but rather genuine political organizations. Their major concern was less a general program than the urgent problem of caring for the population. In the large factories of the Ruhr region and elsewhere, these organizations grew up mostly on the factory level, and in more rural regions where small industry prevailed, on a municipal level. Thus in the Bremen region, local "Alliances to Fight Fascism" were formed. Social Democrats, Communists, Christians, and eager young people who had had nothing to do with traditional parties, all worked together in these groups.

Thus, spontaneously, a democratic, anti-fascist organization had formed, on which the occupying powers could have relied, had they been concerned with "freedom" and "democracy." This fact could not be denied, though it was distorted, by the occupying powers. An activity report of the "Manpower Division" of the British military government said: "Immediately following the collapse of Germany, self-appointed groups of people, who did not represent the majority of the workers, set themselves up as 'industrial soviets' and attempted in some cases to take over the firms."

In Hamburg, where the process can be best documented, 50,000 workers immediately petitioned for recognition of the "Socialist Free Trade Union." By June 18, 1945, the group had been banned by the British military government. In April, similar groups in Bochum, Essen, Gelsenkirchen, Herne, Aachen, and other places in the Ruhr region were broken up or banned. Lucius Clay's political advisor Robert Murphy, in a telegram of June 28, 1945, openly demanded the "negative policy of suppression of all democratic elements" in order to create a "political vacuum."

In the French occupation zone, the Württemberg Trade Union Alliance was founded on May 11, and on June 10, the Free German Trade Union Alliance was founded. In the U.S. zone, as Stuttgart was cleaned up, the Americans attempted to dissolve the Baden-Württemberg Trade Union Alliance again, and blocked all its activities until September, 1946.

The chief historian with the U.S. High Commission, Harold Zink, covered up the reasons for the moves against these organizations and for the ban on the formation of political parties: "The argument was, to proceed by a slow process of reconstruction of labor organizations, thereby significantly reducing or altogether eliminating the risk of Communist takeover of such organizations."

Somewhat less precisely but far more correctly, Field Marshal Montgomery presented the disdainful content of all re-education efforts: "The Russians support the trade-unions. I decided to do nothing. . . . By doing so I hoped that, in the course of time, the right people would come forward out of their own ranks, but if we went too fast, there was a danger that the trade unions would fall into the wrong hands and make trouble." He expanded on this in a May 2, 1946 memorandum: "But if the Germans become restless and major hostilities break out against the occupying powers, then they will get support from political and trade-union organizations, which they could use to carry out their harmful intentions."

Measures against the organizations usually did not take place so brusquely as in Hamburg. They consisted in an amazingly bureaucratic and demoralizing delay in the acceptance procedures which had been set up by Industral Relations Directive Number 16. The dragging-out of these secret authorization procedures for political parties and labor organizations had the goal of placing acceptable persons into critical positions. These positions went almost exclusively to people who had held leading offices before 1945, and thus had dubious loyalties. Many of the really influential but scarcely visible positions were taken over by émigrés who had been prepared for those positions abroad, where their "proper" loyalties were instilled.

Anyone who achieved any sort of position or rank belonged to a lodge, a fellowship, or a more or less informal group around some institution, which looked after him and gave him his career plan. The first round of organizers in Germany were either bought off, like the factory council chairman of Salzgitter A.G., Erich Söchtig, or were quickly obliged to give up active work.

Nothing was better prepared or planned in greater detail by the Allies than post-war Germany's personnel policies. Unless it was a question of émigrés that had to be ordered back home, the military jeeps would drive cross-country with their "white lists," hunting up the designated individuals from every nook and cranny and bringing them into their designated positions. The deployment of these jeeps was based on precise psychological profiles drawn up by social democrats and other émigrés in England and America working with the various Anglo-American psychological warfare units.

War, Hunger, and Demolition: Part of Re-Education

The stress functions necessary for re-education in Lewin's sense were more easily created under the conditions of war than under occupation. The bombardment of cities which were known not to be the site of crucial war industries, but rather of cultural momuments and the population itself, were aimed at breaking down the population's morale. But on the contrary, the bombardment mobilized the civilian population's last will to resist, thereby prolonging the war and the destruction it brought. The bombardment nonetheless had much to do with creating the objective preconditions for re-education.

We can get a sense of the psychological effect of strategic bombing if we imagine ourselves in the bunker of a house in a city under bombing attack, and recall our feelings listening to the howl of the approaching bombs. The urgent wish that the bombs should fall anywhere else—on our neighbors, on our aunt or uncle, only not on this house—was the least of it.

More essential was the impotent feeling of despairing panic, issuing into a speechless, rigid form of cold terror. These moments of raging, despairing, total impotence respecting the apparently arbitrary bombing raids, were the "psychologically" right times for re-education. The actual detonation of the bombs changed this feeling of impotence into quick, determined actions to aid the victims. But soon the sirens sounded again, and the old fear returned. These periods of tension and relief produced the psychological "hot and cold bath" which was to wear down people's fighting—and general— morale.

The bombing of cities also had "real" results. Loss of capacity of German industry from the effects of the war was only 8.1 percent, and an estimated further 7.3 percent was demolished after the war. This should have meant a burst of prosperity unleashed by the conversion of industrial capacity to peacetime production. The purpose of the so-called dismantling threat in the Western zone was precisely to prevent this from occurring, and was not aimed at the actual destruction of industrial capacity. The Morgenthau Plan's well known threat to make Germany into a pasture, likewise served more to produce the fear required for the re-education effort, and was not an actual Allied plan.

One of the documents already under consideration by the American State Department in 1944 was a memorandum establishing a long-term strategy for Germany. The memorandum made it clear that a reconstruction of Europe without German industry was out of the question. The securing of influence in Europe was an urgent priority, while the dismantling threats and the economic chaos in the occupied areas—which more or less directly included France and Italy—was of primarily "psychological" importance.

These psychological considerations led to Directive JCS 1967 of the High Command of the American occupying troops: "You will take no steps which

a) could lead to the economic re-establishment of Germany or b) are intended to maintain or strengthen the German economy."

That the demolition campaign of the Allies was primarily designed for its psychological effect is shown not only by its modest scope, but by how it was implemented. There were no clear plans or regulations. No one really knew its purpose. For that reason, the wildest rumors spread about the supposed Allied demolition plans, causing confusion, excitement, and resistance measures, which immediately proved to be unnecessary as new rumors went into circulation.

The real effect of the bombing lay in the destruction of living quarters and infrastructure. Of the 15.8 million residences which had existed in Germany before the war, more than 25 percent were completely destroyed. Five to six million homes were more lightly damaged, and could be reconstructed. Only one-third of all homes remained intact.

The indigenous population was not alone in competing for homes. Approximately 8 million displaced persons, which included foreigners conscripted by the Nazis for slave labor in Germany, were left to their own devices by the Allies and crowded especially into the villages. The so-called alien workers, drawing conclusions from how they were treated in the work camps, prepared to get similar treatment from the civilian population. To heighten the effect, SHAEF provided them with liquor and goaded them to take their own revenge on German civilians for what had been done to them. Statements from the military government announced that the alien workers would be put into the intact dwellings, while their owners would be quartered in the work camps. As far as is known, such relocations never took place. But the harsh reality was the plundering and robbing carried out by bands of these pitiful creatures, against whom the German population could not defend itself without being immediately punished by the occupying powers.

These unfortunates were finally driven back into the work camps by the occupation troops and put under strict guard. Those who did not "voluntarily" go to work in Belgian and French mines were, over the course of the next 10 years, moved back to their homelands.

In addition to the captured workers were 17 million "Germans of foreign citizenship," 8 million of whom crowded into West Germany. They were joined by 2 million refugees from the Soviet occupied zone. The distribution of these masses of people was quite unequal. Whereas the population of the French occupied zone increased by only 4 percent, in the American zone it increased by over 20 percent, and in Schleswig-Holstein by over 63 percent. Thus, the most seriously affected were the sparsely populated rural regions least prepared for such an onslaught. The resettlement of the various groups was directed by the psychological warriors to achieve a maximum of friction; mixing religious denominations was carried out precisely for this effect.

The Food Weapon

All these stress factors were only a prelude to the real treatment. "After the First World War, food has proven to be a dangerous political weapon, and during the discussions over the founding of the United Nations Relief and Rehabilitation Agency

(UNRRA), it became clear that food was obviously well suited for this purpose," wrote leftist historian Gabriel Kolko. In keeping with this, Marshall Plan chief Averell Harriman described the control of consumer goods as "one of the most efficacious weapons our arsenal possesses to guide political events in Europe in the direction which suits us."

Psychologists have found that forced hunger is the most powerful means of driving adults into an infantile level of consciousness. Observations showed that under such conditions people tend to lose their acquired morality and will submit to any self-degradation which could lead to obtaining food.

In 1945 there were still food reserves, and despite the flood of refugees distribution did not collapse with the entry of the occupation troops. But by 1946–47 the reserves had been exhausted. The well-calculated starvation of the German population began. As a rule, 2,000 calories constitute the minimum for human subsistence. In the American sector, an *average* of 1,275 calories were available per person; in the British zone, 1,015; and in the French, only 940. The responsibility for this shortage situation was ascribed to the Russians' refusal to sell on the world market any of the raw materials and finished goods available in their zone, in order to use the revenue to buy the necessary food supplies for all of Germany. General Clay had laid the basis for this refusal with his harsh announcement on May 3, 1946 that all reparations to the Soviet Union would be halted.

The only recourses for industrial workers in the urban regions were strikes and demonstrations for a bit more food. They could not believe that the occupying powers were behind the starvation rations, but blamed it on the Nazis still in official positions, and demanded the dismissal of those who out of "incompetence or malevolence" were responsible for the food shortage, such as Minister Schlange-Schöningen in North Rhine-Westphalia. There were violent hunger demonstrations in the urban areas, with up to 100,000 participants in a single city. Like the demonstrations after the reinstatement of Nazis in leading factory positions, these were forcibly suppressed by the occupying powers; the Allies' standard argument was that demonstrations do not make bread. And they did not neglect to point out in their announcements accompanying the tanks: "And don't forget that according to the laws of the occupying powers and the military government, the guilty can be punished with death."

Anti-fascist workers in Germany experienced the post-war period as a singular disappointment, especially those who had expected the victorious powers to make a new republican beginning. The first post-war years took them from one defeat to the next. This process began with the obstruction of their independent organizations and the installation of a leadership dependent on the grace of the allies.

Though some of these did not come until the beginning of the 1950s, by 1948 it was already clear to any relatively alert observer that no real new beginning had taken place in Germany. The cynicism with which 90 percent of the working population's hard-earned savings was devalued, after the mark had already been artificially devalued by the Allied powers' printing of 12 billion marks, while corporations still received 90 percent of face value; the cynicism with which the hoarding of goods—despite inconceivable misery among the population—was rewarded by the high prices caused by the currency reform; these things spoke all too clearly. One result of such policies was the rapid increase in consumption of alcohol in spite of a rapid 18 percent jump in the cost of food, "offset" by a "liberal salary increase" of a total of 4.5 percent.

The rise in living standards over the following years did not redress the psychological damage suffered by the population up to 1948. This is clear from the children of this generation: all the rekindled hopes and dreams for a new beginning, expressed in the initial enthusiasm for reconstruction, were gone. They lost hold of their ideals, goals, and exemplars, preferring to merely do their job. They learned that the important thing is to only think of oneself and seek one's own advantage. It should be obvious that such a way of thinking does not lead to great thoughts, inventions, or contributions to development, nor can it direct a maturing generation toward a future which inspires it to live and create. Whoever is cut off from his past, also loses his future. The psychological energy necessary for truly great achievement can never be mobilized for things merely to one's own petty advantage.

Re-Education and De-Nazification

Actual de-Nazification was at first carried out quite intensively, and by September 1945, more than 136,000 National Socialists were sitting in the old concentration camps. However, it soon became apparent that the occupying powers were going to rely heavily on old Nazis. In early 1947, two-thirds of the Nazis interned in 1945 were set free. De-Nazifying approximately 8 million party members would, of course, have been a big job. But the fact that no effort at all was apparently intended, shocked many occupation officers. U.S. officer Arthur D.

Kahn, for example, recounted in his book *Officers, Cardinals, and Concerns* the outrage he felt when the general director of the armaments firm Opel A.G., who as early as 1932 had conferred with Hitler and had published appeals for supporting National Socialism, was fined a total of $200. The same penalty, along with the loss of his job, was meted out to a postman who had been a member of the NSDAP in 1939–40.

Injustices of this sort were common, and the U.S. military government made no attempt to cover them up. Robert Murphy, for example, justified them with the cynical statement: "It is not the Americans' intent to destroy the basis of private property with a thorough de-Nazification."

Against initially strong resistance, former Nazi professionals were reintroduced into three areas in particular: civil service, the economy, and the media. In the staffing of the newly formed state governments and economic councils, "mass rehabilitation of Nazis" took place. A typical example is Arnold Gehlen, one of the most intelligent and devoted ideologues of the Nazi regime, but who had never occupied an official position. In 1947 he was entrusted with the training of the top echelons of federal officials at the college for administrative science in Speyer. His cousin, Gen. Reinhard Gehlen, was able to peddle his experience from the Nazi secret service to the Americans.

The personnel at the "Office for Organization of Consular Economic Representation," (later to become the Foreign Office), was typical: 60.3 percent had earned their spurs under Ribbentrop. Old party members made up 65.3 percent.

Of course, it was also necessary to bring in entirely new people. The Allies used three different

methods of recruitment. The first was to select suitable people from the POW camps for special training. This was under way during the war. The second
could only begin in 1945. In this case, suitable persons from the National Socialist youth-elite corps
were sought out and put into academy-like estab-
lishments for reorientation by a correspondingly
elite staff of Allied teachers. The third method was
a comprehensive exchange program enabling tal-
ented young Germans to study in the United States
or England, where they were grouped into more
or less informal "fellowships."

The re-education of prisoners of war was already
under way in England by 1941. The British War
Ministry assigned this task to the Psychological Warfare Executive (PWE). The first step was to set up
a screening camp. From the interrogations of Hess
and other psychiatric studies of the attitudes and
reactions of "genuine" Nazis, they derived criteria
by which they believed suitable candidates could be
selected for re-education. The purpose of the
screening centers was to "use de-Nazification in order to select de-Nazified future leaders and civil
servants from among the Germans," according to
H. V. Dicks. At the same time, material was to be
collected for later used in propaganda operations.
Rees pointed out in this connection that "military
and other battle units"—which emphatically included POW camps—"are unique experimental
groups, and on the other hand, it is possible to lead
them in a manner scarcely possible in civilian life."

Those first chosen were immediately involved in
practical activities. Under the guidance of advisors
from émigré circles, they published a camp newspaper: *The Weekly Post,* "Newspaper for German
Prisoners of War in England." From 1943, they

regularly prepared radio broadcasts designed to damage fighting morale at the front and among civilians. The radio broadcast project grew to such proportions that it had to be consolidated into its own camp, Camp 7 in Ascot. Other prisoners were then required to criticize the camp newspaper and selected radio broadcasts. Their reactions were carefully studied by the relevant agencies in order to shape military propaganda.

The anticipated need for leadership cadre in occupied Germany could not be met from these circles alone. Therefore, the Control Office for Germany and Austria (COGA) decided to intensify and professionalize the re-education program. One result was the establishment of the "Wilton Park" POW Camp 300 near London. Its task was to take prisoners specially selected as candidates for leadership positions and "reschool" them in intensive courses.

It is notable in this connection that the selection methods employed were identical to those used by the Nazis to select their own cadre, according to Rees. Individuals with stable personalities, with a sense of self-worth, and with firm convictions were not sought, but rather, quite explicitly, individuals with weak egos. Such individuals were most easily manipulated by an emotional "hot and cold bath" of hostile attack and friendly, motherly warmth until, in total uncertainty, they gave themselves over completely to the group, which could control them with the promise of protection and security. Those moved into Wilton Park were generally given a so-called "Labour Party identity"; other POWs characterized Wilton Park as the "dream factory" and the "democracy mill."

Wilton Park was directed by Prof. Heinz Köppler. Born in 1912 in Prussia, he studied history in Berlin, Heidelberg, and Kiel. In 1933 he received a stipend from Oxford, became a citizen in 1937 and began his rapid rise in the academic world. In 1939, he also became a departmental director within the PWE. On the basis of the Churchill memorandum, he wrote a program for post-war Germany in which he announced the idea of determining German post-war history through the molding of public opinion. In June 1947, he expanded on his program in a speech before graduates of the Hanover Technical University, and proposed to rework the "fundamental questions of European civilization" and "to venture the reconstruction of European life." He wanted nothing less than an alternative to previous Western culture.

At Wilton Park, courses were established for every 300 individuals, broken down into 14 to 16 groups, each of which had a different responsibility. One group had to write evaluations of the political press, another dealt with organizational questions, another worked up a cultural program, and so forth. Each group was assigned a tutor.

As a rule, each course lasted for six to eight weeks. Successful prisoners could take several courses in a row. Well-known experts were invited to lecture, and lectures were discussed in workshops under the tutors' supervision. Then the tutors held sessions in which the participants could submit questions in writing; then group discussion took place once again. A series of such cycles were summarized in a group game, the so-called "Brain Trust Exercise." The high point of every course was the Brain Trust of the German parties, in which mock elections were held with the German Social Democrats, Christian Democrats, Liberal Democrats (predecessor to the Free Democrats) and Communists. With astonishing regularity, the SPD received approximately 45 percent of the votes in the mock secret balloting, while the other parties had to settle for equal portions of the remainder.

The teachers at Wilton Park, representing the international elite of psychological warfare, came from England, Switzerland, and the United States; later, civilians such as trade-unionist Viktor Agartz were flown in from Germany. After 1947, women also took part in the courses.

Group Dynamics in Action

A total of 12,000 Germans passed through Wilton Park. It was their springboard into future top positions in the parties, the labor unions, and the media. Later, in order to maintain the effects of re-education, so-called Wilton Park Friendship Societies were founded. These represented the most important informal channels for the secret background information on which the "leading forces" believed themselves to be dependent. Because it is not verifiable, such secret background information is an excellent means for exercising control over people who consider themselves to be masters of their own fate.

In addition to the general group-dynamics methods of Rees, Bion, Trist, and others, what was decisive for the success of Wilton Park was the ideology lived out by the inmates. It was not merely for purposes of introducing a sense of being "the chosen," that everything said at Wilton Park was treated as "top secret." No note-taking was allowed. Professor Köppler never tired of drumming it into participants' heads that "Free societies are based on the decisions of a minority which we call the political elite. In the final analysis, a society rests on the decisions of amateur, not professional politicians."

Thus course participants received a unique opportunity, not only to become acquainted with the elite, but to feel as though they belonged to it. In this connection, Köppler constantly held up to Wilton Park inmates the "aristocratic form of life" as a model for emulation. Aside from teaching more refined forms of interaction, the philosophic content of the courses was to inculcate the teachings of John Locke. Only with this training could one truly assume and maintain the correct "stance." The content of the exalted "democratic" ideal was reduced to questions of style. Political content dwindled in importance in comparison with matters of form. Content was merely the lever for lifting oneself into a position of power. The brain-trust meetings were scarcely concerned about which political standpoint was taken and defended. The important thing was the method by which any position could be sold to the majority.

Participants came to see themselves as the real democrats, who did not obstinately cling to any one doctrine, but were free to change position at will as in a Jesuitical exercise. From there they could drive the fanatics and rigid doctrinaires from the field, clearing the way for a pragmatic approach with the broadest possible support. Their sole political obligation was to belong and remain loyal to the group, to which they owed their position and which had begun to assume a sort of mother role.

The training of later "leading" politicians in these groups is reponsible for the glibness and chronic dishonesty of post-war politics in Germany, and the absence of concrete development programs and clear aims for future political work. Everything becomes submerged in empty prattle about "freedon and democracy," which seems to have lost any practical significance.

While Wilton Park provided a supply of compliant politicians for various "democratic" parties, in the United States the groundwork was being laid for post-war German culture, or what passes for such. The United States had no German prisoners of war until 1943. In March 1943, Assistant Secretary of War John J. McCloy commissioned Frederick Osborn of the Murphy & Company bank, director since 1941 of the Special Service Division, to work up a study on prospective re-education measures. Osborn passed the assignment to the military expert S. L. A. ("Slam") Marshall, who 19 days later produced a study titled "Indoctrination of Enemy Prisoners." Marshall emphasized that the "social attitudes of the prisoners of war" should be studied in advance in English camps. Similar studies were produced by David P. Page, Ed Davidson, and Cyrus Brooks.

K. Bondy, who had found refuge at Harvard, wrote a study which earned him the chance to establish an Institute for Psychology at the University of Hamburg, which only a few years ago attracted attention for its work on active brainwashing. Bondy published numerous essays on re-education of prisoners of war. His close co-worker was G. T. Seger, a former SPD parliamentarian from Magdeburg, who contributed his personal experience from the Oranienburg concentration camp, from which he had been released in 1935, afterwards settling in the United States. Seger and Bondy founded the Council for a Democratic Germany, which set itself the task of alerting the U.S. administration to the necessity for re-education in Germany. One other member of the Council's executive committee was Louis P. Lochner, who in his capacity as Associated Press correspondent had been with the Nazi troops in every battle up through 1942, and who published Goebbels' diary in 1948. Secretary of State Stimson, who was responsible for the American side of the Strategic Bombing Survey, was one of the first to support the Council's re-education plans, with the proviso that they "promote the external security of the United States in the post-war world and ensure the success of the USA's post-war plans."

The first project followed the English example— the publication of a newspaper to propagandize for the "American way of life." *Der Ruf* (*The Call*) was "prepared and published by German prisoners of war for German prisoners of war." A "Special Project Branch" was formed expressly to run the paper, and whose task was to prepare "small groups for various purposes in post-war Germany," "to train [them] in theories of the social sciences." The editoral staff was brought to the Van Etten camp in Elmira, New York, "where specially selected prisoners were sent for re-education."

Reich-Ranicki reported that "failed revolutionaries" were sought who were depressive to the point of persecution neurosis, with openly existentialist attitudes. One such person was ex-Communist Alfred Andersch, who had "turned" while at the Dachau concentration camp in 1933, subsequently serving as an inconspicuous office worker from 1933 to 1940. In 1944, while in the construction corps of the army in Italy, he was able to escape to the American side. Another was H. W. Richter, the brain of the group, who had been expelled from the Communist Party in 1933 and escaped from Germany in 1943. The editors of *Der Ruf* also included René

Hocke, later correspondent for *Süddeutsche Zeitung*; Curt Vinz, owner of the Nymphenburg publishing house I. Wilimiz; and Erich Kuby. Controllers of the groups were Robert Pestalozzi and Walter Schoenstedt, former associates of Münzenberg's anarcho-Communist newspaper *Unsere Zeit*. This well-known Communist from Weimar, Germany, walked around camp wearing a U.S. Army captain's uniform.

When the paper was moved to Fort Phillip Kearney in 1945, the editors received additional intelligence assignments, such as oversight of all other camp newspapers, working out personnel proposals, commenting on the material prepared by the OSS/OWI for psychological warfare in Germany and Japan.

The same editorial staff also started up an independent tabloid aimed at the younger generation and which, under a U.S. license, was able to apppear in an edition of 100,000 on paper whose quality was extraordinarily high for Germany at the time. Its publisher was an earlier associate, Erich Kuby. After the 17th edition, the editorship was changed to transmit a "left" image. Writers for the paper included famous representatives of the "third way" such as Ignazio Silone, Arthur Koestler, Simone de Beauvoir, Jean-Paul Sartre, Lord Beveridge, and Harry Ehrmann of the New School for Social Research. These authors, together with Otto Suhr, Ernst Reuter, and the ex-Communist in U.S. service Ruth Fischer, called together the "Congress for Cultural Freedom" in Berlin, the launching pad for the "counterculture" revival in Germany.

The older group around Andersch and Richter started out with a "counter-paper" named *Scorpion*. They came across as too "nihilistic," however, and soon lost their U.S. license. Eventually, in September 1947 the Fort Kearney group landed at the estate of a woman, Ilse Schneider Lengyel, who, among her other charms, had adequate stocks of food. There, in the vicinity of Füssen, they founded Group 47, and with grants from the Ford Foundation, the Rockefeller Foundation, and the McCann advertising agency, were able to award their first cultural prize to Heinrich Böll, a literary newcomer. The group received a special license from the military authorities which allowed its members to move from one zone to another in Germany without restraint on any available mode of transportation—an extraordinary privilege at that time.

Next this group, together with Waldemar von Knöringer and H.-J. Vogel of the SPD, formed the Grünwalder Circle "against creeping fascism." That was the seed form of the later "New Left." Since 1958, Richter has acted as the top West German brain behind the "Ban The Bomb" movement. He founded the Easter March organization in Munich and in 1959 initiated the European Congress of Opponents of Nuclear Weapons in London, where he was elected president of the European Federation Against Nuclear Armament.

It is only once we consider the re-education plan that it becomes clear why, after the unconditional surrender, the total German army, from anti-aircraft assistant to reserve member, a total of 12 million men, was crammed into prison camps. There could be no other reason, since the capitulation and occupation did away with their purpose, namely to prevent prisoners from re-entering the war as enemy combatants. At the end of 1948, there will still 2.4 million men spending their most productive years behind barbed wire: 30,976 in U.S. camps, 435,295 in British, and 631,483 in French (as well as 890,532 in Russia and 300,000 in camps of other war participants).

The most important re-education method in the camps was hunger. Especially notorious was the American camp at Heilbronn. The camp resembled a collection of chicken coops, where meals consisted of egg powder and prisoners dug the ground for earthworms. The reason for this treatment was that a starving man will usually experience anyone who gives him food as a liberator, even if it is the same person who had previously let the individual starve.

Naturally, there was special treatment for officers, particularly young officers ready to cooperate. (The older ones were treated as fixed in their views and of little use.) An academy founded by CIA official Otto Molden, later called the Austrian College, in the isolated Alpine village of Alpach, brought together bright, young officers from every country which participated in the war. Old antagonisms were to be overcome in discussions over a common postwar perspective, and new acquaintances were to be made. The ruling philosophical direction was the so-called Viennese School; from the beginning the entire enterprise was under British influence. Alpach's best-known product is Sir Karl Popper, who began his career there as an assistant.

Another re-education establishment was the University for Labor, Politics, and Science at Wilhelmshaven, which became a model for trade-union educational centers. It was founded on the initiative of Captain Conder and Colonel Dillon, and was organized on the model of an English college. The idea was to set up a special educational center for participants in the war whose education had been interrupted. The SPD supported the activity from the beginning. According to Maria Meyer-Sevenich, it aimed at an education "in order to shape social institutions in the spirit of the new democracy. . . . It will not just be to impart knowledge; it will be to live in community. People who have gone through this communal experience will be the bearers of a new spirit." The facilities chosen were isolated barracks where, in seclusion, "self-government" could be practiced in village parliaments, village executives, and village courts. As in Wilton Park, "Brain Trust" and democracy games were played. The organization was taken over in 1962 by Göttingen University, with the intention of going after Germany's only center of scientific research.

One experiment in Wilhemshaven was the joint lecture series of Prof. Wolfgang Abendroth and Rüdiger Altmann, where participants were drilled in the structure of political post-war propaganda in Germany. Students were presented with opposing "left" and "right" positions, and were encouraged to take sides. What they were not supposed to notice, however, was that the opposing sides were so chosen that no matter which side they chose, the basis for both contrasting positions was the same. The special method of this indoctrination method had been worked out by the Frankfurt School's radio research program in the United States. It was proudly claimed that this method was superior to the one-sided forms of Eastern indoctrination. One application of this method in post-war history was the "positivism debate" in German sociology, which made Germany's best students, who could not stomach Anglo-Austrian empiricism, susceptible to "New Left" propaganda. Political discussion in the Federal Republic has almost exclusively followed this pattern: alternatives offered as opposites are judged according to the very same cultural and epistemological groundwork. Wilton Park perfected the application of this method.

Bibliography

American Journal of Orthopsychiatry, Vol. XV, No. 3, July 1945.

Clay, Lucius D., *Decision in Germany*, New York, 1950.

Dicks, H. V., *Fifty Years at Tavistock*, London, 1970.

Deuerlein, E., *Potsdam 1945*, Munich, 1968.

Drenker, Alexander, *Diplomaten ohne Nimbus!*, Zürich, 1970.

Hammond, Paul Y., "Directives for the Occupation of Germany, the Washington Controversy," in H. Stein, *American Civil-Military Decisions*, University of Alabama, 1963.

Kahn, Arthur D., *Offiziere, Kardinäle, Konzerne*, Berlin, n.d.

Kolko, Gabriel, *Politics of War*, New York, 1968.

Niethammer, Lutz, "Zum Verständnis von Reform und Rekonstruktion in der U.S.-Zone am Beispiel der Neuordnung des öffentlichen Dienstes, in *Vierteljahresheft für Zeitgeschichte*, Vol. 21, 1973.

Proudfoot, M., *European Refugees, 1939–1952*, Evanston, Ill., 1956.

Rees, J. R., *The Shaping of Psychology by War*, New York, 1945.

Secretary of State of Foreign Affairs (ed.), *An Account of the Industrial Relations in Germany, 1945–1949*, London, 1950.

Zink, Harold, *The United States in Germany 1944–1955*, Princeton 1957.

6

Old Wine in New Casks: The German Secret Services

As has been shown in the previous sections, there was a rapid consolidation of the old international fascist networks in occupied Germany during the Cold War. The same individuals who during the war had been involved in numerous negotiations on the post-war period in the United States, in Great Britain, in Switzerland, in Sweden, Paris, or Moscow with the various factions of the Nazi leadership now arrived as the occupiers of Germany and had the decisive power over the political and economic reconstruction, the treatment of the Germans, and the personnel of the various new institutions and parties to be formed.

First, the tremendous wealth which the Nazi leadership had hoarded from their spoils had to be brought to safety, and—months before the war's end—arrangements were also made for the leadership of the National Socialists, the SS, the secret service, etc. to be "successfully" installed elsewhere.

Organizations for Escape

Immediately after the war, two organizations became active, "The Spider" (Die Spinne) and "Odessa" (Organization der ehemaligen SS-Angehörigen—Organization of Former SS Members), which had the task of making possible the escape of National Socialist war criminals, SS leaders, and high officials of other Nazi organizations into foreign countries, simultaneously maintaining the interconnections within these farflung networks of these "old boys." Later, came other organizations, such as the HIAG (Hilfsgemeinschaft auf Gegenseitigkeit der Soldaten der ehemaligen Waffen-SS e.V., Society for the Aid of Former SS Soldiers, Inc.), and "Quiet Aid" (Stille Hilfe) of Princess Ysenburg, organizations which often overlapped in their personnel.

How was the escape organized? Hundreds of escapees assembled at previously arranged locations, and were taken by the assistance organizations, in close connection with their foreign friends, via different routes abroad. One of these routes was the so-called Cloister Route, where the "clients" were disguised in monks' robes and moved from cloister to cloister through Austria to Italy. At a time when ordinary citizens were not allowed to leave their occupied zones, the specialists in Odessa were supplied with border passes for all occupied zones. Thus, the former SS member Eric Kern, alias Eric Kernmayr, travelled without difficulty as the middleman for the Spider group back and forth between Munich and Salzberg, the same Kernmayr who would become the editor of the neo-Nazi *Deutsche Wochenzeitung* and the head editor of the *Deutsche Soldatenzeitung*. He was also the founder of the influential "Gmünd Circle" of former SS members in Salzkammergut, which, based in Austria, never had to undergo any "de-Nazification" or any other form of cleanup.

Otto Skorzeny, the head of the Special Commandos during the Third Reich, had a special role within the escape organizations from his base in Madrid, where he moved following his acquittal at Nuremberg. Another important figure was the Austrian Bishop Hudal in Rome. As the long-time confidante of Pope Pius XII with the rank of titular bishop and rector of the Instituto Santo Maria dell'Anima, it was possible for him to furnish passes for his future "clients," and to seek aid for the escape of hundreds of Nazis to the Middle East and South America from such organizations as the Refugee Bureau in the Vatican, Caritas, and the Red Cross. Bishop Hudal was a fanatical supporter of Hitler. Like many Austrians, he saw in Hitler and the Greater German Reich a continuation of the Holy Roman Empire of the German Nation, and was enthusiastic that finally the "great ethnic idea" had been reawakened and that the "unity of the Germans in language and culture" could now be accomplished. In his 1936 book on *The Foundations of National Socialism,* he expressed the same racial theories as were espoused by the fascists in Germany (and other countries) at that time.

Odessa could count on the support of a great number of collaborators. Every 25 miles along the German-Swiss border there was an "interface." In Lindau am Bodensee, Odessa had formed an import-export business, with branches in Cairo and Damascus. Bregenz and Lindau were important locations because they lay within the Germany-Austria-Switzerland triangle; once "clients" were in

Austria, further escape via the airports in Geneva or Zürich to other destinations was virtually assured. There was no lack of money, passports and visas. Swiss, Austrians, French, British, and Americans were all well informed about these operations and some actively helped out. Extremely close relations existed even during the war between the American OSS in Europe under Allen Dulles, stationed in Berne, Switzerland, and leading National Socialist officials (see Chapter 3). If, however, some leading officials were "unintentionally" confined at the Allied international internment camps, this was no disaster. The British internment camp at Wolfsberg in the Steiermark had the reputation of being a springboard for leading SS personnel. Even Otto Skorzeny, who after his acquittal in Nuremberg was automatically re-arrested as an SS man, managed to quickly escape, while thousands upon thousands of small-time party members rotted in Allied internment, often for years at the point of starvation, quite unable to manage such an elegant, quick "escape."

The Quiet Aid organization was officially founded in 1951, and pretended to be a corporation which dealt with the "old boys" who were in prison. Its founder, Princess von Ysenburg, came from one of the oldest oligarchical families of Germany. At her home in Isartal, the various threads for the financial and "moral" support of Nazis, and not only those in prison, came together. The princess naturally had close ties to the other "old families". That is why she arranged to free her relative Prince Josias zu Waldeck-Pyrmont, who was being held because of his role as SS Obergruppenführer (Senior Group Leader), one of the major posts at

Buchenwald. Prince zu Wladeck-Pyrmont recriprocated by concerning himself about financial support for Quiet Aid. With his approximately 4,000 square miles of land and his houses, castles, and so forth in Lahntal, he was one of the richest men in the country, whom neither the currency reform nor the other post-war confusions could harm in any way. Princess Ysenburg's friend Luise von Oertzen, the president of the German Red Cross, was also quite helpful. Previously, she had received the Golden Party Badge from the NSDAP and now repaid the favor.

More important for Princess Ysenburg, perhaps, was the fact that she had become friends with American High Commissioner John McCloy and his wife, which not only meant prosperity but also valuable further connections in the United States. The value of these connections was soon revealed. The Princess wrote an article in *Reichsruf,* the newspaper of the right-radical German Reichs Party (Deutschen Reichs-Partei, DRP). The first Chancellor of the Federal Republic, Dr. Konrad Adenauer, had wanted to take action against this newspaper because of its open Nazism, but his efforts were blocked by his State Secretary, former SS member Hans Globke, who worked closely with McCloy. Globke recommended his associate Dr. Rudolf Aschenauer to Adenauer to take care of the "negotiations" with the DRP. At that time, Dr. Aschenauer himself was on the executive committee of Quiet Aid. The organization was always in close contact with Nazi underground cells and other right-radical organizations both in Germany and foreign countries, and cultivated excellent relations with the West German Ministries of Justice and the Interior, which is not exactly surprising if one considers that more than fifty percent of the administration was carried over from the pre-occupation days.

Financial Arrangements

In the currency reform of 1948, the "little people" lost the last remnants of what they had been able to salvage from the postwar ruins. For such people, it was literally the "zero hour," while the leaders of the "Third Reich" had long before carefully taken care of themselves, primarily through numbered accounts in Switzerland.

SS Gen. Carl Wolff, who at the bidding of Himmler and Schellenberg during the war had negotiated for months at a time with Allen Dulles and the German expert of Swiss intelligence, Max Waibel, over a separate peace, did not overlook this opportunity to make appropriate financial arrangements. Somehow, millions in the bank account of the "Friends Circle of the National SS Commander," of which General Wolff had been in charge, vanished without a trace.

The legendary SS treasures, which were supposedly dropped into some lake or other or buried in frantic haste in the region of the Alpine Redoubt, were merely a rumor used to divert attention away from the really big operations being run through Swiss, New York, and London banks. A good deal of money was, of course, put aside in these primitive ways, as revealed in a list giving the total value of the treasure buried by the Reichssicherheitsdienst (State Security Service) near Altaussee (Salzkammergut): 50 kilos of gold bars, 50 cases of gold coins and other gold objects, 2 million American dollars, 2 million Swiss francs, five cases of jewels and jewelry, a stamp collection worth 5 million gold marks, and so forth. But the majority of these "salvage operations" took place through the above-named official banking channels.

The rescue of the profitable "Operation Bernhard" in the postwar period is interesting in this respect. An operation under this code name was begun in 1940 by the chief of the Secret Service, Reinhard Heydrich, to mass produce foreign pounds sterling and dollar banknotes. This gigantic counterfeiting operation was designed to solve the acute currency shortage of the Nazi Secret Service, which consumed millions in its worldwide activities. Heydrich assigned the job to Austrian Wilhelm Hoettl, who led the Italy Division of Bureau VI of the Foreign Section of the Secret Service; under him, among others, was Gestapo boss Herbert Kappler in Rome. Later Hoettl took over the Balkans special office, from which he controlled the operation of the Gestapo in Budapest, where Adolf Eichmann and Kurt Becher carried out their dirty work. Hoettl was thus hardly a small fish. He had direct ties to certain Vatican networks, and in 1943, as Ernst Kaltenbrunner's agent, he was in frequent contact with Allen Dulles in Berne.

At the Sachsenhausen concentration camp, Hoettl assigned Bernhard Krüger the task of finding prisoners with experience in counterfeiting and bringing them to Sachsenhausen, where they were to carry out their work in strictest secrecy. Friedrich Schwend worked as the distributor of the counterfeit money, and from his headquarters in Labers Castle in Meran in the South Tyrol oversaw a huge network of agents which included both "Aryans" and Jews. One of the "full Jews" was Georg Spencer Spitz, a friend of Hitler's photographer Heinrich Hoffmann. Operating in Holland, Belgium, and

France, Spitz is said to have alone put £3 million into circulation. A total of 5.4 billion counterfeit marks were supposedly disbursed to the population of Germany. Hoettl and company of course managed to put aside a "nest egg" for themselves.

Friedrich Schwend put 1.5 million Swiss francs in a Liechtenstein bank and bought himself into a Vienna export and import company, Transdanubia. He also invested 100,000 Reichsmarks in securities and bonds, including those from the Steyr-Puch firm, the largest Austrian armament company, which would later make some big deals with the old boys in Latin America. His co-worker Spitz left the firm after 1945 and went to work for American intelligence. He had also taken care of himself, putting money into the Munich Bank Lenz & Company. Through this bank he gained control of the gambling casinos built after the war in Baden-Baden, Weserland, Bad Neuenahr, Bad Dürkheim, and Constance. Another "distributor" in Schwend's network, Friedrich Karnatz, moved to Chile and soon became a member of the board of the Deutsch-Südamerikanische Bank, a subsidiary of the Deutsche Bank. In short, while the German population suffered an unimaginable famine, the terror of occupation, and psychological bombardment through the de-Nazification measures, the real criminals were building up their new lives abroad.

Hoettl himself did not find it necessary to move to South America; U.S. intelligence furnished him with a handsome house directly on Altaussee, from where he directed operations for the Spider organization. Allen Dulles showed great appreciation to his old friend, and actually visited Hoettl in Salzkammergut in the first few months after the war. After 1950, Hoettl went to work for the "Gehlen

Organization," which operated as a part of American intelligence. Like Hoettl, Gehlen had received a handsome house from Dulles on the Starnberger Lake. Hoettl's principal area of activity was the Austrian region around Salzburg, Linz, Graz, and Klagenfürth. From there he also performed his old Balkan supervisory job, but now for Dulles.

Because of his experience in the Third Reich, Hoettl was one of those intelligence specialists without whom the Allied intelligence organizations simply could not manage. Hoettl was the contact man to the networks run by Jesuit general Count Vlodzimierz Halke von Ledochovsky, with whom he had worked for years during Hoettl's Balkan and Eastern European stints. Dulles had been kept very well informed about all these activities from 1943 on, and Hoettl had also given him a running account of his discussions with Adolf Eichmann in Budapest. Those discussions reveal the monstrous hypocrisy of the Allies' assertion that they did not learn until after the war—when the concentration camps were discovered—of the atrocities being committed by the Nazis. Not only did they know, they also had the exact locations of these camps— yet they did not bomb the gas chambers of the camps or the rail lines which led to them, over which millions of human beings were carried to annihilation. Instead they bombed cities such as Berlin and Dresden, where there were mostly women, children, and old men, since everyone else was at the front.

Traffic in Human Beings

Other foreign transfers of Nazi money were carried out through an incredible traffic in human beings. The International Red Cross in Geneva received 5

million Swiss francs from foreign Jewish fortunes
which served as escape money for Nazi criminals
for whom a second career had been arranged. In
exchange, selected Jews were released from German concentration camps after 1944 to go Switzerland, from where they could embark on their
further journey to the United States.

Such transactions took place within the framework of the increased efforts for a separate peace
led by Heinrich Himmler and Walter Schellenberg,
who were already making arrangements for life
after the war. Through Dr. Kersten, Himmler's
doctor living in Sweden and member of the Swedish
royal house of Count Bernadotte, Himmler and
Schellenberg established contact with the Swiss Alt-
bund president Dr. Jean Marie Musy, who himself
had connections with the Chief Rabbi, Dr. Stern-
buch.

The first negotiations between Himmler and
Musy took place in October, 1944 near Vienna;
after further meetings it was finally agreed that
every two weeks, a transport containing selected
Jews from the concentration camps would be allowed to go to Switzerland. For 1,200 to 1,300 Jews
every two weeks, Dr. Musy was to take into his trust
a certain sum from the Jewish side which was later
to be handed over to the Germans. These sums,
totalling over 5 million Swiss francs (official), were
transferred to the International Red Cross.

In parallel with this operation between Himmler
and Musy, Kaltenbrunner was also working out quite
similar deals. In this case, Hungarian Jews were
concerned, who would likewise be allowed to travel
to Switzerland, as long as corresponding amounts
of money were furnished for post-war use by the
Germans. Kaltenbrunner and von Ribbentrop soon

sought to put an end to Himmler and Schellenberg's competition. They alleged that telegraph messages had been decoded according to which the negotiations of Himmler and Musy were plotting to "work out asylum rights for 250 Nazi leaders in exchange for the release of Jews." Despite this ferment within the Nazi camp, both operations continued in a limited way. In the chaos of the last months of the Third Reich, every faction in the leadership tried its best to organize its various networks abroad.

The Case of Reinhold Gehlen

A competition between the Anglo-Saxons and the Russians over Hitler's former intelligence officers was soon acted out before the eyes of the Germans at Flensburg: An Allied Surveillance Commission under U.S. Gen. Lowell W. Rocks and a Soviet commission under General Major Trussow searched for the files and personnel of the German intelligence network.

Meanwhile, a whole section of National Socialist intelligence found a haven in south Germany with the Americans: the Fremde Heere Ost (Foreign Army East) division of Gen. (ret.) Reinhold Gehlen. This intelligence network, operating under the Reich security office (Reichssicherheitshauptamt, RSHA), had been responsible for intelligence on the enemy in the East, which included the Abwehr (counterintelligence) activities of Abwehr chief Canaris and later Schellenberg as well as Gestapo and SS activities in the East. This section had active connections in many East European and Russian networks of Nazi collaborators such as General Vlasov's Russian units, which had fought on the side of the Third Reich. Like many other leading intelligence agents of the Third Reich, Gehlen had recognized, at the latest after the Battle of Stalingrad in 1943, that the war could not be won, and began to consider his post-war career.

After extensive preparations and numerous tactical maneuvers, Gehlen had a final discussion of the situation with his close associates General Wessel and General Baun in Bad Elster in Saxony. There they discussed the final details of how the complete archives of Fremde Heere Ost could be transported to safety, so as to be able to use the files again immediately after the war. Gehlen planned to hand himself over to the Americans along with the entire Fremde Heere Ost network, and had already put out the appropriate feelers. From these early contacts, Gehlen knew of the plans for the occupation of Germany and had all the material moved into the American occupation zone in South Germany.

For this extremely delicate operation, the Regensburg cathedral's pastor, Dr. Rudolf Graber, later bishop of Regensburg and confidant of the Regensburg Prince von Turn und Taxis, was asked to be the mediator. This nominally Catholic network, which Gehlen used near the end of the war, was later to become known through its connections with the Catholic, right-radical organization "Tradition, Family, and Property." Bishop Rudolf Graber belonged to the circle of so-called Catholic anti-Freemasons around Manfred Adler as well as to other, predominantly right-radical Swiss groupings. That a Prince von Thurn und Taxis should be involved here should be no surprise, since for hundreds of years, this family, through its monopoly of news and postal services, firmly controlled part of Europe's intelligence network.

As prearranged, Gehlen turned himself over to

the Americans shortly after May 8, 1945, and was first sent to Brigadier Gen. Edwin L. Sibert, who had been informed of this operation two years before, having worked together in Berne with Allen Dulles and his German advisor Gero von Gaevernitz. In August 1945, Gehlen was transported with his co-workers to Washington, while Silbert combed zealously with Baun through the American occupation zone for secret service personnel in order to immediately start working with them.

The Gehlen Organization

Meanwhile in Washington, Gehlen developed new concepts for operations against the East with his new employers and with Swiss intelligence. A decisive role in the personnel and technical questions of this secret work was played by none other than Max Waibel, the German expert in Swiss intelligence during the war and subsequently the military attaché of the Swiss embassy in Washington. The Gehlen Organization was incorporated into the CIA as the German Group and in 1955 entered the "German service"—under the name Bundesnachrichtendienst (BND, Federal Intelligence Service).

The Gehlen Organization was given a large estate in Pullach near Munich for its use, where its members produced reports on the Soviet occupied zone as well as the Soviet Union and Eastern Europe. First they concentrated on the thousands of prisoners of war who were just beginning to return from the Soviet Union; then they intensified their worldwide activity, re-establishing connections to the networks which escaped from Germany to Argentina, Brazil, Chile, and other South American countries, and were now occupying leading positions in important organizations.

Gehlen himself cultivated close connections to Bonn through regular meetings with Globke, Adenauer's State Secretary in the Chancellory. Adenauer's interest in Gehlen was characterized by one of Adenauer's assistants as follows: "Gehlen seemed interesting to Adenauer in two respects. First, Adenauer could keep up to date on developments in the East zone. That was especially important for Adenauer because his two most dangerous opponents, Jakob Kaiser in the Christian Democratic Union (CDU) and Kurt Schumacher in the Social Democratic Party (SPD), were very well informed about the Soviet zone. Second, Adenauer immediately recognized that through his information, Gehlen exercised influence on those to whom he delivered this information—the Americans."

Additionally, Adenauer wanted to have at least some control over Gehlen's Swiss connections to Max Waibel through regular exchanges of information. Only after 1948 did the Gehlen Organization work "officially" with Swiss intelligence. Close connections also existed to relevant networks within Spanish, Italian, French, and other intelligence organizations.

The Gehlen Organization soon had connections with Nazi International networks throughout the world, and—as noted in the Thurn und Taxis case—served less the North German faction of Chancellor Adenauer than the networks of the South German oligarchy, which was nominally Catholic and, by reputation at least, anti-Freemasonic.

Adenauer had a constant if latent mistrust of Gehlen until their public break during the so-called Spiegel Affair, and his mistrust was further strengthened during his first U.S. visit. At that time

Adenauer was expressly warned by the head of American military intelligence, Maj. Gen. Arthur Trudeau, against the "Nazi Gehlen" in many conversations. When Gehlen heard of these conversations, he immediately alerted Allen Dulles, who in turn intervened with President Eisenhower to have Trudeau immediately transferred. In light of these facts, *Die Zeit* editor Countess Marion Dönhoff's evaluation of Gehlen is very revealing. In 1968 she wrote: ". . . his [Gehlen's] political sentiments were absolutely beyond reproach": Gehlen had always kept out of anti-Communist groups!

While a "southern faction" had been formed in post-war politics, there was formed a corresponding "North German Hohenzollern- and Freemason-faction," controlled by other oligarchs and foreign intelligence groups.

The Case of Otto John

The north German group can be best described with reference to the case of the first president of the Federal Office for Protection of the Constitution (Bundesverfassungsschutz—BVS), Otto John.

Otto John was the official Nazi representative in the top management of Germany's Lufthansa Airline in the Third Reich, and for this reason continually traveled abroad. After 1942 he also made contact with British and American intelligence, and met regularily with their contact people. He was on the periphery of the July 20, 1944 conspiracy's assassination attempt against Hitler, which was largely made up of individuals who wanted to overthrow Hitler in favor of a Hohenzollern monarchy.

After July 20, John moved to Great Britain, where his friends in the secret service received him with open arms. He was immediately assigned to the

Psychological Warfare Division and worked there with Sefton Delmer and with the Calais black-propaganda broadcasting station. Like John, Delmer was part of the circle around the Hohenzollern prince Louis Ferdinand. Since the 1920s Delmer had also been a close friend of the late Prince Bernhard of the Netherlands; Bernhard was active during the war as an SS member with the I.G. Farben firm, and was generally known as the "Nazi Prince." At times John also worked in the re-education center of Wilton Park as an "educator" and after 1945 ran a division of the "Control Office for Germany and Austria," which played an important role in the "de-Nazification of Germany."

John's task was to seek out useful co-workers who would be helpful to the British during post-war reconstruction. Additionally, John soon became leader of Camp Number 11 in Bridgend, Great Britain, where the British held captured generals, admirals, SS-leaders, and other leading individuals of the Third Reich. Through this screening process, John assembled part of what would later become the leadership of the German army. The other part had been sought out by Gehlen and U.S. general Julius Klein; it included Gehlen's old friends Adolf Heusinger and Hans Speidel, who were to assume high positions in the German army.

John's role becomes more graphic when the activities of his friend Sefton Delmer are further examined.

Before the war, Delmer was an officer in the British secret service stationed in Berlin, working nominally for Lord Beaverbrook's newspaper empire. Delmer was given the job of putting together the forces which would most persistently work against German industrialization from inside Germany. He had contact with almost every pre-war German political grouping, and went on campaign tours with the leaders of these groups. First with Field Marshal Ludendorff, then later, in 1931, he became acquainted with SA leader Ernst Röhm and through Röhm he gained personal contact with Hitler and other senior Nazis. He was apparently one of the most fanatical followers of Hitler.

In 1931, Delmer wrote after a meeting with Hitler: "Following this conversation I had frequent opportunities to speak with Hitler—in an official as well as unofficial capacity. But on each of these opportunities it happened the same way. I raised a question. He answered, and his answer grew into a speech, while ever new thoughts streamed through his imaginative and tremendously alert, clear mind."

The British were pushing the Hitler option not only out of personal affinity, but also for quite concrete reasons. (Hitler repeatedly and solemnly affirmed to Delmer the "division of labor" which he proposed: England as the sea power and Germany as the European land power which would incorporate the Russian "land mass" and Russian natural resources.) Funds were delivered from the Schroeder Bank in Cologne to the bankrupt Hitler. (The branch office director of the Schroeder Bank in New York was Allen Dulles.) Through Delmer, the money of Beaverbrook and other British Hitler fanatics also flowed to Germany. In the critical year of 1932, as the NSDAP began to suffer massive electoral losses, Delmer traveled from city to city during the election as the only foreign journalist accompanying and advising Hitler. He confessed quite openly that his personal as well as business interests bound him to the would-be Führer.

Delmer had close ties as well to Professor Lindemann, the later Lord Cherwell. This professor provided Delmer with psychological studies on the German population. An advisor to Winston Churchill, Lindemann was also responsible for the bombing of the civilian population of German cities, the purpose of which was to utterly destroy the last remains of German culture—not a stone was to be left standing. Later, Delmer was put in charge of the "Special Operations Against the Enemy States and Their Allies," and it was in this capacity that he oversaw the black propaganda radio station Calais. Delmer's aim with this "military broadcast station" was to refine and improve the methods of Goebbels, the "little doctor" whom Delmer admired as extraordinarily brilliant.

On the invitation of the first President of the Federal Republic, Freemason Theodor Heuss, Otto John finally returned from the Calais propaganda station to the Federal Republic in 1949. Heuss knew John from their participation in a discussion group in the house of Klaus Bonhöffer, who was killed in the last weeks of the war. This discussion group, to which the Dominican father Laurentius Siemer, the former Chancellor Heinrich Brüning, and others belonged, supported the British proposal to choose Otto John as president of the soon-to-be-established Federal Office for Protection of the Constitution (BVS), exactly as did Adenauer's old rival, Jakob Kaiser.

Adenauer's Battles

Adenauer defended himself against the "British stooge," as he called John, and sought to put in his own people, an effort which failed because of the intervention of the British high commissioner. Meanwhile, John had become friends with American High Commissioner McCloy. Adenauer became all the more angry at being characterized by John and Prince Louis Ferdinand as "American property." Adenauer had refused to give John his letter of appointment for a year, then forced John to investigate a series of his "pan-German" Hohenzollern friends. Adenauer demanded from John a report on the supposed Eastern contacts of the "pan-German" CDU member Jakob Kaiser, who Adenauer suspected of leaking plans of the European Defense Community to the East Germans.

Afterward, Adenauer instigated the investigation of John himself and his Eastern contacts and the "rumor" that John had a well-stuffed Swiss bank account. It was this faction, advocates of a neutralized, reunified Germany, which sought to sabotage Adenauer's policy of integration into the West in every possible way.

The task of the BVS is counterespionage and defense against those within the Federal Republic hostile to the constitution. With Otto John as president and with section leaders who had been slipped in early by the Gehlen faction, it was a foregone conclusion that the Federal Republic would become a playground for intelligence agents from all over the world.

The founding of the Federal Republic in 1955 did not put a stop to these activities at all. Astoundingly, the following took place on the tenth anniversary of July 10: the president of the BVS vanished and appeared a short time later in East Berlin! Although other Germans who had been active in the Calais broadcast station and Wilton Park, for example Edler von Putlitz, had moved to East Berlin after a "short stay" in the Federal Republic, still the change of residence of the leader of a counterintelligence agency was certainly a sensation. John remained in East Germany a total of 17 months. During that time he held press conferences, gave speeches, and appeared on television, advocating reunification and the pan-German way "against the Cold War policies of Adenauer."

When John returned to West Germany after 17 months, Adenauer's suspicions were indeed confirmed about John's Eastern contacts, but a loud faction publicly claimed to be able to prove John's innocence. A federal court determined that John had gone to East Germany voluntarily, and that his claim to have been taken there in a drugged state was not credible. In any case the "pan-Germans" used the controversy about him to their own purposes.

Posser and Heinemann of the Legal Office also fought for John. That is not astonishing, since Gustav Heinemann, along with his All-German People's Party, had entered into an alliance with the Soviet-financed German Confederation of Col. (ret.) Josef Weber, in order to fight Adenauer in the election campaign.

The Freemasons, too, took up John's defense, including the former FDP ministers Dehler and Stammberger. Dr. Gerhard Schröder, a prominent minister in Adenauer's cabinet, also interceded for John. Before the war Schröder had been the financial advisor of Reichsbank president Hjalmar Schacht, and then was employed in a leading position by Fritz Thyssen, who together with Schacht joined the well-known Niederdorf "celebrity" transport which left the Third Reich during the last days of the war and went over to the Americans. Schacht too had advocated the restoration of the Hohenzollern monarchy. (Prince Louis Ferdinand, the heir to the Hohenzollern throne, was married to the Russian Grand Duchess Kyra. According to tradition, the head of the House of Hohenzollern was the head of German Freemasonry.)

But all these intercessions were to no avail. John was found guilty by the federal court and put into prison. A short time later he withdrew from public life to live in the Hohenburn Castle in Igls, a resort in the Tyrol.

Early on, Gehlen had taken care that he would have a certain amount of control over the proceedings in the BVS in Cologne. John's representative Albert Radke, a retired colonel, was from Operation Gehlen, and one of the two division directors was Richard Gerken, who until 1945 was a leading associate with the Nazi security police in the Netherlands.

Military Counterintelligence

The battle around the third pillar of the secret intelligence service began when the re-armament of Germany was already being planned during the official "de-Nazification" period. The Allies arranged a military contact station, which was to be located in Bonn under a code name (since only recently had the law for the elimination of militarism been passed).

Interestingly enough, Countess Dönhoff, who had come over to West Germany—on horseback from her estate in East Germany—as late as 1946, intervened in the debate over the personnel of this agency. After her move to the West, she had first been with the Metternichs, and was brought to Hamburg as the managing editor of the British-controlled newspaper *Die Zeit*. The Countess wanted to see her old friend and former tank corps general Count von Schwerin appointed head of the military contact station. This proposal was immediately accepted by the British High Commission. The count was known to the commission as the leader of the England-America group in the Fremde Heere Ost department. The present leader of the Institute for Peace and Conflict Studies in Hamburg, Count Baudissin, was a member of the Dönhoff-Schwerin group.

Adenauer also attempted to fight this appointment, but he was forced to yield to British and other pressure. Yet he was soon able to put Theodor Blank, a man he could trust, into the position, a move which was decisive for his policy of rearmament and integration into the West. Yet Schwerin was able to empower two individuals with developing the secret military intelligence service, which was later to be called Military Counterintelligence (Militärischer Abschirmdienst, MAD). The two were the former major Joachim Oster and Friedrich-Wilhelm Heinz, an old warhorse from German counterintelligence.

In a certain sense, however, Adenauer seemed to be sure of his influence, since it had originally been his idea to create an independent secret service alongside the existing one. The reason was that Adenauer "wanted to be informed about the military situation in East Germany, before West Germany had completed its remilitarization," and he wanted to be informed by "an intelligence service which was not dependent on the Americans," as was the Gehlen Organization on the CIA.

Joachim Oster's father was the leader of the central section of the Nazi foreign counterintelligence bureau and one of the close confidantes of Abwehr head Admiral Canaris. The younger Oster brought Friedrich-Wilhelm Heinz out of the old Abwehr networks. While Oster organized the central office of the new bureau, Heinz took over the agents in the field. Heinz had been a member of the national leadership of the Stahlhelm, the World War I veterans' organization, later joined the NSDAP, was soon working against the "south German group" around Hitler, and was for that reason expelled from the party. He then worked for Canaris as a group leader in the Field Counterintelligence Division and became, in 1941, a regimental commander of the Brandenburg Division.

As a monarchist and through his close connection to Canaris, Heinz worked in a leading position in the resistance group Schwarze Kapelle (The Black Orchestra) until being arrested by the Gestapo. After 1945 he first stayed in the Eastern-occupied zone, then moved to the West to form an intelligence service with an individual from Holland. His specialty was information on the placement and strength of Soviet troops in the East zone, which he passed on to the intelligence services of Holland, the U.S.A., and France. He brought the intelligence networks which he had cultivated with him to his new job. A short time after his appointment, however, a scandal was created against him to incriminate him as a Soviet agent. In December 1954, he disappeared into East Berlin, but he swore on his return that he had been kidnapped. Whether or not that was true, he was subsequently dismissed.

Joachim Oster is said to have had an "extraordinarily loyal" relation to the then SPD head and opposition leader Kurt Schumacher, who had control from Hanover over an independent intelligence network in East Germany through the Berlin Ostbüro of the SPD. But Oster also maintained "loyal relations" to Defense Minister Franz-Josef Strauss and Strauss's foster-father Josef Müller, who had been Canaris's contact with the Vatican.

Even here, Gehlen did not sit idly by. Agents of Gehlen soon moved to the top within Theodor Blank's "Blank Office," as the defense ministry was known, since under the occupation the Germans were not allowed to officially have such an institution. The former Gehlen representative Gerhard Wessel and the former Gehlen organization boss Adolf Heusinger arranged for the appropriate flow of intelligence to Pullach exactly as did the later chief of the office, Col. Josef Selmayr, who had come as a Southeast Europe expert from Operation Gehlen. Wessel soon took over the leadership of the sub-section responsible for military intelligence in the defense ministry, and Col. Ernst Ferber, a member of Operation Gehlen, became personnel director in the Ministry for Protection of the Constitution.

How far the infiltration of all the services went is shown by a brief depiction of the "Affair Felfe."

Felfe moved, with two friends he had known from the NSDAP time in Dresden, into Organization Gehlen in the beginning of the 1950s. All three, Felfe, Clemens, and Tiebel, had first served in various functions for the NSDAP in Dresden, then, beginning in 1943, all three worked together in Berlin in the Swiss Section of the National Security Department of the SS. After the war, they worked for the British secret service and then were recruited into the Soviet service. Although then-Interior Minister Gustav Heinemann knew in April 1950 of the Soviet connection, Felfe and his two comrades were taken into Operation Gehlen. Gehlen was so enthusiastic about the "former" British and Soviet agent Felfe that he made him his Soviet Union section leader in Department III for counterintelligence. Thus a man was sitting in a position in the counterintelligence department of the foreign intelligence service of the Federal Republic who, until his arrest in November 1961, passed on all information to the Soviets. And Felfe was not the only case.

Licensing of Parties: The FDP Example

Since the Germans were to be spoon-fed democracy, no German in 1945 could do anything without a license from the occupying powers. Not only were the reconstruction of the press and radio, with their great influence on public opinion, completely under the control of the Allies, but also the reconstruction of political parties. But here, as with the takeover of the secret services, the principle was that the old Nazis had special rights. The case of the Free Democratic Party, which today behaves in such a liberal manner, is especially revealing.

Following 1945 the FDP was not only a collecting place for leading Nazis, but it was generally known as the party which stood up for the HIAG and other front organizations of the SS. The North Rhine-Westphalian and Hessian regional section of the FDP proposed a program in 1953 which they intended to be understood as a "call for a national assembly" and which they called the "German Program." The program contained the following: "The German Reich, as a decentralized unitary state of the tribes and regions, will give to those tribes and regions, as bodies for self-government, the possibility of unfolding their unique characteristics. On the foundation of a just division of tasks between the Reich and its members, there is no room for a multitide of governments and parliaments." The creation of this "German Reich" would be made possible through an "understanding with Russia."

Shortly before, in 1952, Werner Naumann, the spokesman for the "right" in the FDP, explained what was essential:

> National Socialist thought, which has deci-
> sively influenced our people and 12 years of
> German policy, has been further developed
> by us. . . . We need a new style, new slogans,
> new concepts, and a new language if we are
> to reform our people politically and push them
> ahead. This style will not be emphatic, prop-
> agandistic, or overstated, but strictly factual,
> a faithful image of our position.

Werner Naumann had been undersecretary under Goebbels, and in Hitler's Last Political Testament had been selected as Goebbels' successor. Together with the Essen lawyer Dr. Ernst Achenbach, who held an influential position as chairman of the foreign-policy committee of the FDP and the Committee for a General Amnesty for War Criminals, Naumann organized a conspiracy for infiltration of parties by leading National Socialists. Achenbach served in that effort as the contact man with industrial figures.

During the Nazi period, Achenbach had held an influential position in the foreign ministry, and after the war maintained connections to the Nazi networks throughout the world. During the war, he had been the political advisor to the German ambassador in Paris, Otto Abetz, under whose lead-

ership at that time in Paris Ernst Jünger, the leading
"Conservative Revolutionary," also worked. Achenbach was named as the leader of the "Naumann
Circle," but in contrast to those more politically
exposed, he was not arrested by the British in their
spectacular "anti-Nazi" action in 1953.

Naumann had attempted, together with the networks of former subordinates from the Reich propaganda ministry, to form a group which would
serve as a gathering place for a great nationalistic
opposition. He placed Dr. Friedrich Middelhauve,
his closest co-worker, as an advisor to the second
national chairman of the FDP, and the FDP soon
became a collection of right-wing groups of all colors.
Naumann had close relations to Middlehauve and
to Dr. Erich Mende, who, as member of the National Committee of the FDP, was the leading fighter
for former soldiers and war criminals in the Bundestag (and today is suitably praised in the *Nationalzeitung*). Naumann consulted with Mende before
he met the former SS generals Hausser and Gille
in 1952. The idea was the creation of a new "German Reich," which, it was hoped, would come
through an understanding with Russia on the question of "German unity."

The FDP became the political arm of the "old
boys." In a 1957 enlistment brochure of the Mutual
Benefit Society of the Waffen SS, it stated:

> In the Bundestag, in the regional parliaments,
> and everywhere else, it was the FDP which
> always stood up for us unequivocally. . . . We
> have in the past weeks had negotiations with
> important individuals of the Lower Saxony
> FDP and have been asked in a comradely man-
> ner to work with them. We can work unre-

servedly with them on the organizational
reconstruction of the party on the regional
level. A man we can trust will be put up for
parliament in a sure district. In every conceivable way we are offered possibilities for
cooperation with a new FDP. . . .

Since any political activity in occupied Germany
was possible only with the express approval of the
Allies, and against the background of real de-Nazification, the suspicion is naturally aroused that
the occupying powers consciously encouraged the
return of the old Nazis into political affairs. In fact,
this suspicion is grounded.

After the original quick trials, there came, on
May 8, 1947, an equally quick absolution for all
repatriated prisoners of war. As a side effect of this
"generous act," many former leading National Socialists, who had until 1945 occupied the highest
positions in the party and who had then taken flight
to foreign countries, could now return as "war prisoners," and were additionally qualified to claim repatriation compensation and other financial
benefits. They did not have anything to fear from
courts, de-Nazification hearings, or trials. With that
action, an additional door was opened which allowed the occupying powers to incorporate the old
Nazi apparatchiks into the "reconstruction."

In this light, it can be added that sixty percent
of the diplomatic apparatus of Nazi Joachim von
Ribbentrop's foreign ministry was incorporated into
the foreign ministry of the Federal Republic—and
that specific periods in the later history of the Federal Republic show that this apparatus knew how
to use its old foreign networks.

Recent studies on the reconstruction of the German judicial system from 1945 to 1949 demonstrate that the same thing happened in this sphere.

In Bavaria (and the same is true in the other zones), not a single judge was tried for his activity in the Third Reich, not even the judges of Hitler's People Courts. Judges and prosecuting attorneys had the choice, after the flurry of de-Nazification died down around 1947–48, of either petitioning to retire "with honor" or entering again into judicial service, and, as the historian Dr. Korts states: "On grounds of the seniority system, they were predestined for first-class careers." In a smooth and shameless manner the judicial apparatus of the new state was furnished with the personnel of the old!

The Continuity of the "Conservative Revolution"

Toward the end of the Third Reich, not only the networks of National Socialists organized themselves into a Nazi International; the Conservative Revolution or "German Movement" carefully worked on the continuation of its intellectual tradition and on the necessary organizational substructures. Moeller van den Bruck's book *The Third Reich* had been the battle cry of the German Movement before the National Socialists made that term their own. The present intellectual leader of the Conservative Revolutionaries, the director of the Siemens Foundation, Armin Mohler, expresses this concept in his book *The Conservative Revolution*: "In *The Third Reich,* Moeller van den Bruck contrasts to the universalistic Holy Roman Empire of the German nation and to the lesser German 'transitional empire' of Bismarck a portrait of a Final Empire in which the contradictions of socialism and nationalism, of 'left' and 'right' are sublimated and find a comprehensive unity." Without any interruption, the German Movement pulled together in their various outward forms in order to realize this Final Reich through the destruction of the Third Reich.

Before the war, these circles became known as the "socialists within the NSDAP" around the Strasser brothers, but Hans Zehrer's "Black Front" circles (see Chapter 8), to which Sigmund Warburg, Ernst Jünger, Graf von Moltke, Otto and Gregor Strasser, Ernst von Salomon, Giselher Wiersing, and other belonged, must also be noted here. The Strasser faction had attempted to push the ideas of Naumann, Masaryk, and Moeller van der Bruck into the ascendency in the NSDAP, until in 1934 it finally became clear that the south German faction around Hitler was firmly in command. Shortly thereafter, Straser, Röhm, and others were either murdered or forced into exile. Some, however, decided to cooperate with the Nazi state.

The partisans of the Conservative Revolution, especially Ernst Jünger, advocated quite concrete "territorial divisions," which were taken up again in practically the same form after 1945. In the circles of the Conservative Revolution, the dividing line between the Catholic South from the Protestant North was understood more as the line of Roman conquest rather than as the "German line of destiny." Mohler advocates the idea that "a space which has never been incorporated into the West by the Roman legions has different political possibilities from any which was once within the Roman orbit." Concerning friends and foes and therefore concerning possible alliances, Mohler says, "against the civilized, capitalistic West, against the Roman-Catholic South, for and with the Germanic-pastoral North and the barbarian-Bolshevik East."

The meaning of these ideas is important because they are appropriate for bringing together and fusing the "Right" and the "Left." The National Bolshevists within the German Movement around the Strasser brothers wanted a connection between the goals of radical socialists and radical nationalists, which was to be reached through an alliance between the two "proletarian" nations of Germany and Russia against the "capitalistic" West. Gregor Strasser spoke of an "anti-capitalist longing" which gripped the entire German nation.

The Third Way

A "third way" was sought, beyond Western capitalism or Eastern Communism, a "third front" or "third party," which would gather under the banner of the peasant revolution: in the Black Front. As already cited in Chapter 1, the standpoint of the Black Front was summarized by a National Revolutionary in 1932, and is still valid today for the Conservative Revolution:

> The Black Front can be clearly situated if we dispense with the bourgeois-democratic schema of "left" and "right." Let us imagine the German parties and political currents to be shaped like a horseshoe, whose bend represents the Center and at whose end-points are the KPD and NSDAP respectively; the space occupied by the Black Front lies inbetween those two poles of Communism and National Socialism. The opposites of "left" and "right" are dissolved by their entering into a kind of synthesis, while strictly excluding the "bourgeois." This position between the two poles is the best characterization of the tensile nature of the Black Front. . . .

One of the most important advocates of the "third front" or "Black Front" was Hans Zehrer. Zehrer was head of the most important newspaper of the Black Front in Weimar Germany, *Tat*, in Jena, which was published by Diederichs, a leading Freemasonic publisher where the Thule Collection and a large number of Eastern Buddhist and German mystical texts were also published. Included within Zehrer's circle of activity were persons who were taken up in the post-war period into the world of the German press, promoted especially by the British occupiers. This becomes understandable if we read Zehrer's statements in *Tat* in 1931, where he anticipates Pan-European disciple Winston Churchill's *Mitteleuropa* (Central Europe) concept of a "Bavarian-Austrian-Hungarian Confederation." Zehrer demands that Germany must take up definite alliances for Central Europe and the Marches.

> The federation corresponds in foreign policy to the idea of the Reich, but not the Second Reich . . . but rather the idea of the Third Reich in the sense of Moeller van den Bruck. The liberal idea of the nation state collapses, the idea of the federal Reich opposes it, which will dissolve the Reich first into the federation of separate regions but which must additionally take on the care and responsibility for the space of Central Europe. This will be the task and the problem of the federation: to acquaint ourselves with the Eastern space from the Artic Ocean to the Black Sea, to travel through that space, to fill that space with its ideas, to find German ruins and ancient settlements in this space, to awaken, to seek bases, to fill this space. . . .

The leadership of this movement and this intellectual tendency could be "guaranteed only through elites and oligarchs," Zehrer wrote in conclusion. Zehrer "spent the winter" with a group of likeminded individuals at Sylt, after he had taken on various short-term positions in Nazi Germany. After 1934, the Underberg and von Opel families, the publishing families of Govert and Rowohlt, the writer Ernst von Salomon, and later Axel Springer all belonged to the Sylt group.

Other members of the *Tat* circle had fled the country with Otto Strasser, the leader of the Black Front who had worked with the *Tat* circle, the Landvolkjugend (Youth of the Country) and the Bündischen Jugend (Youth of the Federation). Ernst Jünger worked with the German embassy in Paris under Otto Abetz, with whom Dr. Achenbach, already discussed, was active, while some followers of the Conservative Revolution such as Hjalmar Schacht had participated in the destructive madness and had helped organize it until a few months before the end of the Third Reich. All were in favor, however, of a return of the Hohenzollern monarchy.

After the war, the Conservative Revolutionaries came back together from every direction and immediately assumed important positions in the newly created state. Otto Strasser considered National Socialist rule as a necessary historical phase before the coming "New Order." National Socialism was "one of those periods, appearing to contemporaries and the survivors as a hideous time of destruction, of the fall of a world ready for collapse, which exactly because of its task of destruction is incapable, which intrinsically must be incapable, of building up and forming the New Order which is forcing its way up into the world." And Hjalmar Schacht was confident that "out of the misery of these two wars" a "moral new orientation of mankind will arise, which will be stronger than all technology."

Guiding the Press

Hans Zehrer was first made editor by the British of the British-controlled daily newspaper *Die Welt*, but was forced by overwhelming protests against his well-known pro-Nazi attitudes to give up the position. He was later cleared, however, by the Protestant Church and by Bishop Lillje, and was able to take the position of editor with the Protestant newspaper *Sontagsblatt*. In 1946, Zehrer returned, if only briefly, to the political scene as he wrote, with Adolf von Thadden (the later founder of the National Partei Deutschlands—NPD) the program of the Deutschen Rechtspartei (German Right Party), which demanded a return of the monarchy and "the national unity of the whole German people on the hereditary land which was cultivated by their ancestors." After this interlude, he was fetched back to Hamburg again by the British as editor. There he built up a newspaper empire under Freemasonic control with Alex Springer that, in parallel to the publishing empires of Rowohlts, Goverts, Suhrkamps, and so forth, fought sharply against Adenauer's policies. In place of Adenauer's conception, he supported a reunification of a neutralized Germany under the "pan-German" faction, and, along the lines of the old national-conservative conception, viewed Adenauer's attempted Western integration of the Federal Republic as a catastrophe.

Only much later were *Die Welt*, Springer, et al. to acquire an anti-Soviet image. Many co-workers of the Black Front were moved up into leading positions. Giselher Wirsing was a foreign-policy expert in Zehrer's circle who had been editor of the Nazi newspaper *Münchner Neueste Nachrichten*, and had been a close associate of Walter Schellenberg, with whom he negotiated in the later days of the war in Hitler's name with the Swedish and British for a separate peace. After the war he became the editor of the newspaper *Christ und Welt/Deutsche Zeitung* and continued there for 17 years.

Otto Strasser himself continued in exile until 1955, from where, first in Switzerland, later in Canada, he directed his international network with the help of numerous friends.

In March 1955, he returned to the Federal Republic. Many groups of the national opposition which were fighting against Adenauer's Western integration saw in Strasser the potential leader of a "national collective movement." Strasser founded the German Social Union and the "Alliance for German Renewal" which was to serve as a nonpartisan organization to "continue the spiritual preparation for the new order." Strasser's program stipulated a "sovereign Germany" in "the three zones of Bonn, Berlin, and Pankow," the construction of a German national army ("armed neutrality"), and a new national order in economic and social policy. In October 1958 Strasser organized a "Congress of European Neutralists" in Heidelberg in order to create an effective "third force" in German politics which could implement the reunification.

In the overheated atmosphere around the rearmament in the Federal Republic and through the anti-nuclear movement of these years, the National Bolshevists of the Conservative Revolution received a great stimulus. Participants in the congress included Soviet-influenced groups such as the Congress of German Unity, the German Bund, the Standing Congress Against Nuclear Rearmament, and the Pan-German Union. Foreign fascist groups were sent in to participate, as were reporters of various national-neutralist publications, along with observers from the Soviet zone, representatives of the National Front, the Liberal Democratic Party, the National Democratic Party of Germany (NDPD), the Soviet agency ADN, and so forth.

The NDPD had been founded in 1948 in the Soviet zone, and was a National Bolshevist party which was in favor of reunification, a general amnesty for National Socialists, and German-Soviet friendship. Their chairman, Vinzent Müller, also founded the "National Front" in 1950, in which all the "old boys" could gather and exercise a powerful influence in the Western zones. On the steering committee of the National Front was from the beginning one of the most decisive national revolutionaries of the Weimar time, Ernst Niekisch, who exercised from this position important influence over the financing and direction of "nationalist" and National Bolshevist organizations in the West. The conveyor of money for all these "nationalist" groups, which had their source in the East, was Werner Schäfer, who had been a concentration camp head during the Third Reich—in Oranienburg! Because of his extreme brutality, he was soon made the commandant of the infamous Moorland slave-labor camp in Emsland.

This confused conglomeration of left and right becomes explicable if the aforementioned principle of the Black Front is recalled. According to his own writings, as early as 1920 Otto Strasser had met with Comintern chief Zinoviev as well as Hitler, and had combined elements from Bolshevism and Hitlerism.

A statement of Armin Mohler is interesting in regard to the present situation. Mohler said that "National Bolshevism will always have its roots in Germany north of the Main River and east of the Rhineland." Mohler saw in the "messianic tones" of the two "prophets" of the Conservative Revolution, Nietzsche and Dostoevsky—"each thereby indicating with the finest individuality the position of his country"—the crucial reference points for Conservative Revolutionaries in East and West. In Nietzsche's literary remains was found a four-point program for German politics. The first point was called "The Sense of Reality"; according to the third, "We need an unconditional agreement with Russia, with a new common program which does not allow any British ideas to come to dominance in Russia. No American future!" According to the last point, however: "A European future is unstoppable and the unification in a Christian perspective a great misfortune. . . ." And Dostoevsky wrote, "Two great people, us and them, are predestined to change the face of Europe."

East Bloc Connections

Those in the East did not hesitate to take advantage, exactly like the Allies in the West, of the Nazis' secret-service and intelligence networks. Very early there were close alliances between certain Comintern networks and the networks of the Nazi secret service and party apparatus. In 1931, Communists and National Socialists worked together—the joint work by Joseph Goebbels and Walter Ulbricht in 1931 on the Berlin transportation workers' strike should be recalled. A graphic picture from more recent times is the fact that on Goering's yacht, which is now in the possession of *Stern* magazine reporter Heidemann, who dug up the bogus Hitler Diaries, people of the type of SS General Wolff met with Leopold Trepper, the leader of the Comintern resistance group, the Rote Kapelle. And that is no isolated example.

The Ryazan School played an important role in German-Russian relations. Captured German officers, among whom was Field Marshal Paulus, commander of the German Army at Stalingrad, were taken to this Red Army school. Some of the individuals of this group later went to the East German military academy at Dresden, which is today called "the long arm of Ryazan" and which is still an important German-Russian contact point. Another important institution was the Antifa School in Krasnogorsk. Beginning in 1942, it was directed by Wilhelm Zaisser, who had been in the Soviet Union at the espionage academy of the Red Army and belonged to the faction of the Moscow police minister Lavrentii Beria.

Many German war prisoners, who, according to Soviet plans, were to assume important positions in the German post-war government, went through Zaisser's Antifa School. In Krasnogorsk, Zaisser also recruited a group of former Abwehr officials and fuctionaries out of the Gestapo, the SD, and the SS. One of the most well-known of these was Lieutenant General Bamler, former section leader in the Abwehr, a friend of Admiral Canaris, and a confidant of Heydrich. He had been taken prisoner in 1944. Even during his Abwehr service in Paris, Bamler had had contacts with the Paris cell of the Rote Kapelle.

After 1945, Wilhelm Zaisser was the first head of the ministry for state security in East Germany, sharing the leadership with his old friends Ernst Wollweber and Erich Mierlke. Zaisser had enough experienced German secret service agents available to build up the ministry. Even Gestapo head Müller had offered his service to the Soviets in 1945. He conceived a central security ministry that would borrow its organization from the Soviet state police and from the foreign-service sections of the Gestapo, and would also employ the infiltration techniques of the old Communist Party apparatus. After a short transitional period, the ministry for state security could take up its work.

Many resistance fighters or even fellow travelers may have been astonished at the individuals whom Zaisser had gathered together. For example, the former Canaris ally General Bamler advised the ministry, and some former Gestapo functionaries such as the SS Obersturmführer Louis Hagemeister, the earlier director of the espionage/counter-intelligence central of the Nazi Reichssicherheitsdienst office, was now to take over the interrogation office of the East German Staatssicherheitsdienst (State Security Service—SSD), in the regional government in Schwerin. SS Untersturmführer Johann Sanitzer became a major in the SSD regional government at Erfurt; earlier he had been the leader of the Gestapo headquarters in Vienna.

As in the old days in the Nazi Reichssicherheit office, where strict party discipline was not absolutely necessary to a successful career, it was not essential here for the people of the SSD who moved up quickly to be members of the ruling Socialist Unity Party. Good technocrats were preferred.

The group around Vladimir Semyonov, the chief Soviet diplomat in East Berlin who in 1942 controlled German émigré networks from Stockholm and later was a messenger for the Soviet Union for many years in Bonn, included Zaisser and Liberal Democratic Party functionaries like Kaster who, like their friends in the West, worked for the establishment of a reunited, non-Communist, neutralized Germany.

Hermann Moritz Wilhelm Kastner played a central role. Kastner was the founder and chairman of the Liberal Democrats after the war. He had come in contact with the Western secret service through Meissen bishop Wieneken, but supposedly worked with the West only after 1948. Wieneken became acquainted with the Slovak Dr. Carnol Tarnay, who worked for the CIA and who from then on exchanged information with Kastner via West Berlin. Semyonov had close relations to Kastner. Kastner also had close relations to the Soviet supreme commander in Germany, Army General Zhukov. Kastner was a possible partner for a definite Russian faction just in case a neutralized, reunified Germany came into existence.

In the Soviet Zone, the pro-Soviet faction under Ulbricht stood directly opposed to the neutralist faction around Kastner. These two factions also existed in the Soviet Union, in one form or another. Kastner declared to the Stockholm newspaper *Aftonbladet* in 1950: "Attempts to bolshevize Germany would fail; communism is not the sort of thing that can be exported from Russia to Germany." After Stalin's death, the Soviet circles around Semyonov as well as the Western reunification faction wanted to politically activate Kastner. Semyonov is said to have recommended dismantling the hegemonic position of the SED leadership under Ulbricht and creating an entirely new government in East Germany; and Semyonov is said to have offered Kastner the leadership of the government on June 13, 1953.

The East German uprising of June 17, 1953, however, destroyed Semyonov's dreams along with the corresponding conceptions in the West.

Conservative Revolutionaries in the West

Otto Strasser's "German Social Movement" was not the only organization on the side of the Conservative Revolution which over and over again sought to effect a coalescence of the left and the right. The Socialist Reich Party (SRP), founded in 1949, was important as a temporary measure.

Zehrer and von Thadden's German Right Party (DRP), which later called itself the German Reich Party, was able to elect six individuals to the Bundestag in the first German parliamentary elections. All six came out of Lower Saxony. Chairman of the DRP faction was Dr. Franz Richter. Only in 1952, when Richter went over to the SRP, did it come out that his real name was Fritz Rössler. He had entered the NSDAP in 1930, and had served as the leader of the national center for Reich propaganda at the end of the war. As a supposed Sudeten German, he had gained a rapid influence with the Sudeten Germans after the war and became, soon after his entry into the DRP, the chairman of the party. In 1949, Rössler alias Richter was taken for six weeks to the famous British re-education center of Wilton Park, and from then on carried out with renewed élan the activities of the radical right.

Adolf von Thadden is the second prominent figure in the DRP. Acquainted with Sefton Delmer and Otto John, he was variously criticized by other right-wing politicians since he had "on orders of the British shoved himself into the reconstruction of the DRP." He was also criticized for having worked with the Polish security service; after the Soviet invasion he had remained in the part of the Eastern zone that was administered by the Poles, and worked there as an estate director. In 1946, he worked with Hans Zehrer to write the program for the DRP. Among the founding individuals of the DRP was Otto-Ernst Remer, a former SS member who had by no means given his all at the front, but rather had early made his way to the West in order to work from December 1946 to February 1948 for the U.S. Army—writing a history of the war!

The SRP and the DRP

In 1949, the Socialist Reich Party was founded, which was later outlawed along with the Communist Party of Germany (KPD) under the law for protection of the constitution. Otto-Ernst Remer was the second chairman of the SRP. Its program arose in the British internment camp at Staumühle. There Dr. Bernhard Gericke wrote a book *The European Revolution*, expressing his "theses for the renewal of political life in Germany," which simply restated National Socialist ideas in a cleaned-up version for all of Europe. The SRP is interesting not least because of reports that during the Third Reich, Himmler and Schellenberg had proposed to Churchill and Montgomery that "a new ideology should be cooked up from the best parts of National Socialism and other ideologies" and an SS state superior to the Nazi regime be erected on that basis.

Dr. Gerhard Krüger and Dr. Fritz Dorls were in the same internment camp as Gericke. The "Action Program of the Socialist Reich Party" of 1949 demanded the

> unification of all Germans in an organic German Reich. Every attempt to create a partial German state in the East or West as a satellite of alien powers must be viewed as an intensification of the fateful split of the Reich and therefore must be rejected. The claim, inherited by the Germans through history and culture, through human and ethnic rights, to the collectivity of its national space is inalienable. . . . The SRP affirms in the Reich concept the ethnically and historically conditioned form of order of the Germans. . . . The SRP acknowledges one authentic ethnic socialism of all Germans which has grown up out of the spirit of our time.

The hard core of the extreme right from the British internment camp soon controlled contacts to the Eastern sector. Dr. Dorls was in touch with Soviet officials in Berlin-Karlshorst, the Soviet headquarters in East Germany, and through his activity as editor of the Lower Saxony CDU party newspaper, maintained simultaneously close connections to Count Westarp, who later entered the SRP but at this time still worked in the press office of the Lower Saxony regional government. Dorls and Westarp were in the confidence of the Lower Saxony CDU regional chairman, Dr. Günter Gereke, who a short time later moved to the Soviet zone and there became active for the National Front. Wolf Graf von Westarp had been a member of the Allgemeine SS and was put into the press office in 1945 immediately by the British. Later he became a member of the editorial board of the East-financed newspaper *Die Nation*. The German representative of the post-war fascist Malmö International, Karl Heinz Priester, of Wiesbaden, was also a member of the SRP.

Although the Anglo-Soviet connections of this party were quite obvious, they were not once mentioned during the trial of the party before the Federal Constitutional Court. The grounds for outlawing the SRP were limited to the fact that they were identical in personnel and ideology, among other things, with the NSDAP.

The SRP branch in Hanover had close connections with Berlin-Karlshorst. In August 1951, the Berlin regional leader of the SRP resigned from his position because he was in disagreement with negotiations for financial support which the SPD members Count Westarp and Dr. Krüger had under discussion with Soviet contacts. It is therefore not surprising that the quite open contacts between the SRP and the Communist Party (KPD) in the West zone, especially with the vice-chairman of the KPD and member of the Bundestag Kurt Müller were controlled from Hanover. The old tradition of the NSDAP-KPD alliance was continued in the so-called Unemployed Committees, which existed until 1952 in Lower Saxony and North Rhine Westphalia. In the Bundestag, Dr. Dorls and Rössler, alias Richter, voted with the Communists against the proposal made by the other parties on the question of German Unity.

After the prohibition of the SRP as a successor

party of the NSDAP, the right collected in the German Reich Party (DRP), which was working for the same "third way" and also advocated a neutralized Germany. Additionally, this party advocated direct discussions between Bonn and East Berlin. Adolf von Thadden was again on the steering committee of the DRP. Exemplary of the position of this grouping was a telegram of the former Hitler Youth leader Herbert Freiberger in 1956 to the Soviet ambassador in Bonn, Valerian Sorin, which said that the policies of Dr. Adenauer vis-à-vis the Soviet Union are "strongly disapproved of by many millions of Germans" and that efforts would be made to "create the preconditions for a German reunification." Freiberger was the chairman of the DRP in Lower Saxony.

The chairman and vice-chairman of the district of Greater Berlin of the DRP had direct contact to Field Marshal (ret.) Paulus, who was living in Dresden, and to the National Front in East Berlin. At the Pan-German Soldiers' meetings, which regularly took place in East Berlin, they had made contacts with the Dresden Paulus Group. Others also cultivated connections to the Dresden Group, including the former Federal Republic minister Theodor Oberländer.

The forum on fundamental principles held on the DRP Party Day in September 1956 had the theme of "Germany between East and West" and demanded a "confederation of both states." The kind of confederation they comtemplated is clear from the anti-Western statements of participants who declared:

We should proceed from the fundamental principle that the so-called liberation of the central German region according to the rules of the game of economic and political managers should never take place with the purpose of replacing what is presently there in central Germany with the world of unscrupulous business and profit calculations of all sorts of firms.

On the original DRP steering committee of three, along with von Thadden, was General (ret.) Andrae, whose Anglo-Soviet profile as a "pan-German" is so typical of the post-war history of Germany. Andrae was the former German commandant on Crete, had been taken prisoner by the British, and then turned over to the Greeks. He was released in 1952, plunged into the world of the right of the DRP, and devoted himself more and more strongly as time went by to collaboration with shadow newspapers such as the *Nationaler Rundschau*, which were notoriously financed by the East.

With the introduction of the five-percent clause, putting a floor on the vote needed to enter a legislative body, the DRP was able to get into the regional assembly in Rhineland Pfalz in 1959 with 5.1 percent of the vote. The election theme of the party could have been written by anti-nuclear activist Bertrand Russell or the present-day peace movement. The DRP used protests "against procurement of land for NATO air bases" in exactly the way that the worked-up "fear of stationing of nuclear weapons" is used, and campaigned against the "occupation climate" of the Federal Republic. Their featured speaker of the day was Col. (ret.) Hans-Ulrich Rudel, who had just returned from Latin America.

The Continuities

The program of the DRP is still current today since the left and right have, throughout the post-war period, supported this very program, in one form or another: The Germans have the right "to build a Reich in Central Europe, the hereditary settlement land of their state. . . . Only after the restoration of the Reich is the unification of Europe possible." Point two of the program was: "Foreign troops maintain the division of Germany. Therefore, removal of all occupation troops! The reunification is only possible if Germany is prepared to remain neutral and not to take part in military alliances with world powers. Let Germany be open to East and West!"

Conservative Revolutionaries also permeated other parties and political groupings. The German Party (Deutsche Partei—DP), whose chairman, Dr. Heinrich Hellwege, had been appointed to the British zone advisory council in 1946. A member of the first and second Bundestags and later the prime minister of Lower Saxony, he desired a restoration of the monarchy and close collaboration between Lower Saxony and England. In 1952, Hellwege demanded that a "conservation revolution" should renew all those forces that had been absorbed by the Nazis in 1933 and thereby turned into their opposites. The Nazis had proven to be reactionaries because they had not freed themselves from the "nationalistic frame of mind of the nineteenth century." The century of nation-states and class struggles was now over; "today we live in the century of great expanses and of socialist cooperation."

Also a member of the German Party was refugee-politician Dr. von Merkatz, later chairman of the

Pan-Europa Union, as was the former commerce minister Dr. Seebohn.

Since we have not referred to the major parties such as the Social Democratic Party, the Christian Democratic Union, and the Christian Socialist Union, two things must be indicated: first, that many politicians of the small parties named such as the DRP and DP went over to the major parties after the dissolution of the other parties in the 1960s, and second, that the same kinds of fights on these fundamental issues had taken place from the beginning in these major parties.

It is not true that the theses presented here merely belong to the past; the horseshoe image is still used today as a political concept by the Conservative Revolution, in order to build up a "Fourth Reich." Quite openly, Armin Mohler says today that the enemies of Germany are those who "have instituted and maintained the split in Germany" and that "Germany will [make] itself into the spokesman of those in the world [who] seek to defend themselves against the great homogenization under the Soviet Star and the Stars and Stripes"—which particularly includes for Mohler Khomeini's Iran and Qaddafi's Libya! In order to create a new Reich today, the left and right must be transcended, and a new Black Front created. For, as Mohler says in the afterword of his book *The Conservative Revolution*: "It struck the author how much of what is said and done in today's rebellion, despite the fact that all that could be heard in the foreground was the vocabulary of 1789, comes very close to that which was reconstructed in the foregoing book. No present-day rebels may be aware of this connection. That strengthens the author in his conception of the necessity of such efforts."

Since 1945, the work for the new Reich has been

carried on in a variety of external forms. In 1984, the work has come decisively closer to its goal.

The message in a lead article in the Swiss newspaper *Die Tat* in December 1946, "The New Antiquity," was at that time a sort of strategic directive:

> Revolution means: re-volution, to roll back, the coming again of an earlier condition. In the beginning was the word, and the present teaches us to pay more attention to the original sense of the word "revolution." Europe, which has experienced for the past 150 years an era of revolution, of rolling back, has in this time overcome and negated the legacy of many centuries. This legacy is the Western community, in the spirit of Christianity. But today the cross is decayed and the disintegration of the Western community is proceeding of itself with startling rapidity wherever we look. Old idols, which were long believed to have been preached to death, seek their fallen temples. The Western superstructure, that community of Roman, German, and Slavic peoples, who recently were rooted in Christianity, is dissolving, like snow in the sun. In the new blaze of a Saturnian star that proclaims the beginning of a new antiquity, piece after piece of the thoughts of Western thought binding the peoples are melting away. Naked and isolated, the black craigs of nations appear out of the ebbing sea that has concealed them for centuries. The people seem to listen within, and to grow back into themselves.

A re-Asianization in Russia, the article claimed, has already begun despite Bolshevism, in Germany a re-Germanization, in Italy a return to the Caesar cult, and so forth. It then cites the key ideas of the Ernst Jünger circle, that nation-states must be dissolved into the tribes and regions (Franconia, Silesia, Tuscany, Brittany), that is, into ever-smaller unities. This is to take place, however, so that from there, the Swiss and their allies may be able to create something greater that goes beyond nation-states. Within this retrograde motion is said to be already hidden the turn in the opposite direction. And at the end of the Swiss article of 1946, we read: "*Homo revolvens* plays his part in the great world theatre: He will not rest until the contents of museums are exchanged. Then the sacrificial stones will again stand in the meadows and the crosses in the showcase. . . ."

Bibliography

Brockdorff, Werner, *"Flucht vor Nürnberg"—Pläne und Organisation der Fluchtwege der NS-Prominenz im "römischen Weg,"* Munich-Wels, 1969.

Dulles, Allen, *Germany's Underground,* New York, 1947.

Frieser, Karl-Heinz, *Die deutschen Kriegsgefangenen in der Sowjetunion und das Nationalkomitee "Freies Deutschland,"* Inaug. Dissertation, Phil. Fakultät, Würzburg, 1981.

Funke, Manfred (ed.), *Hitler, Deutschland und die Mächte,* Düsseldorf, 1978.

Grabbe, Hans-Jürgen, *Unionsparteien, Sozialdemokraten und Vereinigte Staaten von Amerika 1945–1966,* Düsseldorf, 1983.

Höhne, Heinz, *Canaris—Patriot im Zwielicht,* Munich, 1978.

Jenke, Manfred, *"Verschwörung von rechts"—Bericht über den Rechtsradikalismus in Deutschland nach 1945,* Berlin, 1961.

John, Otto, *Zweimal kam ich heim, vom Verschwörer zum Schützer der Verfassung,* Düsseldorf, 1969.

Mader, Julius, *Die graue Hand—Abrechnung mit den Bonner Geheimdiensten,* Berlin, 1960.

Nollau, Günther, *Das Amt. 50 Jahre Zeuge der Geschichte*, München, 1978.

Pomorin, Junge, Biermann, *"Geheime Kanäle"—der Nazi-Mafia auf der Spur*, 1981.

Schacht, Hjalmar, *My First 76 Years*, Bad Wörishofen, 1953.

Schellenberg, Walter, *The Schellenberg Memoirs*, London, 1956.

Skorzeny, Otto, *Secret Missions; War Memoirs of the Most Dangerous Man in Europe*, New York, 1950.

Steininger, Rolf, *Deutsche Geschichte 1945–1961*, Frankfurt, 1983.

Walde, Thomas, *ND-Report, die Rolle der geheimen Nachrichtendienste im Regierungssystem der Bundesrepublik Deutschland*, Munich, 1971.

Wechsberg, Joseph (ed.), *The Murderers Among Us: The Simon Wiesenthal Memoirs*, New York, 1967.

Ziegler, Jean, *Das Schweizer Imperium*, Hamburg, 1982.

Zolling, Hermann, and Höhne, Heinz, *Pullach intern. General Gehlen und die Geschichte des Bundesnachrichtendienstes*, Hamburg, 1971.

7

The Nuremberg Trials, Hjalmar Schacht, and the Cold War

Dealing with the Nuremberg Trials of 1946 is a highly ambiguous matter. There was the spectacular trial of Goering and associates, against the major war criminals. But there was also the second round of trials, against the Nazi doctors and judges, against the industrialists Flick, Krupp, and the executives of I.G. Farben, against the SS shock troops, the Wehrmacht High Command, against the Wilhelmstrasse foreign ministry, and so forth—twelve trials in all.

The international military tribunal judging Goering and associates was conducted by many of the participants with the high-minded intent of preventing one of the darkest chapters in man's history from ever recurring, yet it acquitted one of the most evil Nazi criminals of all, economics minister Hjalmar Schacht. The later trials, the so-called trials of the "minors," presided over by three American judges, sought to try and punish others who were co-responsible for the horrors of war and genocide, but it suffered from a series of intensive operations to cover up findings proving closely intermeshed collaboration with the Nazis on all sides. What could have been a new beginning was sabotaged.

Preparations for the Trial

Before the war's end, discussions had begun over whether to hold such a trial. Allied opinion was sharply divided. As anger began to rise over the barbaric war, many began to favor a "short trial" for Germany's entire leadership, including its military leadership, in the event of a German surrender. This question came up directly in talks among Stalin, Roosevelt, and Churchill at the so-called "Tripartite Dinner" arranged by the Soviet Embassy in connection with the Teheran Conference. Stalin demanded that Germany's entire military leadership, which he estimated to number between 50,000 and 100,000, must be immediately liquidated after the capitulation. Roosevelt assented to this at the time, whereas Churchill sharply protested against what he called the cold-blooded execution of soldiers who had fought for their country.

These positions shifted as the war drew to a close. While the Americans and Russians were increasingly distancing themselves from the idea of liquidation, in favor of putting the German leadership on trial, Churchill made a sudden 180-degree turn, vehemently calling for the liquidation of the top leadership. Churchill had his reasons for this new attitude; for one thing, he did not welcome the prospect of a community of principle between the Americans and the Russians on this question, which might result in a trial that would set a dangerous precedent in international law. Moreover, liquidation was more in keeping with Churchill's enthusiasm for the brutal Morgenthau Plan. At the end of 1944, it looked as if Churchill would be able to get his way; at the Quebec Conference, he and Roosevelt hastily signed the Morgenthau Plan for the transformation of Germany into a politically splintered, impoverished, de-industrialized pastureland, as well as Lord Simon's and Morgenthau's joint project for executions without due process. There is in fact evidence that at this time Roosevelt went so far as to seriously consider having the entire German population sterilized. Roosevelt's legal advisor Samuel Rosenman reports that Roosevelt had fun drawing a sketch of a machine that could carry out mass sterilization operations.

Already on Sept. 5, 1944, U.S. War Secretary Henry Stimson had written to Treasury Secretary Henry Morgenthau to confront Morgenthau with the glaring flaws in his plan. Depriving Germany of all its industries would affect the other European nations as well, and would condemn millions of Germans to death by starvation. Economic oppression of this magnitude would be dangerous, "because it does not prevent war, it only paves the way for the next one." Stimson, declaring to Roosevelt that the proposed liquidation of industry would be a crime against humanity and a sheer act of revenge on the part of the war victors, wrote: "It will make more of an impression on our posterity if we put these people on trial in a manner in keeping with our advanced level of civilization. . . . We should therefore participate in an international tribunal which should be devoted to putting on trial the highest echelon of the Nazi leadership."

As Stimson and Secretary of State Cordell Hull received word of the proceedings in Quebec, they mounted a common front against Morgenthau as a meddler in foreign policy. Yet before a battle broke out within the Cabinet, Morgenthau very suddenly became discredited. The Morgenthau Plan and the Quebec agreement were leaked to the press, unleashing a storm of American protest which swept Morgenthau away. Roosevelt speedily distanced himself from Morgenthau's concept, later spoke of "grave mistakes" launched in Quebec, and maintained that he could not recall having signed Morgenthau's memorandum.

In general, within the policy-making circles of Britain and the United States, unbending hatred for the Nazis criss-crossed with open sympathy for this "master race which unfortunately failed." Those who were assuming a militantly anti-Nazi stance in order to cover up their own collaboration, vied with those who wanted the horrors of the war to be quickly forgotten, so as to get to work reconstructing Germany's industry and agriculture.

Eventually, the approaching Cold War rapidly put a brake on this infighting. Decisions had to be made, and quickly. It had been decided that the Central European industrial heartland was to be built up into a strong bulwark against the Bolsheviks. In his book *War or Peace* John Foster Dulles described this quite graphically: "A revived Germany can be a great trump card in the hands of the West. While it pulls East Berlin into the Western sphere of power, it can gain a predominant strategic position in Central Europe, which undermines the Soviet military and political position in Poland, Czechoslovakia, Hungary, and the neighboring countries."

The London Accord

On Aug. 8, 1945, Justice Robert Jackson, later to be chief U.S. Prosecutor at Nuremberg, helped to bring about the conclusion of the London Great Power accord on the apprehension and trial of the leading war criminals. As the site of the trial, he chose Nuremberg, the city where the Nazis had celebrated their greatest triumphs, held their party meetings with mass torchlight processions, and in 1935 announced the infamous racial laws. Of this once magnificent medieval city, in which men like Albrecht Dürer, Adam Krafft, Hans Sachs, and Peter Henlein lived and worked, practically nothing but the Palace of Justice and the adjacent prison was left.

In his report to the President on preparations for putting National Socialist criminals on trial, he wrote:

> Doubtless what appeals to men of good will and common sense as the crime which comprehends all lesser crimes, is the crime of making unjustifiable war. . . . But International Law as taught in the Nineteenth and the early part of the Twentieth Century generally declared that war-making was not illegal and is no crime at law. . . . This, however, was a departure from the doctrine taught by Grotius, the father of International Law, that there is a distinction between just and unjust war. . . .
>
> The reestablishment of the principle of unjustifiable war is traceable in many steps. One of the most significant is the Briand-Kellogg Pact of 1928, by which Germany, Italy and Japan, common with ourselves and practically all the nations of the world, renounced war as an instrument of national policy, bound themselves to seek the settlement of disputes only by pacific means. . . . Unless this Pact altered the legal status of wars of aggression, it

has no meaning at all and comes close to being an act of deception. . . . This Pact constitutes only one in a series of acts which . . . brought International Law into harmony with the common sense of mankind, that every unjustifiable war is a crime. . . . We therefore propose to charge that a war of aggression is a crime, and that modern International Law has abolished the defense that those who incite or wage it are engaged in legitimate business.

With this line of argument, Jackson had forged a link to that rich humanist tradition of the seventeenth century which in the sphere of law is inseparable from the names Leibniz, Grotius, and Pufendorf. Hearkening back to Grotius is particularly appropriate, because with his work *De Jure Belli ac Pacis* (*On the Law of War and Peace*) it was Grotius who laid the basis for the Peace of Westphalia and thus for the resolution of the Thirty Years War; at that time as well, the world had faced the rubble-heap inflicted by barbarism.

Along with the London accord came a statute for the court which contained the most important norms of law. They dealt with punishable offenses and punishments as well as certain general questions of justice, and specified the applicable rules of procedure. The decisive article in the statute, on which the indictments hinged, is Article 6, under the general heading "Jurisdiction and General Principles," which runs as follows:

. . .The following acts, or any of them, are crimes coming within the jurisdiction of the Tribunal for which there shall be individual responsibility.

(a) *Crimes Against Peace:* namely, planning,

preparation, initiation or waging of a war of aggression, or a war in violation of international treaties, agreements or assurances, or participation in a common plan or conspiracy for the accomplishment of any of the foregoing;

(b) *War Crimes:* namely, violations of the laws or customs of war. Such violations shall include but not be limited to murder, ill-treatment or deportation to slave labor or for any other purpose of civilian population of or in occupied territory, murder or ill-treatment of prisoners of war or persons on the seas, killing of hostages, plunder of public or private property, wanton destruction of cities, towns or villages, or devastation not justified by military necessity;

(c) *Crimes Against Humanity:* namely, murder, extermination, enslavement, deportation, and other inhuman acts committed against any civilian population, before or during the war; or persecution on political, racial, or religious grounds in execution of or in connection with any crime within the jurisdiction of the Tribunal, whether or not in violation of domestic law of the country where perpetrated.

Leaders, organizers, instigators and accomplices participating in the formation or execution of a common plan or conspiracy to commit any of the foregoing crimes are responsible for all acts performed by any person in execution of such plan.

Arguments Against the Trial

Opponents of the Nuremberg Trials have always raised the objection that the trials violated the most elementary principles of law, specifically the principle of *nullen crimen sine lege, nulla poena sine lege*, which is to say, there can be no crime or punishment unless defined by a pre-existing law. The relevant laws for the trials at Nuremberg were only resolved upon after the events in question had taken place. The defense argued that such a procedure ran counter to the law of all civilized nations; since no legal statute had determined the concept of a war of aggression as of the time of the allegedly criminal actions, and no punishment had been established for the perpetrators, no court of law could be convened to judge and sentence the criminals.

The Nuremberg Court examined all these arguments, and after careful evaluation rejected them as unfounded, instead fully associating itself with Jackson's argument on this question. The relevant passage in the judgment reads:

> The working out of the statute took place in the exercise of the sovereign power of the legislature of those countries to which the German Reich had unconditionally surrendered; and the indubitable right of those countries to mandate laws for the occupied areas is recognized by the civilized world. The statute is no arbitrary exercise of the power of the victorious powers, but is, in the view of the Tribunal, as will be shown below, the expression of the timely creation of statutes of international law; and in so far as that is true, the statute in itself is a contribution to international law.

Even after the London accord was signed, opposition continued to be voiced against the trials.

In the United States, criticism was particularly strong, as shown by the statements of U.S. Supreme Court Chief Justice Harlan Stone, who made no secret of his low regard for the Nuremberg Trials. In view of this mood, it was certain that a morally steadfast man who conceived of the trials as a "mission" for the future good of mankind would have to contend with difficulties, animosities, and obstacles within his own camp.

On Dec. 4, 1945, a report appeared in the American Army journal *Stars and Stripes* sharply attacking Jackson. The attack should be seen in conjunction with the resignation of the acting prosecution spokesman, "Wild Bill" Donovan, the head of the Office of Strategic Services (OSS). Their self-estimations illustrate the sharp difference between the character of the two: while Jackson said, "Time will show whether you are right or I am," Donovan's view was, "Time will not care one way or the other whether we are right or not."

In the courtroom, their methods were equally disparate. Jackson set himself to work on the extensive documentary material, with which he intended to prove the guilt of the leading Nazis, certainly a laborious task which attracted no publicity but was appropriate to the gravity and import of the trial. Donovan had no intention of missing out on the glamor and glitter of the trial, and even thought up the idea of presenting a Nazi "witness for the prosecution." For a time, he succeeded in interesting Reichsmarshal Goering in his scheme, and Hjalmar Schacht himself offered under certain conditions to speak as a crown witness. But Donovan ran into strong opposition from Jackson, who under no circumstances wanted to create even the impression that he had entered into some deal with

Goering by promising leniency or any other advantage merely in order to impel him to "tell all." When Donovan saw that he could not get his way, he resigned in a rage, "because he wanted to have nothing more to do with the trial."

In fact, the negative news coverage must be seen as part of the psychological warfare against Justice Jackson. The portrayal of the mass murderer Goering as "highly intelligent," "artful," and so forth was intended to finally free the "idealist" Jackson from his "mission." Part of this perversity was the IQ testing of the accused, whose meticulous results were distributed by the Anglo-Americans, with the conclusion that Schacht, Goering, and Austrian Nazi leader Artur Seyss-Inquart were geniuses! For the moment, no commentary was made on this subject, yet this episode explains a great deal about the singular admiration not infrequently showered on these butchers.

An indirect broadside against the trial was delivered by Winston Churchill in his famous speech at Fulton, Missouri on March 5, 1946, which signaled the start of the Cold War. The speech was intended to announce to the world the disintegration of the Allied victors' coalition. Churchill, at that time already voted out of office, advised Britain and America to be cautious and defense-ready toward Moscow: the Soviet Union now constituted a growing provocation and danger to Christian civilization. "From Stettin on the Baltic Sea to Trieste on the Adriatic, an Iron Curtain has descended across the continent of Europe. . . . This is certainly not the free Europe we fought to build." Half a year later, on Nov. 6, U.S. Secretary of State James Byrnes, in his well-known Stuttgart speech, promised the Germans a quick return to German self-determination and economic reconstruction. He did not add that he meant only the reconstruction of West Germany, at least not in public; to journalists, he confided at the time that he had given up hope of a reunified Germany.

With these speeches, political lines were drawn which threw overboard the concept of a political community of principle, the basis on which the Nuremberg Trials were first brought about. A man like Jackson was no longer in demand in this political Ice Age.

Meanwhile, as the Cold War emerged, the Nazis and their friends around the world welcomed a splintering of the Allied coalition. When Goering read Churchill's Fulton "Iron Curtain" speech, he declared: "In the summer of last year, I had no hope of living to see the autumn, the winter, and a new year, and now, if I can make it until next fall, then it seems that I will experience many more falls and winters and summers." He added, with a sardonic laugh: "The only members of the Allies who still hold to the alliance are the four prosecutors, and they are united only against the accused."

Jackson's Statement for the Prosecution

If people later attached so much hope to the events at Nuremberg, it was above all because of the highly moral, politically civilized standard which Jackson established in his speech. He evoked the best humanist traditions of the West and showed himself firmly resolved to counterpose law, as a moral necessity for mankind, to the horrible crimes of the Nazis and the inhuman devastation of the war. In his eyes, the first task of the trial consisted in laying the foundations for a law of war and of war-avoidance, solely in the interests of the self-preservation of humanity. The core of his indictment was to bring forth the accountability of the Nazi leaders, and to present the assemblage of their actions as a coherent conspiracy on behalf of a war of aggression and as a conspiracy to commit crimes against humanity. In his opening statement to the tribunal, Jackson declared:

> This Tribunal, while it is novel and experimental, is not the product of abstract speculations nor is it created to vindicate legalistic theories. . . . The common sense of mankind demands that law shall not stop with the punishment of petty crimes by little people. It must also reach men who possess themselves of great power and make deliberate and concerted use of it to set in motion evils which leave no home in the world untouched.

Jackson rejected any notion of the collective guilt of the German people, an accusation from which many other participants at Nuremberg, especially on the judge's bench, could not free themselves. Jackson's outlook culminated in the statement: "Truly, the Germans—no less than the world outside—have a score to settle with the accused."

On the question of procedure, Jackson stated:

> In general, our case will disclose these defendants all uniting at some time with the Nazi Party in a plan which they well knew could be accomplished by an outbreak of war in Europe. Their seizure of the German state, their subjugation of the German people, their terrorism and extermination of dissident ele-

ments, their planning and waging of war, their calculated and planned ruthlessness in the conduct of warfare, their deliberate and planned criminality toward conquered peoples—all these are ends for which they acted in concert; and all these are phases of the conspiracy, a conspiracy which reached one goal only to set out for another and more ambitious one. . . .

The case as presented by the United States will be concerned with the brains and authority in back of all the crimes. These defendants were men of a station and rank which does not soil its own hands with blood. They were men who knew how to use lesser folks as tools. We want to reach the planners and designers, the inciters and leaders without whose evil architecture the world would not have been for so long scourged with the violence and lawlessness, and wracked with the agonies and convulsions of this terrible war. . . .

Experience has shown that wars are no longer local. All modern wars become world wars eventually. And none of the big nations at least can stay out. If we cannot stay out of wars, our only hope is to prevent wars. I am too well aware of the weaknesses of juridical action alone to contend that in itself your decision under this Charter can prevent future wars. Judicial action always comes after the event. . . . This trial represents mankind's desperate effort to apply the discipline of the law to statesmen who have used their powers of state to attack the foundations of the world's peace and to commit aggressions against the rights of their neighbors. . . .

The real complaining party at your bar is Civilization. . . . Civilization asks whether law is so laggard as to be utterly helpless to deal with crimes of this magnitude by criminals of this order of importance. It does not expect that you can make war impossible. It does expect that your juridical action will put the forces of International Law, its precepts, its prohibitions, and, most of all, its sanctions, on the side of peace, so that men and women of good will in all countries may have 'leave to live by no man's leave,' underneath the law.

The question now became whether the judges would apply this standard in their verdict, or whether they would find the charges too sweeping, too vague, to allow them to render a judgment.

The Conspiracy Question

The panel of judges at Nuremberg had discussed the prosecution charge of a conspiracy to conduct a war of aggression. Continental Europe generally lacks a concept of conspiracy as a criminal action; the Russians temporized on the subject of the concept while the French rejected it. In Anglo-American law, this concept has long been known and is well established, being defined as agreement or consent between two or more persons in order to commit a crime. The accused is convicted if it is proved that he actually and voluntarily participated in a plan to commit an act known to him to be a crime. This definition is not so far from the continental European concept of guilt, if a limitation is made to the basic concept which can be summarized in the question: What degree of closeness to the crime must be proven in order to declare an accused as guilty?

However, there was also no unified position in the Anglo-American camp. Especially from the British, there was opposition to the conspiracy approach, even though the criminal nature of conspiracy has been developed in their Common Law since at least the 13th century. The German Section of the Foreign Office warned against using conspiracy as a charge in a memorandum of June 30, 1945: "Criminal conspiracy would become an arbitrary phrase in foreign relations and would necessarily contribute to the founding of strange and curious measures." Four weeks later, the advisory historian of the Foreign Office, E. L. Woodward, wrote that it was not practical to charge the Germans with a conspiracy to a war of aggression:

> There was no conspiracy. The great powers knew exactly in 1937 that Germany was rearming. It is therefore unrealistic and will seem so to future historians to speak of a plan or a conspiracy of the Germany. . . . The great powers silently tolerated that the Germans violated agreements, they concluded treaties with the German government nonetheless. . . . How difficult it is to prove "intention" by means of documents is well known; we should limit ourselves to the war crimes and atrocities committed by the Nazis and leave their foreign policy out of it. . . .

Jackson had stated at the London Conference why he attached such great value to the conspiracy findings. For Goering, Gauleiter General of Poland Wilhelm Franck, security chief Ernst Kaltenbrun-

ner, Field Marshal Wilhelm Keiter, or Plenipoten-
tiary General for the Utilization of Manpower Fritz
Saukel, he did not need this charge. These men
had themselves committed so many crimes that their
conviction was hardly in doubt. But what about
Krupp or people like Hjalmar Schacht? Schacht, as
Jackson said in the meeting of July 16, "is either a
major war criminal or nothing. . . . Only a theory
of a common plan or of conspiracy will catch him
and his kind. . . ."

If agreement was finally reached in London on
the principle of conspiracy, the controversy broke
out again during the deliberations of the court. For
months, this discussion played the central role. In
fact, what was decided here was how the Nazi leadership was to be evaluated *politically*, determining
the severity of punishment.

The French justice Donnedieu de Vabres argued
most vehemently against this charge as "underde-
termined," failing to allow a firm specification of
the time, place, or method of the crimes committed;
instead only principles, perhaps passages out of
party programs and quotes out of *Mein Kampf* were
brought out, and then the assertion made that these
form the essential parts of a conspiracy. But generally there had not been a well-determined, un-
alterable plan, he contended. A guilty verdict
because of "conspiracy" could therefore only follow
ex post facto, and would thus be a violation of the
fundamental principles of law.

Donnedieu de Vabres also took the point of view
that the charge of conspiracy was totally superflu-
ous for a guilty verdict since it could be easily proven
that the accused had committed quite concrete
crimes in unleashing a war of aggression. Since the
accused planned the war, prepared for it, brought

it about, and conducted it, it is more intelligent to proceed according to the principle "the conspiracy goes over into the crime," and to punish them for what they had done, not that which they had possibly conspired about. Also, he had the conception that a conspiracy presupposes an equality of stature among the participants. But the Führer Principle of the Nazis flatly excludes that. Rather, every foundation for the conspiracy theory must be withdrawn and the 22 accused convicted and punished appropriately for their precisely defined crimes.

The Russian judge Gen. I. T. Nikitschenko rejected these explications as irrelevant. He proposed that the judges should act as practical men and not as a "debaters' club." For international law, the conspiracy was an innovation and doubtless would lead to judgments *ex post facto*. But he did not understand why the Western judges were so excited about that. There was much that is innovative in this trial: thus certain specific crimes were defined for the first time, and it was prohibited for the accused to justify themselves by the claim that they were merely following orders, but that didn't cause anyone any particular problems. According to the Russian view, it is the job of the judges to establish new legal norms. Why not admit that that is what they were doing? Nikitschenko added that the crimes were so unique and extensive that the court is justified to pioneer new areas, through conviction on the basis of conspiracy in violation of international law. Colonel Volchow, the Soviet delegate on the Tribunal, repeated that the unprecedented atrocities of the Nazis, for example, mass extermination, were so complex that the crimes could not be dealt with unless they were condemned with something as comprehensive as conspiracy.

The British judge Birkett spoke most emphatically on retaining the charge of conspiracy. The principal purpose of the trials is to prove the existence of a common plan in respect to a conspiracy. If this charge were to be dropped, the heart of the general charge would be torn out and the process would be without value. Some of the defendants could be found guilty, of course, without appealing to conspiracy; "however, the Nazi regime would be acquitted."

Yet Birkett maintained that the conspiracy charge should be restricted to conducting a war of aggression and limited to the years 1937–45. This conception was incorporated into the final judgment, which states:

> The prosecutors asserted that any important participation in the affairs of the Nazi Party or the government is a proof for participation in a conspiracy which is criminal *per se* and therefore presents a criminal conspiracy. The concept of conspiracy is not defined in the statutes. Yet according to the view of the tribunal, the conspiracy must be clearly defined in reference to their criminal intentions. There must not be too great a temporal gap between the decision and the act. If the plans are designated as criminal, then this cannot merely depend on declarations in a party program, as they are to be found in the 25 points of the Nazi Party of the year 1920, and also not from the later expressions of opinion in *Mein Kampf*. The tribunal must investigate whether a concrete plan for carrying out the war existed and determine who had participated in this plan.

With that, the court had decided against Jackson's essential thesis, according to which a long-term Nazi conspiracy existed. Temporarily, the conspiracy was limited from 1937, the year of the Hossbach Conference—at which Hitler laid out for the Nazi economic and military leadership his war plans—to the end of the war, and in content to the "planning of concrete crimes" without regard to general programmatic assertions.

In restricting the conspiracy charge to certain operations beginning in 1937, the court was forced to delimit the evidence of crimes against humanity. The statute had intended that such crimes had to be committed in coincidence with other crimes which were expressly cited in the statute; thus criminal acts could not be condemned which were committed before late 1937. Since no evidence was presented to the court on concrete plans for the enslavement or murder of Czechoslovakian, Austrian, or Polish populations, plans which were a part of the preparations for attack on these countries, not a single defendant was convicted under the crimes against humanity charge for crimes he had committed before 1939. In addition, no defendant had to answer before this court for any crimes which had been committed in Germany before the beginning of the war, and which were committed without knowledge of Hitler's criminal intentions. With this single stroke of the pen, the tribunal swept at least one-third of the evidence from the table and saved defendants such as Schacht and von Papen from harsh punishment.

The Controversy over Schacht

The dilemma of the Nuremberg Trials is personified by former Reichsbank president and economics minister Hjalmar Schacht. The key to a successful conclusion of the trial, that is, a politically realistic judgment of the Nazi regime, of the extent of its crimes, and its long-term planning, as Jackson had intended, lay in an evaluation of the role of defendant Schacht. In contrast to the other major defendants, Schacht dispensed with the racialist-cultist zeal of the Nazis. Quite coolly, in discussions around a conference table, Schacht had laid the foundations for not only Auschwitz but for the military campaigns of the Nazis as well.

It was known that Schacht had helped bring Hitler to power, that he had made Hitler "socially acceptable" among industrialists and the nobility. What did not enter into the discussion at Nuremberg, however, was the fact that Schacht was the center of extensive international connections because of his position as a founder and member of the board of directors of the Bank for International Settlements (BIS) in Basel, and was able to control crucial changes of political climate which originally made the Nazi seizure of power possible.

Long before Nazi hegemony, Schacht had his feelers out to the Anglo-Americans in order to determine, in advance, how they would act toward Hitler as the Reichschancellor. The answer he received was entirely positive, for at the same time that Germany was being squeezed financially, the preparations were being made for Hitler's appearance. Such preparations go back to the middle of the 1920s, and indeed, Schacht had already in the beginning of the 1920s formed close connnections with the Dulles brothers who, like himself, were at the Versailles reparations negotiations. The contact was never broken and was to prove indispensable for Schacht and the Nazis.

It was this international faction that was determined to subject Germany to the kind of austerity only a demagogic dictator could impose. The internal looting of Germany's living standards, labor power, and capital base under Hitler led inexorably to a drive for conquest of Western Europe and the territories to Germany's East. The great industrial installations that could have been turned to humanity's benefit were assigned, under the compulsion to turn the austerity outward and find new looting grounds, to fuel the Nazi war machine. The Schacht-imposed principle of *primitive Bauarbeit*—labor-intensive production—led inexorably under the Nazis to the slave-labor camps, and, for used-up slave laborers and other "useless eaters," the death camps.

One of the most important international contact points for Schacht was British central bank chief Montagu Norman, who was openly sympathetic with the Nazis and, since the time when both were on the board of directors of the BIS, had been a friend and advisor to Schacht. Schacht and Norman had frequently met before the Nazi seizure of power for secret conferences in Badenweiler. *Before* the seizure of power, Norman had provided all the support for the Nazis that he could, and refused any credit to the Weimar government for overcoming the financial crisis. This connection ran through the Stein Bank of Cologne, the London Schroeder Bank, and the Bank of England, on whose directorate was F. C. Tiarks, the director of the British Schroeder Bank who acted as a middle man and who was also a partner of the Stein Bank in Cologne. We also find the Dulles brothers here, for Foster represented the legal interests of the U.S. Schroeder Bank, and his brother Allan was on the directorate of this bank. Foster was also a leading spokesman and financial supporter for the isolationist America First organization, which was riddled with Nazi supporters, and wrote apologies for the Hitler regime.

Exemplary of the international connections behind the Nazi seizure of power is the tie of the Hitler financier Fritz von Thyssen—who, through the Keppler Circle, together with Schacht had convinced German industrialists of Hitler's merits—to the U.S. investment bank Dillon, Read.

On Jan. 10, 1925, Dillon, Read loaned a Thyssen firm $12 million, and one year later loaned the Rheine Elbe Union $25 million; six months later the Thyssen factory received another $5 million. In 1926, a series of the largest mining firms of Germany merged, including the firms named above, into the Vereinigte Stahlwerke, A.G., a gigantic trust overseen by von Thyssen. He received $30 million from Dillon, Read on June 26, 1926, and another $30 million in July 1927. A year later, Dillon, Read invested $15 million in the Gelsenkirchen Bergwerks A.G., a principal component of the steel trust, and $16 million in Ruhrchemie A.G. and Ruhr Gas A.G., both businesses contracted by the Thyssen factory. The Siemens firm received no less than $24 million in 1925–30 from Dillon, Read, while the Deutsche Bank received $25 million in September 1927.

If the Anglo-Americans were to avoid fouling their own nest, it was evidently decided, this whole body of evidence had to be excluded. The prohibition of the *tu quoque* (accusations which are equally valid against the accuser), which at Nuremberg was scrupulously observed with the other defendants, hung invisibly in the air around Schacht. That body of evidence was a precondition for understanding the entire conspiracy from the seizure of power by the Nazis to the concentration camps.

Schacht before the Court

Before the trial, the victorious powers were not in agreement over whether Schacht should be put on the list of major war criminals. The Americans and Russians were in favor, the British were vehemently opposed. Indeed, the British were generally averse to putting any name from German industrialist circles on the list, while Jackson insisted that at least representatives of Krupp, I.G. Farben, and Flick be brought before the court. The French swung the vote on this question in favor of placing Schacht on the list, for they harbored at this particular time considerable hatred against German industrialists.

Schacht behaved in Nuremberg from the very first day as though he had nothing to do with the whole proceedings, as though his transfer from a concentration camp (where Hitler had put him in 1944) to the defendant's box had all been an error and was totally unjustified. He was outraged that he had been placed in the same position as "these monsters." He did not speak a single work to Goering, "that murderer and thief." He turned away, full of contempt, from Kaltenbrunner, that "hangman with a law degree," and also wanted to have nothing to do with the "parvenu and careerist" von Ribbentrop.

From the beginning, Schacht played on his international connections, on his extensive knowledge of events on the international level of diplomacy. He appealed, for example, to acting U.S. prosecution representative Donovan, in a let-

ter describing the background of the Nazi regime
and indicating that he would rather go into such a
comprehensive summary with a man of Donovan's
judgment than with the German defense attorneys.
A man such as Schacht, who had been indispensable
for the fascist preparations and conduct of the war,
could presume to give the court assistance on the
international collaboration of the German industrialists and not even shy away from referring to
assurances which departing U.S. Ambassador Dodd
had given him in Berlin concerning the post-war
period. Schacht was also one to whom the then-
acting U.S. Secretary of State Sumner Wells had
stated in the spring of 1940 that the United States
was not interested in the overthrow of the fascist
regime. Finally, Schacht could have documented
conversations from the years 1942–43 with American bankers to whom he had offered, in Basel, to
continue the war in common with the Greater German Reich against the Soviet Union.

How arrogantly this defendant could behave toward the court and how double-edged his testimony
was for the Allies, is shown in Jackson's interrogation of Schacht. The American prosecutor went
into Schacht's role in the partition of Czechoslovakia, whereupon Schacht became outraged that
the British and Americans wanted to pose as the
protectors of this country, for it was well known
that in 1939, the Western powers, a few days before
Munich, had demanded that Czechoslvakia capit-
ulate to Hitler. As Jackson, with complete justification, referred to the fact that Schacht had
confiscated all the assets of the branches of the
Czechoslovak central bank immediately after the
occupation of the Sudetenland, Schacht parried,
with equal justification: "But pardon me, he [Hitler]

did not take it with force. The Allies gave him that country." And the dialogue continues:

Schacht: I cannot answer your question for the reason that, as I have already said, there was no "taking over"; rather, it was a gift. When someone gives me a gift such as this, I accept it with thanks.

Jackson: Even if it doesn't belong to those giving it away?

Schacht: Well, in that case, I naturally have to leave that up to the judgment of those giving it away.

Exemplary of Schacht's confidence in his escape from punishment was an episode on the periphery of the trial: In a pause in the proceedings one day, an American guard noticed how defendant Albert Speer, Hitler's architect and slave-labor coordinator, was industriously drawing something. Questioned by the guard, Speer replied: "You see, Schacht has commissioned me to design a villa which he will have built after the trial is over." Schacht later confirmed Speer's words with a nod of his head.

Schacht was obviously an extremely painful sight for the Anglo-Americans. The longer the trial extended, the more this "highly respectable man in the high, stiff collar" was able to build a wall between himself and the "Nazi oddities" whose bloody atrocities were all too obvious.

Schacht's Policy

When the Nazis took control, they could count again on financial support, especially from the United States and Great Britain. With these funds and with his gigantic public works program, Schacht was able in a relatively short time to take millions of unemployed off the streets. Freeways and dams were

built, swamps drained, and other labor-intensive
projects launched. This program encompassed
however only 20% of the Nazi economy, with the
other 80% flowing into a gigantic rearmament program unprecedented at that date.

At Nuremberg, the American prosecutors had
dated the Nazi conspiracy from 1920, the year of
the founding of the Nazi Party, citing the party
program and Hitler's later *Mein Kampf*. This was
accurate as far as it went; but so long as primary
attention was directed merely to the paramilitary
internal structure of the NSDAP and the military
and racialist statements of the program and *Mein
Kampf*, a look at the international financial forces
behind Hitler, and the conceptual authors of *Mein
Kampf*—Haushofer and his British co-thinkers Halford Mackinder and Houston Stewart Chamberlain—would be ruled out.

These geopoliticians advanced an extreme Mal-
thusianism which must necessarily end in a search
for new living space. In the strategic considerations
of these people, the "Eurasian Heartland"—the Soviet Union—played a central role. If one does not
take this absolutely central motor of the Nazi ideology into consideration, then fascism will always
be viewed as a mere "sociological phenomenon."

The conspiracy the American prosecution wanted
to prove is established precisely by this fusion of
the Nazis with the British geopolitical concept of
conquest of the Eurasian heartland. Out of this
ideological brew, the Nazis drew their strength; and
against this background, the political-economic decisions of the Nazis can be portrayed coherently,
down to the very last battle of the war.

The attempt was made at Nuremberg to prove

that Schacht had always known that Hitler's rearmament program would end in war. In speeches from
the year 1935–36, Schacht clearly acknowledged
that he was quite familiar with the connection between his policy and the impetus toward war. Again
and again he complained that Germany "had too
large a population in too small a space, that this
fact weighed upon him like a nightmare." The proposal which came from America, that the problem
be solved through a severe restriction of the birth
rate, was rejected in outrage by Schacht—he did
not name those American friends who had suggested it; he saw the solution only in overcoming
the "political apportionment of possession" ("*politische Besitzverhältnisse*"), which could mean nothing
other than the creation of new "living space." He
wrote in 1936 in an article in a Reichsbank publication: "Here it must be asserted that the attempt
to shrink a great people down through external
force must lead with necessity to social misery and
unrest, *eventually however to an explosion. . . . Peace in
Europe and therefore the whole world rest*s *on whether
the crowded masses in Central Europe receive the possibility of life or not.*" Such a statement can only be
taken as a sheer threat, especially in a year when
the German air force was making its first test flights
in the Spanish Civil War.

Schacht further wrote: "A great question which
must be taken up in consideration of the population
density is whether the people have completely utilized the existing space at their disposal. . . . Germany has with enormous expenditures of capital
and labor taken everything from its land that is
possible. The results of the last three years show
that the upper limit reached in 1933 cannot be gone

beyond. *The German man cannot produce sufficient foodstuffs for the German people from the land which is presently given to him."*

Here is expressed the great Malthusian theme of over-population, coupled with the battle for survival which is always the first move of predatory military actions. Schacht adopted a moderate tone in these years, and an expedition toward the East was not yet discussed. He demanded instead the restoration of former German colonial possessions for overcoming the *"Lebensraum* dilemma."

But how serious could these demands have been, given Schacht's knowledge of the other European powers' jealous clamp on their overseas possessions? Hitler's aims, as expressed in *Mein Kampf,* were direct: "As much as we recognize the necessity of coming to terms with France, it still remains utterly ineffective if this were to exhaust our foreign policy aims. They can and will have a point if they form a cover for our flank for an enlargement of our living space of our people in Europe. . . . If, however, we speak today of new territory, we are thinking primarily only of Russia and the border countries subordinate to it."

In contrast perhaps to many industrialists and Nazi sympathizers in Germany, Schacht was thoroughly familiar with Hitler's *Mein Kampf.* The above passages and similar ones could not have escaped Schacht's attention, since he was interested in all questions of foreign policy; nor those passages in which Hitler so clearly said, "Now the time has come to finally stop the colonial and trade policies of the pre-war period and to move to the territorial policy of the future." Schacht could derive no hopes from meetings with Hitler that Hitler did not mean exactly what he said. Schacht's proposals on a new division of the colonial sector must be seen as a diversionary tactic from the real plans which the Nazis were considering, without in the least implying that Schacht did not have in secret his own conceptions of the "opening up of living space," or, as he called it, overcoming "political apportionment of possession."

The mass deportation of prisoners of war, Jews, and political prisoners into German slave labor camps was the direct consequence of Schacht's economic policy. Schacht's primitive accumulation, the plundering of domestic resources without any hope of replacement, necessarily forced the Nazis to war and predatory expeditions. The crimes against humanity which the Nazis committed were the lawful consequence of Schacht's bestial measures.

Because the prosecution neglected to consider the economic measures which Schacht had set in motion, measures of whose consequences Schacht, as well as his friends in London and Wall Street, were perfectly aware, the Nuremberg plaintiffs could not prove the existence of a long-term Nazi plan and conspiracy for a war of aggression. The potential for doing so was pulverized between the millstones of British geopolitics and American high finance. At least with respect to prosecuting Schacht, Jackson was very much "on the outside looking in." The world of international finance was a "closed society," and Schacht was emphatically part of it.

Schacht as 'Conspirator against Hitler'

At Nuremberg, Schacht liked to play up his own role as a conspirator against the Nazi regime. He did, in fact, have contact with the group of conspirators around Dr. Carl Goerdeler, and he provably made many attempts to establish contact with the Western powers. But should that exonerate him?

Schacht boasted to the court that in 1942–43 while in Basel, he had attempted to persuade American bankers to join with the "Greater German Reich" in a war against the Soviet Union. In fact, it seems that one of his chief aims had been to draw the Western powers into conspiracy for an aggressive war against the Soviet Union. The First Secretary of the American Embassy in Berlin at the time, Donald Heath, claimed that Schacht informed him about the imminent attack on Russia. He reported that "Around June 6, 1941, some two weeks prior to the surprise attack on Russia, Schacht apprised us that Hitler was determined to invade Russia on or around July 20. Schacht assured us that this had to be viewed as an established fact, not to be doubted." (It is doubtful, however, that Schacht, who was out of favor with Hitler as of 1937, knew about the top-secret Operation Barbarossa plan.)

Already in March, 1939, Goerdeler and Schacht had established contact in Ouchy, Switzerland, "with a man who maintained very good relations to the English and French governments," in order to let London and Paris know that Hitler was determined under all circumstances to move eastward toward Danzig and Warsaw to annex the rich black soil of the Ukraine and the oilfields of Rumania and the Caucasus.

Since it has also been documented that the English and French likewise planned a surprise attack on the Caucasus oilfields, it appears that the conspiratorial group of generals had already resolved by the summer of 1939 to conclude some sort of behind-the-scenes deal with the Western powers and to negotiate a price for Hitler's overthrow. The central point is that, as the currently accessible materials on the German underground plot show, if Hitler had been overthrown and the Nazis wiped out, the conspirators were expected by London, Paris, and Washington to pressure Poland into making territorial concessions. In other words, the principles of foreign policy of Hitler's Germany would have remained the same, regardless of what regime was in power.

Seen in this light, Schacht's conspiratorial doings are exposed as merely an attempt to distance himself from the Nazis, whose ideological, anti-Semitic orientation did not suit him, but whose foreign-policy convictions he shared. Schacht, not wishing to go along with Hitler on a policy whose groundwork—in the sense of Jackson's accusation of long-term conspiracy and planning—he himself had laid, now had to look around for other confederates. The conspiratorial, criminal content of Schacht's policy, which aimed at a war of aggression, never changed.

Schacht's conspiracy against Hitler bore all the characteristics of the idea of universal fascism as proclaimed by Mussolini: "Either we succeed in giving unity to politics and life in Europe, or the axis of world history will finally shift to the other side of the Atlantic, and Europe will play a second-rate role in history," or as preached by Richard Coudenhove-Kalergi, leader of the fascist Pan-European Union, who in 1922 called upon Mussolini to announce a European Monroe Doctrine, "Europe for the Europeans."

Schacht's ideas fit in with that Euro-fascist attitude which prevailed following Germany's attack on the Soviet Union in 1941. There were high hopes for a continental anti-Bolshevik crusade; but Hitler rejected this idea, saying it was aimed against German supremacy, and raged against a "shameless Vichy newspaper" which had dared to describe the war against the Soviet Union as Europe's war. "We are not fighting for a new European order, but for the defense and security of our vital interests."

In the Euro-fascist camp, National Socialist policies were considered egotistic and imperialistic. The French Euro-fascist Pierre Drieu la Rochelle summed it up as follows: "German policy in all conquered European countries has been fundamentally guided by prejudice, by old methods of war, and by diplomacy. It was not capable of developing something new out of the fabulous opportunities presented to it. It proved incapable of transforming its war of conquest into a revolutionary war. . . ."

Of course, whether Hitler carried out the invasion of the European countries and, above all, of Russia with support from Americans and English or in the context of a supranational Euro-fascist crusade could make no difference with respect to the charge of conspiring to plan a war of aggression. The problem was, however, that Schacht could not be convicted without revealing in the courtroom the ambiguous role of the victorious Allied powers. And precisely in this lies the whole tragedy of the Nuremberg process.

Schacht was acquitted at the Nuremberg military tribunal, against the votes of the Russians and the Americans (the Soviet members of the Tribunal insisted on publishing their dissent). For the second and third leadership levels of the Nazis, that acquittal meant new hope for a quick rehabilitation, and they were not disappointed.

The Later Trials

The later trials took place as the Cold War began to break out, offering incentives to the U.S. State Department for concealment and rehabilitation of Nazi criminals, under the rubric of using such types against the Soviet bloc—a policy which had extremely destructive effects on the course of German history.

The question of how Hitler could have attained power, who had prepared the way for him nationally and internationally, was a question which involved the long-term design of National Socialist policy, and was therefore no longer of interest at these trials. A lasting contribution was made by putting individuals on trial for crimes against humanity—as in the case of Nazi practitioners of euthanasia. But examination of the trial documents makes it impossible to avoid the impression that the only issue now was to recover as elegantly as possible from these vexing proceedings, and to create as quickly as possible a technical-administrative and political foundation in occupied Germany that would counter the Red menace as efficiently as possible. In 1950, the Nuremberg defense counsel Carl Haensel wrote concerning this phase of the proceedings:

> The phase in the Nuremberg proceedings that manifested Renaissance natural-law judicial methods seems to have lapsed once again. The classical form in which the international proceedings were carried out before the international military tribunal . . . has been reduced to a trial procedure that has even given up the externally maintained unity of intent of

the court. . . . The strength of this eruption of natural law which ended the international proceedings with thirteen death sentences has . . . died away, and a death sentence or a conviction for conspiracy to breach the peace will no longer be handed down.

The protocols of the London Conference exhibited with special force the fundamental conception of the American chief prosecutor Robert H. Jackson that an international tribunal of law would be established for the punishment of not only the war of aggression, but for every breach of peace, every "plan for making an illegal war." The publication of this verdict and its codicils . . . makes it possible to trace how this great idea of Jackson's has been transformed.

The original intent of Justice Jackson and his co-thinkers, to set forth in broad strokes the anatomy of an inconceivably unjust state, to uncover the driving force and motives, to punish the principal instigators at all levels of the system, had given way to an excruciating effort to adjust the Nuremberg trials to fit the changed post-war political realities. By virtue of the Cold War, a tendency had set in within the United States which, if not in sympathy with the Nazi criminals, believed that the Germans could not become good allies of the Western powers if German generals were sitting in confinement.

A brief examination of the proceedings against the I.G. Farben company will show how the proceedings at Nuremberg were transformed. The firm's international connections make it easy to recognize how directly these international ramifications shaped the Nazi regime and, in the long run, guided its course.

The International Connections of I.G. Farben

For many years, especially in the United States, the German industrial giant I.G. Farben had cultivated close international business connections. Even during World War II these connections continued, especially with Rockefeller's Standard Oil Company and the Nickel Trust—both of which also conveyed strategically important products to the Nazis during the war, products that were denied to America's ally Britain. This went so far that on Capitol Hill, Sen. Harry Truman quite accurately charged Standard Oil with treason; he declared on March 27, 1942: "Even following our entry into the war, Standard Oil has made every effort to secure German control over vitally important war materials."

At the interrogation of the I.G. Farben directors at Nuremberg, it was documented how the Nickel Trust, which controlled 85% of world nickel production, supplied the Hitler regime with nickel for political-military reasons. On Sept. 29, 1947, testimony of I.G. Farben director Paul Häfliger was read which stated that in 1934, one year after Hitler's seizure of power, an agreement was concluded between I.G. Farben and the Nickel Trust which sanctioned I.G. Farben to supply approximately half of the German requirements at a 50% foreign-exchange saving.

A lack of political foreknowledge cannot be presumed on the part of the Nickel Trust. One of Häfliger's memoranda of Oct. 19, 1939 states: "The Nickel Trust must be concerned not to allow its basic attitude to become public. Typical, for example, was its behavior when in the spring of this year at Ottawa as well as in the British Parliament interventions were made to at least reduce exports to Germany. The Trust understood even in time of crisis how to divert the action from behind the scenes with misleading statements and thereby prevent any results."

In the same memorandum Häfliger proposed inducing the Finnish government to reserve for Germany the major part of nickel production at Petsamo, Finland. The Nickel Trust had owned the concession for these mines since 1934. The trust had no objections whatsoever to Häfliger's autocratic actions: "Knowing the personalities and the basic attitude of the Nickel Trust previously shown," he wrote, "I take it for granted that such an arrangement will be welcomed cordially by the Trust. And for its part will perceive the supplying of Germany as a desirable protection against a possible Russian attack. . . . Obviously the Trust will endeavor to abstain as much as possible from anything that could frustrate further cooperation with us after the war."

Who were these personalities whose basic attitudes Häfliger knew so well? The most important was John Foster Dulles, director and trustee of the Nickel Trust and its chief counsel in all matters outside the American continent.

Another connection of I.G. Farben in the United States is significant: the previously mentioned investment bank Dillon, Read. At the outbreak of the Second World War, the president of the bank, James Forrestal, was chosen by I.G. Farben to head its largest enterprise in the United States, the General Aniline and Film Corporation. Under Forrestal's direction, General Aniline supplied German fascism via the South American route with militarily important products during the first year of the war.

Forrestal became the U.S. Defense Secretary in 1947-49, while the vice-president of the bank, William Draper—one of the twentieth century's most rabid advocates of reducing the world's population of "lesser races"—headed the U.S. economic policy division in occupied Germany and was assistant defense secretary of the United States in 1947–49. Forrestal appointed to a senior Defense Department post a certain Howard Peterson, who had argued I.G. Farben's most important legal cases in the United States between the two world wars. Is it an accident that Howard Peterson, the lawyer of I.G. Farben, was chosen as the judge in the Nuremberg trials against the directors of the Farben Trust? Or that (unlike Goethe's house), during the massive American bombardments of the city of Frankfurt, the I.G. Farben headquarters, a gigantic building in the middle of Frankfurt, did not receive a single hit?

The Trial Against I.G. Farben: Indictment and Verdict

Under such conditions, the trial could not go too badly for the I.G. Farben defendants.

No indictments for plotting a war of aggression were brought against the company's supervisory board of directors, even though the chairman of the board, Carl Krauch, had demanded on April 28, 1939: "Today, as in 1914, the German political and economic position appears ... to demand a rapid development of war through anniliating attacks at the very beginning hostilities. . . . The creation of a unified large-scale economic bloc of the four European anti-Comintern partners is required, which Yugoslavia and Bulgaria must soon join. The bloc must extend its influence over Romania, Turkey, and Iran."

This thinking corresponded exactly to that of Carl Duisberg, the chairman of the I.G. Farben board, president of the Reich Association of German Industry, and a Pan-Europa member. Duisberg had dreamed earlier of an economic bloc from Bordeaux to Odessa, whose centerpiece would be the German Reich.

In the spring of 1940, I.G. Farben was able to propose a 100-point comprehensive plan for a "new order" for "Establishing a European Grand Economic Sphere." On March 27, 1941, Continental Oil A.G. was founded, which, together with the Deutsche Bank, was to be primarily concerned with the Caucasus petroleum refining area. The president of the executive committee was I.G. Farben director Ernst Rudolf Fischer; the board chairman of Continental was Karl Blessing, a member of the Reichsbank directorate who later became the postwar Bundesbank's president. Hermann Josef Abs, the dean of West Germany's post-war banking community, was also involved in the operations of Continental A.G.

In view of these deliberate policies for dividing up the spoils of the East, it is inconceivable that the leadership of I.G. Farben—particularly Hermann Schmitz (a director of the Bank for International Settlements), Baron Georg von Schnitzler, August von Knieriem, Paul Häfliger, Max Ilgner, Wilhelm Mann, and Heinrich Oster—were not tried for plotting a war of aggression. A summary of the indictment is contained in the Dec. 28, 1948 dissenting opinion by Judge Paul M. Hebert:

Under Count Three of the indictment, all defendants are charged with having committed war crimes [using I.G. Farben as an instrument] and crimes against humanity as defined in Article II of Control Council Law Number 10. It is alleged in the document that defendants participated in the enslavement and deportation to slave labor on a gigantic scale of members of the civilian populations of countries and territories under the belligerent occupation of, or otherwise controlled by, Germany; that the defendants participated in the enslavement of concentration-camp inmates, including German nationals; that the defendants participated in the use of prisoners of war in war operations . . . and, that the defendants participated in the mistreatment, terrorization, torture, and murder of enslaved persons. . . . [committing] war crimes against humanity.

The court acquitted the board of directors of I.G. Farben on these charges, primarily on the ground of insufficient evidence that the I.G. Farben defendants had on their own initiative employed prisoners of war in an illegal manner. It was also not proven that the members of the board of directors had participated in connection with the procurement or employment of forced labor. It could not be established that the accused had participated on their own initiative in the employment of concentration camp inmates. Finally, it was stated in the verdict: "We cannot arrive at the determination that they were criminally responsible for the indicated instances of mistreatment of the laborers utilized in the various I.G. installations. Nor do we hold the accused responsible for the incidents in the buildings of Auschwitz."

This verdict was not unanimous. Judge Hebert's statement appended to the verdict, in which he declared he would write a dissenting opinion, contained the following crucial passage:

> Admittedly, Farben would have preferred German workers rather than to pursue the policy of utilization of slave labor. Despite this fact, and despite the existence of a reign of terror in the Reich, I am, nevertheless, convinced that compulsion to the degree of depriving the defendants of moral choice did not in fact operate as the conclusive cause of the defendant's actions, *because their will coincided with the governmental solution to the situation,* and the labor was accepted out of desire for, and the only means of maintaining war production. . . .
>
> I concur in the conviction of those defendants who have been found guilty under count three, but the responsibility for the utilization of slave labor and all incidental toleration of mistreatment of the workers should go much further and should, in my opinion, lead to the conclusion that *all of the defendents in this case* [insofar as they belonged to the board of directors] *are guilty under count three* . . . [emphasis added].

Consolidation

In January 1951, soon after the follow-up trials were completed, the U.S. High Commissioner for occupied Germany, John J. McCloy, declared a general amnesty. One example of the drastic relaxation of penalties and punishments is the trial of the notorious SS Einsatzkommandos (Special Force Commandos): Of the original 13 death sentences pronounced, only 4 were carried out, and the other 9 were reduced to prison sentences. All remaining prison sentences were obligingly set aside by McCloy. As early as 1951, the first prisoners were freed; in 1958, Ernst Biberstein was one of the last to leave imprisonment.

The SS Einsatzgruppen were formed four weeks before the Nazi attack on the U.S.S.R. through an agreement between the Reichssicherheitsamt and the Armed Forces High Command (OKW). The groups were about 800–1,200 men strong and their officers came from the Gestapo, the Sicherheitsdienst (secret service, SD), and the SS. The task of the Einsatzgruppen was to destroy partisans and members of the Resistance and exterminate entire sections of the occupied populations.

The SS murderers Heinz Jost and Franz Six, who were originally condemned in the trial of SS Einsatzkommandos to prison sentences of from 20 years to life, now found lucrative positions in the West German business sector. Since 1960, for example, SS Brigade Leader Six occupied the company-wide directorship for the Porsche diesel auto company at Friedrichshafen, a subsidiary of Mannesmann A.G. This employment, however, was only a cover for work in the Federal intelligence service (Bundesnachrichtendienst, BND)—the West German equivalent of the Central Intelligence Agency—to which Six had belonged since his release from prison in 1952. The BND employed no fewer than 4,000 former SS officers and SD agents.

Despite the incontrovertible evidence concerning the slaughter carried out by the Einsatzgruppen which was presented before the Tribunal, by 1951 SS units were being resurrected, in the guise of "social help associations," such as the Hilfsgemein-schaft auf Gegenseitigkeit ehemaliger Angehöriger der Waffen-SS, HIAG. The members of these SS units demanded their full rehabilitation with in-creasing loudness. On Oct. 6, 1959, the HIAG was declared an "organization in the public interest." After frequent discussions between political offi-cials in Bonn and the leadership of the HIAG, the Bundestag resolved on June 29, 1961 that all for-mer full-time members of the SS Verfügungs-truppe, later the Waffen-SS (the Armed SS), who could prove as of May 8, 1945 that they had a minimum of ten years' service with Hitler, would become "entitled to pensions." With this measure, the last barrier to penetration of the Bundeswehr and the police by former SS members was opened.

In the judgment against the OKW, all 13 field marshals and generals who had been accused were acquitted of the charge of crimes against peace, on the grounds that punishment for conducting a war of aggression must be limited to the politicians in charge.

Given this line of argument, it was only a small step to putting the blame for all the horrors of the war on the German people, which happened as a result of the altered U.S. post-war policy toward Germany, under the slogan of "collective guilt." This "collective guilt" finds no support whatever in the evidence produced at the trials.

In the wake of this change in U.S. policy, an alliance came about that the European facists had hoped for up to the last moment of defeat: that the Third Reich could perhaps succeed at five min-utes to midnight in forming an alliance with the

Anglo-Americans. For many of these "universal fascists," who had streamed into the Waffen SS until the very end of the war, it seemed unthinkable that the West would look on while Eastern and Central Europe were bolshevized. Thus they awaited a military alliance with the Western powers in order to jointly drive back the Red Army.

This hope was carried out in a different way. The alliance between fascists and Anglo-Americans did come about. The Cold War made it possible. It was the Cold War which diverted the United States from promoting the bold economic and political post-war reconstruction of Europe and the underdeveloped world, and which justified in the name of "anti-Communism" an alliance with many of the Nazis whose ties with the East remained.

Bibliography

Ahrens, Hans D., *Demontage—Nachkriegspolitik der Alliierten,* Munich, 1982.

Buck, Andreas, "The Nuremberg Trials—How the Crime of Genocide was Judged and Punished," in *New Solidarity,* Feb. 22, Mar. 4, and Mar. 7, 1984.

Deschner, Günther, "Die Fracht der Tante Ju, die beinahe Geschichte machte," in *Die Welt,* Oct. 1, 1983.

Drieu la Rochelle, Pierre, *Secret Journal and Other Writings,* Cambridge, Mass., 1983.

Dulles, John Foster, *War or Peace,* New York, 1950.

Fall 9—Das Urteil im SS-Einsatzgruppenprozess, Berlin, 1963.

Fall 12—Das Urteil gegen das Oberkommando der Wehrmacht, Berlin, 1961.

Gisevius, Hans Bernd, *Bis zum bitteren Ende,* Munich/Zürich, 1982.

Grüncler and Manikowski, *Das Gericht der Sieger,* 1967.

Hitler, Adolf, *Mein Kampf,* Boston, 1943.

Jackson, Robert Hougwout, *U.S. State Department—Trial of War Criminals, Documents. . .*, Washington, 1945.

Kempner, Robert M. W., *Ankläger einer Epoche,* cited in Gerd Ressling, "Jagd auf die Mörder im Staatsauftrag," in *Rheinische Merkur,* Oct. 14, 1983.

LaRouche, Lyndon H. and Goldman, David P., *The Ugly Truth about Milton Friedman,* New York, 1980.

Loth, Wilfried, *Die Teilung der Welt—Geschichte des Kalten Kriegs,* Munich, 1980.

Maser, Werner, *Nürnberg—Tribunal der Sieger,* Munich/Zürich, I977.

Neulen, Hans Werner, *Eurofaschismus und der Zweite Weltkrieg,* Munich, 1980.

Norden, Albert, *Thus Wars Are Made!,* Dresden, 1970.

Poltorak, Arkadi, *Nürnberger Epilog,* Berlin (DDR), 1971.

Pool, James and Pool, Suzanne, *Who Financed Hitler? The Secret Funding of Hitler's Rise to Power, 1913–1933,* New York, 1978.

Schacht, Hjalmar, "Germany's Colonial Demands," in *Foreign Affairs,* Jan. 1937.

Skorzeny, Otto, *Secret Missions; War Memoirs of the Most Dangerous Man in Europe,* New York, 1950.

Smith, Bradley F., *Reaching Judgment at Nuremberg,* New York, 1977.

Taylor, Telford, *The Nuremberg Trials, War Crimes and International Law,* New York, 1949.

Wheeler-Bennett, John W., *The Nemesis of Power, the German Army in Politics, 1918–1945,* London/New York, 1964.

Das Urteil im IG-Farben-Prozess, Offenbach, 1948.

Das Urteil von Nürnberg 1946, dtv-Dokumente.

Das Urteil im Wilhelmstrassenprozess, Schwäbisch Gmünd, 1950.

It should be noted that the "Nuremberg Court state" has also been one of history's greatest bonanzas for historians and political scientists. "Where else has a country been researched more systematically than was done at Nuremberg?" asks Robert Kemper in his recently published autobiography. In fact, as the Allies moved into Germany they also took possession of the state secret archives, the written history of an entire nation. Almost none of the Allies was able to resist the temptation to join in seizing of these documents.

In this way, a people became deprived of their own history. Since that time, any German historian desiring to do research has had to politely knock on doors in Washington, London, Paris, or Moscow in order to gain access to the plundered documents.

8

The Global Danger:
Today's Nazi-Communists

As international strategic tensions and the world economic crisis intensified since the beginning of the 1970s, so did a systematic activation of an extensive destabilization apparatus within Europe. The 1970s were marked by successive waves of terror and the rapid growth of militant, irrationalist movements—especially the "Green" movement, which sprang up since 1976–77, and after the briefest period of time is in a position to paralyze decision-making in the Federal Republic of Germany. During the course of the terrorist escalation from 1972 to 1977, an international network of left and right terrorist groups were able to lodge themselves within the growing milieu of the various "drop-out" movements.

Over the same period, the activities of international organized crime grew to a similar extent, especially in the narcotics traffic, and it has become increasingly evident that the terrorist infrastructure has extensive overlaps with smuggling in drugs and weapons. In spite of a few tactical successes

319

scored by security agencies, terrorism and the militant organizations surrounding it, as well as organized crime, have proven to be extremely capable of self-regeneration, for at no time have the authorities been able to seriously impair their underlying control structures.

By the 1960s at the latest, research into the background of the Kennedy assassination had already shown that a "Murder, Inc." was operating on the highest level, crisscrossing intelligence channels, financial and political power brokers, terrorist activities, and organized crime.

Aside from initiatives of private entities such as the *Executive Intelligence Review* (*EIR*) and a few others, serious moves by governmental agencies against this apparatus were only resumed during the late 1970s. These initiatives concentrated on terrorist and Mafia-inspired threats to Italy, where a group of young magistrates and public prosecutors began to apply a method which had already been publicly suggested by *EIR* in 1978 following the Red Brigades' murder of Italian President Aldo Moro. According to that analysis, the following elements overlap within terrorism's control structure: certain oligarchical families (particularly in Italy, Switzerland, and Great Britain); their associated financial institutions; elements of various Eastern and Western intelligence services; secret conspiratorial societies, particularly of Freemasonic and other pseudo-religious stripes; the international organized crime network; and the still-extant "Nazi International."

For the first time in post-war history this control structure was brought under public scrutiny in May of 1982 in connection with the scandal surrounding the secret Italian P-2 Lodge. Since then this group of Italian investigative magistrates has circulated further ground-breaking results in connection with the Moro kidnapping, the attempted assassination of the Pope in Rome, and the P-2 Lodge, which have even more precisely zeroed in on the character of this international apparatus.

In the course of these Italian investigations and parallel research by *EIR* concerning the role of the Swiss banker François Genoud, peeling away the outer layers has increasingly revealed that the infrastructure of the Nazi International plays a substantially greater role than was previously assumed. Nodal points of this International were turned up in left-wing and right-wing terrorism and their milieu, as well as in separatist and Islamic fundamentalist movements, in drug and weapons smuggling, and in the business and banking world. In what follows, we shall describe some of the forms and methods of this operation, which is utilized by both Eastern and Western sides for purposes of destabilization.

The 'Bulgarian Connection'

In early 1983, the Italian investigative magistrate Carlo Palermo (weapons and drug smuggling) and Ilario Martella (papal assassination attempt) released results which provide a precise look at the East-West intermeshing of terrorism and organized crime. A year earlier, investigative magistrate Ferdinando Imposimato had taken the first step in this direction in the Moro case, when he spoke of the existence of an "international directorate" from which left and right terrorism, drug and weapons smuggling, political murder and destabilization operations were all steered. In addition to the significance of these researches for his own case—the murder of Aldo Moro—Imposimato had already established the connection between this constellation and the attempt on the Pope on May 13, 1981.

Imposimato's initiative contributed substantially to one of the severest blows against the Red Brigades and its infrastructure, one which succeeded in liberating the abducted General Dozier and capturing the Red Brigades leader Giovanni Senzani.

Palermo's initiative struck to the core of a gigantic drug and weapon smuggling syndicate, at whose apex was the 70-year-old Syrian Henri Arsan and his export-import firm, Stipam International Transport. Significantly, in recent years the firm has been located within a building in Milan belonging to the Banca Ambrosiano, the financial center of the P-2 Lodge. The business accounts of Stipam were handled by this bank.

Arsan's firm dealt not only in giant quantities of small arms, but also in tanks, military helicopters, and other heavy equipment. For transport, ships and railroad trains were made available through close cooperation with the Turkish mafia, which in payment had to acquire and refine raw opium from the Middle and Far East. The Turkish mafia, which itself overlaps with such organizations as the right-extremist Gray Wolves, is the jumping-off point for research concerning the Pope's assailant Mehmet Ali Agca.

Morphine was brought via Trieste into the Trento-Verona-Bolzano triangle, where it was stored and further distributed. Here Sicilian mafia circles took over the further expedition and refining. Northern Italy contains the greatest concentration of military installations in all of Europe. From here was directed the infamous 1973 right-wing "Rosa dei Venti" armed uprising that attempted to overthrow the Italian government.

Another bastion of Arsan's business dealings was Sofia, the second largest center of illegal transactions next to Milan. According to the estimates of Turkish experts, a considerable portion of the illicit sale of weapons would take place via Sofia, whence they were passed into the hands of right and left terrorist groups. In connection with this, there have been repeated references to the role of the Bulgarian export-import firm Kintex.

Judge Martella then picked up the strings of this investigation in connection with the assassination attempt on the Pope. In the wake of Agca's confession, various persons from this "Bulgarian Connection" circle were arrested, including employees of the Bulgarian airline concession in Italy and the Turkish mafioso Bekir Celenk, who according to Agca had offered him a considerable sum for carrying out the attempt.

Another element of this weapons and drug network is the Iranian Sadegh Tabatabai, an arms dealer and confidant of Khomeini. Tabatabai is reported to maintain close relations with the Italian right-wing terrorist Stefano Delle Chiaie, as well as with the Swiss businessman Hans-Albert Kunz. Kunz is considered to be close to Victor Emmanuel of Savoy, in turn a close friend of Licio Gelli, head of the P-2 Lodge. Kunz also maintains relations with the Swiss banker François Genoud, a key figure of the Nazi International. It is interesting to note how these networks have been protected by some West German authorities. Tabatabai was repeatedly given protection by Hans-Dietrich Genscher and his foreign ministry, notwithstanding the fact that he was

convicted of narcotics smuggling on German soil,
and had already previously abetted terrorist actions
and carried out illegal weapons purchases there.
Apparently this was not the first time that Genscher
personally intervened to protect such tools of the
Nazi International. In 1975 Genscher expressly intervened with the Italian government in order to
effect the release of the Gestapo war criminal Herbert Keppler, who at that time was still in the cus-
tody of the Italian authorities. Similar behavior on
the part of the foreign ministry has also been observed with respect to Libyan operations inside West
German territory.

Let us now turn to the key figure in the Nazi
International.

The Case of François Genoud

Two interrelated phenomena have increasingly
dominated society in the post-war period: the Black,
or Nazi, International of the disciples of Adolf Hitler who have never given up their dream of the
"Fourth Reich," and its direct offshoot, international terrorism. Left and right terror, and even
the currently thriving brutal religious fanaticism,
are sides of the same coin. Terrorist formations
have increasingly come to be instruments of the
faction in Moscow whose conscious mission is to
make Moscow into the "Third and Final Rome."
At the hub of all these operations is the mysterious
figure of Swiss-Nazi banker François Genoud. Genoud may not be the real head of the entire operation; we will, however, prove that he is one of its
most important coordinators, along with a number
of lesser-known members of the directorate who
are responsible for the Nazi International's financial and political activities.

Today's Nazi International has at its command an extensive financial apparatus which is primarily fed from the loot amassed by the Third Reich. Between 1943 and 1945, this loot had been invested in not less than 700 private holdings by Hitler's private secretary Martin Bormann, a close friend of Genoud. Of these 700 companies, 214 are in Switzerland, 200 in the Near East, 34 in Turkey, and numerous others in Asia and Latin America. In 1973, ninety tons of the gold in global circulation was in the hands of the Nazis, thanks to the machinations of Hitler's former economics minister Hjalmar Schacht, who, after his acquittal at Nuremberg, directed the reorganization of the Nazi International's finances in collaboration with François Genoud.

The boards of directors of many of these corporations discreetly include Schacht's niece Elsa Skorzeny, wife of the late SS Col. Otto Skorzeny. Otto Skorzeny could always be counted on as Hitler's man to carry out the most arduous command tasks; he rescued Mussolini from imprisonment (for a brief period at least); he ran the commandos in the Battle of the Bulge; and he was also the person who set up the Nazis' escape organization Die Spinne/Odessa and many other organizations after the collapse of the Nazi Reich. Elsa Skorzeny is a member of the directorate of the Nazi International. This directorate oversees financial transactions in North Africa, Latin America, and in the Middle East. Its recent intensification of ties to the Soviet and East German camp was not all that dramatic; since the 1950s, at the latest, many of its members had collaborated with the Soviets, Otto Skorzeny and Otto-Ernst Remer among them.

A glance at Genoud's *curriculum vitae* shows the

continuity in his political career. At every crucial point, Genoud has the right kind of assistance. In Genoud's words, this began with his father, a banker, who had decided to send him to Munich in the 1920s "to further my education as well as to teach me discipline." Years later Genoud acknowledged that when he was not yet twenty years old, he had become "deeply influenced by Hitler."

Genoud also made a month-long trip to India, about which little is known. It is possible that he made a side-excursion to Tibet, like many other Nazi principals before him. Be that as it may, Genoud suddenly resurfaced in Palestine in 1936, where he met up with the Grand Mufti of Jerusalem, thereby laying the groundwork for a friendship and collaboration that lasted until the Mufti's death in the 1970s. Genoud's presence in Palestine coincided with the increasing activity of the Nazis' military secret service, the anti-Jewish agitation financed on a grand scale by the Mufti, and also the Palestinian Revolt of 1936. During the period from the mid-1930s to the beginning of the war, Martin Bormann, Adolf Eichmann, and the Hitler Youth leader Baldur von Schirach also met with the Grand Mufti in Jerusalem, and Schirach visited the numerous pro-Nazi Arab organizations that were sprouting up like mushrooms in Lebanon, Syria, Iraq, and Iran. Friendships were established at that time which have lasted right up to the present, such as with the Syrian People's Party and the Syrian National Socialist Party, the latter led today by the wife of Hafez Assad, Anita Makhlouf. The same holds true for numerous Iranian and Iraqi mullah organizations, including the founding members of the Iraqi-Shiite Al-Dawa'a terrorist organization in Teheran. Al-Dawa'a was founded at the end of the 1950s by

Ayatollah Khoy, the same mullah who had worked for the Abwehr during World War II, and who was responsible for the kamikaze bombings in Kuwait on Dec. 12, 1983.

Following 1939, Genoud was always very secretive about his Nazi activities. Was Genoud already working for the German Abwehr in the mid-1930s? The most reliable reports concerning this, those of the International Union of Resistance Fighters in the Second World War, only take note of his activities in the spring of 1940, when he founded the "Oasis" nightclub in Lausanne with the Lebanese Omar Bey. He is cited as a member of the Nazi Swiss National Front in 1939, and worked closely with the National Union in Switzerland. The National Union was headed by the Swiss patrician Georges Oltramare, whose family still sits on the board of one of the oldest banking houses in Switzerland, the Lombard-Odier Bank in Geneva. The Lombard-Odier Bank was not accidentally the depository of the gold used by Allen Dulles in conjunction with his secret negotiations with the Nazi leadership. Genoud maintained close contact with Oltramare, who under the pseudonym George Dieudonne was editor-in-chief of the anti-Semitic hate-sheet *Pilori* in Nazi-occupied France. He turned up again under the same pseudonym as a radio commentator for Radio Cairo in the 1950s. Around Oltramare were gathered all the young Swiss Nazis who later joined the Waffen-SS, such as Gaston Amaudruz, who joined up with the "Charlemagne" SS division at the Eastern Front, and who was one of the founders of the fascist Malmö International after the war.

Genoud took frequent trips to Berlin, where he was brought into Hitler's closest circles, especially

François Genoud's Career

1929   Meets with Hitler in Munich.

1936   Meets with the Grand Mufti of Jerusalem, Hadschi Amin al Husseini.

1939   Joins the German Abwehr, after which his contact with Martin Bormann and Josef Goebbels became closer.

1943   Negotiates with OSS head Allen Dulles in Berne concerning the post-war period.

1950   Flees after the war to Belgium and then to Tangiers.

1952   Meets in Cairo together with SS Col. Otto Skorzeny, Ahmed Ben Bella, Mohammed Ben Khidder, and the first Fedayeen groups; among them is also Sabri al-Banna.

1956   Wins a legal action in Frankfurt conerning the publication rights to Goebbels', Bormann's, and Hitler's writings.

1959   Founds at Lausanne the Banque Commerciale Arabe with ben Khidder and the Syrian Mardam family.

1962   Works with Ben Bella as a banker in Algiers.

1965   Becomes active in Lebanon with the mafia grouping Casino du Liban.

1969   Legal counsel for three PFLP members brought before a court at Winterthur. Defense attorney is Jacques Vergès.

1970s   Associated with Quaddafi regime, which has just taken power. Turns up as financial advisor to Libyan banks and organizes an international campaign to free the Swiss terrorist Bruno Breguet, who is interned in an Israeli prison.

1980s   Attempts to obtain Jacques Vergès as an attorney for Breguet, who was arrested in Paris in February 1982. Secures Vergès as attorney for the Gestapo officer Klaus Barbie. Involved in the "Hitler Diaries" swindle of *Stern* magazine.

through his good relations with Goebbels' wife. At the outbreak of the Second World War, Genoud was operating as an intelligence contact out of Switzerland and out of Belgium. On account of this activity he was imprisoned for a brief time after the war; he was soon set free through the intervention of the head of Interpol, Paul Kickopf, a former agent of the Abwehr who had resigned in 1942. In 1943, Genoud was incorporated into Martin Bormann's preparations for the period following the expected collapse of the Reich. The goal was a "Fourth Reich," this time on a global scale. Genoud became the key figure in gigantic market transactions on Swiss and other foreign bank accounts. Crucial for Genoud's work was the role of the well-known Swiss banker Dr. Alfred Schaefer, who for decades was chairman of the Union Bank of Switzerland (see Chapter 3). Schaefer was not only Eva Braun's lover before Hitler took her over, but the confidant of Hitler's sister Paula. A multitude of corporations were established, such as the Lausanne-based Diethelm Brothers, which organized the escape of Nazi Luftwaffe Col. Hans Rudel to Argentina.

Rudel later founded the "European-Argentine Friendship Society." Organizations including the journal *Der Weg*, founded not later than 1948, served as the mouthpiece for the Nazi exiles in Latin America. A perusal of this journal reveals that after the war a bitter struggle broke out between the various secret services for control of the old Nazi secret-service apparatus. While Allen Dulles and his friends in the U.S. State Department were shutting their eyes to the emigration of principal Nazis to Latin America, some of the latter were already extending feelers to Moscow. The editorial policy of *Der Weg* favored an alliance between the Nazis and Russia, against the "decadent West and American imperialism"!

The Nazi International in the Middle East

By the mid-1950s, less than ten years after the military dismemberment of the Third Reich, the apparatus for the coming "Fourth Reich" was already in place. In a July 1983 interview with Swiss Radio, SS Gen. Karl Wolff stated, "We are greatly indebted to François Genoud. His contributions following the war were of immeasurable value to us. Without him we would not have survived!"—a compliment of which Genoud is justly proud. In February 1984, he told *Stern* magazine "Everyone has his hobby; mine is to help people like him," by which he meant the SS "Butcher of Lyon" Klaus Barbie.

Genoud has traveled a great deal over the last thirty years in pursuit of his "hobby." Immediately after the war he turned up in Tangiers, the neutral zone where the spies and intelligence services of Asia, Africa, Latin America, and Europe could hold their rendezvous. During the war Tangiers had been a center of the Nazi secret service. Besides Genoud, following the war, General Wolff, General Ramcke, Gen. Hans Rudel, SS Captain Reichenberg, SS Colonel Skorzeny and numerous others took up residence there, and repeatedly turned up as Genoud's closest collaborators. This was especially the case during 1952–56, when the entire pack could be found back together in Cairo, together with their old friends, the Grand Mufti al-Husseini and Hjalmar Schacht.

Before he went to Cairo, Genoud appeared in public once more in 1951, although very discreetly, when he helped found the Black International in Malmö, which was later named the Malmö International. Genoud, who then withdrew from active political life, was the actual godfather of this organization.

Among those present at the founding meeting in Malmö were the previously mentioned Gaston Amaudruz, Per Engdahl from Sweden, the former German SS officers Heinz Priester and Fritz Richter, Pierre Clementi of the French Volunteer Divison of the Vichy regime, Sir Oswald Mosley from Great Britain, and Count Loredan from Italy. Their stated purpose was to found the "European Social Movement" for a "New European Order." This "movement" has been the spawning ground for every neo-Nazi organization of the past thirty years, and Lausanne and Malmö have served as coordination centers, out of which Amaudruz operates his intelligence newsletter *Courier du Continent*.

This newsletter receives regular contributions from former SS officer and concentration-camp administrator Thies Christophersen, who is sought by numerous police authorities because of his evil Nazi propaganda, exemplified by his contention that mass murder was never practiced in the concentration camps. In a 1982 interview with the *Executive Intelligence Review*, Amaudruz said he worked most closly with Christophersen's Society for Biological Anthropology, La Nouvelle École of Alain de Benoist, and its offshoot GRECE, which in turn collaborates with Siemens Foundation chief Armin Mohler, as demonstrated by his attendance at its last annual conference. Mohler, with whom we are already familiar through his book *The Conservative Revolution*, was a Swiss member of the Waffen SS whose dreams of fighting on the Eastern Front were shattered when the Nazis declared him physically unfit for service. It therefore comes as no surprise to find Mohler in the orbit of the recently founded "Republican Party" of Franz Schönhuber, a friend of Genoud and Remer.

In Cairo, Genoud primarily collaborated with Colonel Skorzeny, who had gotten the green light from certain American circles to offer his services to the new regime of Gamal Abdul Nasser. Allen Dulles, John Foster Dulles, and Averell Harriman decided that "It is better to have the Nazis in Cairo than the Communists." The Egyptians, who had not been asked beforehand, quickly found themselves in the clutches of both Nazis and Communists. Taking advantage of the catastrophic shortage of suitable personnel in all areas of the new republic, the Nazis soon settled into key positions of the intelligence services.

This process was coordinated from the West German side by Gehlen's representative in the federal intelligence service (BND), Heinz Felfe, who a few years later defected to the Soviet side. In Cairo, Genoud, Skorzeny, and their friends again rebuilt the old "National Minorities" apparatus formed by the Abwehr of Admiral Canaris, and was later put under the control of Amt IV of Himmler's Reichssicherheitshauptamt (Reich Main Security Office—RSHA). Genoud's old friend, the Grand Mufti, relied on this apparatus for aid in carrying out the 1941 Iraqi coup, as well as for the formation of numerous Muslim military units in the Mideast and Africa, such as the "Saber" and "Dagger" divisions of the Allgemeine Waffen-SS, which were deployed in the Balkans and the Caucasus regions; and the "Arab Legions," which were deployed in North Africa along with Italian armed forces. In Europe, North African Muslims were chiefly funnelled into the "Er Rashid" organization, while other minorities such as Bretons, Basques, and Alsatians were controlled through Fred Moyshes' "Organization of National Minorities," which had existed long before the war, by the Paris-based Nazi intelligence official Dr. Best.

The Algerian agitator Ahmed Ben Bella and his friend Mohammed Ben Khidder, along with a few other friends, were all staying in Cairo at the same time. Some reports claim that Ben Bella, who liked to boast about his participation in the 1944 Italian campaign, had already been recruited much earlier into the German Abwehr and its "Er Rashid" organization. However that may be, Genoud and Skorzeny recommended him to one of their associates, SS officer Gerhard Müller, alias Si Mustapha, former advisor to Egyptian General Neguib. Ben Bella was now one of them.

The importance of such operations for Genoud lay in the possibility of putting state power to work in the interests of the Nazi International. This explains Genoud's enduring relationship to Ben Bella, whom he regularly visited while imprisoned in France. During the Algerian war of independence, Genoud procured weapons through the Nazi International for the FLN and thus became a crucial asset of the so-called Curiel network, which worked within France for the Algerian National Liberation Front (FLN). Most members of the FLN network probably never heard of Genoud, and were definitely unaware of the details of his activities. The secret was hidden behind the apparent neutrality and respectability of a bank which was eager to expand the FLN war chest. Such banks were rare; Genoud, however, headed up one such bank, the Banque Commerciale Arabe, founded by him in 1959. Hundreds of millions of francs flowed into the bank from sympathizers of the FLN. Algerian political leaders only found out later that this was serving the interests of Genoud and the Nazi International more than it was their own.

One of the bank's advisors was none other than Hjalmar Schacht, who was also active as an advisor in many Third World countries such as Iran, Saudi Arabia, and Indonesia. Sitting on the board of the bank were Martial Gaffiot, Gerard-Charles Borguin, the mafia lawyer Max Mosher, as well as Jamil Mardam Bey and, later, his son Zuhair Mardam.

The old Syrian Mardam family were longstanding friends with the Mufti, a friendship going back to Jamil Mardam Bey's work as Syrian foreign minister and also as leader of the Muslim Brotherhood-controlled Syrian People's Party at the end of the 1940s. Zuhair Mardam, who played a key role in the oil business along with the Akram Odscheh from Saudi Arabia, is now with the Saudi-Swiss Finance Corporation. It was not until 1979 that the Algerian government was able to regain control over their bank and their gold which, after the murder of Mohammed Khidder, was under François Genoud's exclusive control.

During this period Genoud established two new and important friendships: Michel Raptis alias "Pablo," and Jacques Vergès. After the war, Raptis became secretary to a founder of the Trotskyist Fourth International, Ernest Mandel, and in this capacity became a leading figure in his own right. Before the war, Raptis had joined the Trotskyists together with an individual who is not unknown today, the current Socialist prime minister of Greece, Andreas Papandreou. After a somewhat miraculous escape from prison at the outset of the war, Raptis wound up in 1952 as Ben Bella's Minister of Planning. A Feb. 5, 1984 interview with Pablo and Ben Bella in the Greek newspaper *To Vema* indicates that they have never broken these ties.

Ben Bella decided in January 1983 to seek refuge at Genoud's residence in Switzerland, at the point it became clear to him that he could never again return to France. Since Ben Bella's release from imprisonment in Algeria, Genoud has helped him build an international fundamentalist network, whose aim is to topple every North African regime.

The paths of Genoud and Raptis criss-cross again and again. In the mid-1960s, while Raptis was busy recruiting European students for military training camps of the Popular Front for the Liberation of Palestine (PFLP) and other Palestinian terrorist groups in Syria, Genoud's Belgian friend François Thiriart of the "Young Europe" movement was meanwhile up to the same thing with his "European Brigades for Palestine." During this time Genoud was in direct contact with George Habash, as he told a journalist of *L'Express* in 1982, adding that since that time he had lost contact with Habash.

Today Raptis also plays an important role in the regroupment of the militant left. In France and West Germany his "International Revolutionary Marxist Tendency" (IRMT) is currently attempting to unite various split-offs from orthodox Communist, Trotskyist and Maoist organization into a catch-all vehicle that will join up with the activities of the Green and "alternative" movements.

The Terrorist Scene

Genoud's public support for the Swiss terrorist Bruno Breguet has also recently caused quite a stir. Breguet came into the limelight in the 1960s in connection with the PFLP, when he was seized by

the Israeli security forces for planting a bomb at
Haifa. The bomb attack was commissioned by Gian-
giacomo Feltrinelli, another key figure in international terrorism. Following Breguet's arrest, Genoud
was active in the background of a campaign of broad
support for the "political prisoner" Breguet. Almost every notable member of the left and left-
extremist delicatessen and intelligentsia participated in this campaign: Jean-Paul Sartre, Simone
de Beauvoir, Michel Foucault, Felix Guattari, Dario
Fo, Noam Chomsky, Günther Grass, Max Frisch,
Friedrich Dürrenmatt, to name a few. It is certain
that Genoud's financial power and extensive Mideast connections were responsible for the Israeli
decision to reduce Brequet's sentence from 15 to
7 years.

After his release in 1977, Breguet plunged back
into the terrorist scene, settling down in Berlin during the outset of the hot phase of the house-squat-
ters movement. Today there is still a circle of friends
in Berlin belonging to this scene, including Breguet's girlfriend, who are suspected of functioning
as a safe-house for Palestinian and Islamic terror
commandos. In the spring of 1982 Breguet was
arrested together with a German accomplice, Mag-
dalena Kopp. They were caught with large quantities of explosives, probably destined for use in a
bombing attempt on the Paris-Toulouse express
train. Kopp is thought to belong to the West German Revolutionary Cells. Breguet, Kopp and others are components of the same network which has
repeatedly surfaced around the international terrorist "Carlos."

The defense attorney for Breguet and Kopp is
Genoud's confidant Jacques Vergès, the French terrorist lawyer who has also taken over the legal de-

fense of Nazi war criminal Klaus Barbie. French security circles and others consider Vergès to be a high-level KGB agent of influence. French experts have also indicated that in 1938 Barbie was transferred from RSHA Division IV to the "Bureau of Jewish Affairs." The leader of this division was Col. Walter Nikolai, founder of the military Abwehr. At that time, circles around Canaris expressed the suspicion that Nikolai worked for Soviet secret intelligence; French sources indicate that Nikolai went over to Soviet intelligence after 1945.

Examining the network of François Genoud with all its left- and right-leaning connections and its multiplicity of political operations in Latin America and Europe, one might conclude that it overlaps with the "Bulgarian Connection," brought to light by the May 1981 assassination attempt on the Pope. This impression would not be entirely wrong. However, the "Bulgarian Connection," along with its component of East bloc intelligence operations, is only one of many flanks in the network of the Nazi International and François Genoud.

Genoud was already involved in trading weapons for drugs during the mid-1960s when he clinched a weapons deal under the auspices of the French gangster Jean-Marie Tine for the Lebanese Casino du Liban, one of the most important Mediterranean centers where the threads of Asia's drug trade and smuggling to Europe and America intersect. The Casino du Liban is financially backed by the powerful Intra-Bank of Beirut, headed by the mafioso Jussuf Beidas. Beidas and Tine are also involved in the "French Connection" of August Ricord in Latin America.

In earlier days this connection went through Genoud's old friend Hans-Albert Kunz, a Swiss

businessman whom the Italian authorities would
very much like to put under cross-examination concerning his involvement in the conspiratorial P-2
Freemasonic Lodge, on the role of Licio Gelli in
countless arms deals, and on the relationship of the
P-2 Lodge to the Pope's assailant Ali Agca. Like
many of his associates, Kunz was present in Cairo
at the same time as Genoud and Skorzeny, and
remained in the Mideast for a long time. He was
advisor to the Libyan King Idris, and in a June
1983 interview boasted that he had mediated the
first agreement between Libya and the Soviet agent
of influence Armand Hammer of Occidental Petroleum.

In recent years, from his position on the board
of the Dreykott company, Kunz has mediated
hundreds of arms deals, especially with Iran. His
agent was the Italian fascist Stefano delle Chiaie,
who is wanted by the police for masterminding the
August 1981 bomb attack on the Bologna train station, which killed more than 80 persons. After delle
Chiaie fled Europe, he collaborated with Klaus Barbie in Bolivia in expanding the drug traffic. What
a small world! Another friend of Genoud and Kunz
is the Swiss businessman Peter Notz, who is still
suspected by the Swiss and Italian police of having
organized the escape of the P-2 Lodge's Grand Master Licio Gelli from a Swiss jail. His regular guests
at Notz's country seat, Gland (between Geneva and
Lausanne), include the Lebanese politicians Sulei-
man Franjieh and Walid Jumblatt. Their last meeting took place in connection with the "national
Lebanese reconciliation talks" in Geneva in November, 1983. The Swiss press took that occasion to
cast some light on a few more aspects of Notz's

business relations in Lebanon, especially with respect to arms deals.

For these kinds of operations Genoud also has a firm of his own, WEFA, located in Basel, which is currently under investigation in France. It is rumored that Genoud is the financial advisor to dozens of Arab banks, especially in Libya. In Spain, one of his most important contacts is Alfredo Fiero, who works for the Spanish export bank Banesco. In late 1983 Fiero and Notz signed an important weapons-trade agreement to aid Ahmed Ben Bella, who maintains extensive operations in Spain, including Spain's Muslim community and the Spanish Communist Party through the "Red Caliph" Julio Anguitar, mayor of Cordova, a city which serves as one of the most significant coordination centers for the Libyan and Iranian terror and destabilization actions conducted against Tunisia and Morocco by Genoud in early 1984.

It is even reported that Ben Bella is preparing to set up a permanent office in the Libyan capital, Tripoli. In early January 1984 Genoud was in Tripoli, at the same time as the Libyan news agency Jana described the founder of *Executive Intelligence Review*, Lyndon LaRouche, as the intellectual instigator of anti-Libyan activities. Genoud's Libyan sojourn coincides with the increasing exposure of his activities, and it is now rumored that he may want to stay away from Switzerland for some time. Perhaps he will ask his friend Qaddafi for political asylum.

The Role of Muammar Qaddafi

A key figure in finance and logistics for the formation of terrorist groups, separatist organizations,

and Green-peace movements is the Libyan head of
state Muammar Qaddafi. Qaddafi plays an extremely menacing role in the destabilization of Africa and several European states. And over the past
few years the Soviet Union has continually expanded its military support for Qaddafi; Libya currently has 5,000 military advisors from the Soviet
Union and its allies. Approximately $12 billion in
weapons and materiel has flowed into Libya from
the Soviet Union over the past seven years. One of
the co-authors of Qaddafi's *Green Book* is an East
German Communist Party operative named
Hannes, who has changed his name to Chalifa Ha-
nesh and is considered a confidant of Qaddafi.

Qaddafi's role in the financial and logistical support of the "peace movement" became public in the
spring and summer of 1982. At a March 1982 meeting in Vienna under the auspices of the Austrian
Society for North-South Questions, Qaddafi received a delegation of Greens and peace activists.
The delegation included Roland Vogt, Otto Schily,
Alfred Mechtersheimer, the South Tyrolean left-
wing extremist Alexander Langer, and the Austrian Socialist Egon Matzner.

In May 1982, the head of the Libyan Embassy
in Bonn, Mehdi Imberesh, appeared along with two
other representatives of the Libyan People's Bureau at an event held by the Greens, who had also
invited European and American representatives.
The meeting was the scene of demonstrative em-
braces between Imberesh, Roland Vogt of the West
German Greens, and Daniel Berrigan, a leading
representative of the American "peace movement."
Shortly thereafter an expanded delegation traveled
to Libya for extended discussions with Qaddafi.

Mechtersheimer, who took part in both conferences with Qaddafi, was so impressed by all these experiences that in May 1983 he warned that the peace movement would run out of steam if it did not take new inspiration from the "universal impulses of the Islamic world"!

The element of "Islamization" of the peace movement and the Greens is becoming increasingly evident. Roland Vogt, for example, has pointed out the significance of such leaders as Ahmed Ben Bella. The Swiss Nazi Ahmed Huber, a journalist who converted to Islam and is a close friend of Genoud and Ben Bella, agrees with Mechtersheimer on the perspective for the Greens: "They are turning away from the right-left mode of thinking. They are developing remarkably original and interesting religious impulses. In a few years the Greens will be completely transformed."

Huber, an admirer of Qaddafi and co-founder of the Swiss-Arab Society, which cooperates with the Geneva-based Islam and the West organization, also sees the Greens' development as one step in a process which, he proudly announces, will sooner or later lead to the "establishment of a Fourth Reich." The "Greater German" Huber is much more comfortable with the German Democratic Republic than he is with the "Americanized," "effeminate" Federal Republic of Germany. As a step toward a "Fourth Reich," he sees a "fully sovereign, nationally independent and reunified Germany" approaching in the next three to five years. With his paeans to the "revitalized Holy Russia," in which he places the greatest trust, the Muslim Huber is very clearly reflecting the currently prevailing irrational fundamentalist direction within the Soviet

Union, a direction being played out fully with their support of Khomeini and Qaddafi, their "Islamic card."

There is also a direct line through Qaddafi to the German National Revolutionary grouping around the magazine *Wir Selbst* and its theoretician, Prof. Henning Eichberg. This grouping is an extremely important connecting link between the new generation of neo-Nazi groups and disoriented leftists and Maoists, Greens and peace movement activists. This magazine, which is financed by Qaddafi himself, ran in its August/September 1983 issue a lengthy interview with Qaddafi, who declared that "I have a very positive evaluation of the Green Movement, especially because it is creating the framework for the peace movement as well as for the protection of the environment, and because it is developing ideas which are also to be found in the Green Book. I hope that out of the Green movement there will develop a movement for the liberation of all Germany. You must find new methods of struggle against oppression in Germany."

The Qaddafi-supported *Wir Selbst* group plays a crucial role in furnishing the ideological impulse for the entire alternative-anarchist, Green/National-Revolutionary spectrum. Henning Eichberg, who once wrote programs for the neo-Nazi German National Party (NPD), has found that both right and left extremist groups are responding positively to his concept of "national identity." His ideas were circulated in the left scene by *Pflasterstrand*, *taz* and other left-extremist newspapers and publishers. The group has already established a solid network of contacts from within the Berlin Alternate List electoral slate, left-wing SPD members and other organizations.

Eichberg's ideas are no less important for the new generation of extremely dangerous, openly neo-Nazi groups, such as the National Socialist Action Front grouping around Michael Kühnen or the Nazi-terrorist group around Odfried Hepp. Eichberg and his pupils are attempting, to form a "broad-based movement" out of "Greens, Socialists, Citizens' Initiatives, and National Revolutionary components."

Eichberg is at the same time one of the most explicit theoreticians of separatism. He is the creator of the idea of "ethno-pluralism." "The revolutionary ideology of the region" is "not 'left,' it is not 'right'; this is precisely why it has revolutionary implications," he preaches.

Members of the *Wir Selbst* group also maintain extensive contacts with European separatist-terrorist organizations. *Wir Selbst* also functions as a launching pad for the international "Society for Endangered Peoples," whose German business manager Tilman Zülch, when asked once about differences between Amnesty International and his organization, explained that "Amnesty is only for the theory, but we are for the weapon!"

One of the participants in the 1983 "Second Armenian World Congress" was the Berlin representative of the "Society for Endangered Peoples," Thessa Hoffman. The congress unanimously rejected a proposal to condemn bloody terrorist attacks such as the one at the Paris Orly airport, in which eight people were killed.

The ideology of extreme regionalism as embodied by Eichberg and his group and organizations like the "Society for Endangered Peoples" is one more example of the ideological intersections between the old and neo-Nazis, Greens and left extremists. Here there is full agreement between persons such as Club of Rome veteran Robert Jungk, Greens like Roland Vogt and Jo Leinen, and old Nazis like the Swiss Amaudruz; all of them glorify such things as the mythologies of old Indian tribes.

The list of separatist-terrorist organizations and initiatives supported by Qaddafi could be drawn out further. An important bastion in this connection is the "International Center for Ethnic and National Minorities" (Ciemen), based at the Benedictine cloister St. Michel de Cuxa in southern France. Ciemen functions as one of the the most important coordination points for southern European separatist organizations. The radicalization of guest workers in European countries as a result of Islamic fundamentalist ideas, also can be placed directly at Qaddafi's doorstep, since it is predominantly directed by such Qaddafi cohorts as Ahmed Ben Bella.

Libya's direct logistical and financial support for terrorist and separatist groups has assumed dangerous proportions. According to American estimates, something like 5,000 terrorists of all stripes and nationalities are processed through Libyan training camps each year. Numerous terrorist and radical organizations are directly financed with Libyan money.

The New Generation of Neo-Nazis

One of the central figures of the neo-Nazi scene is Michael Kühnen and his National Socialist Action Front (ANS/NA) and its electoral organization, Action for Repatriation of Foreigners (AAR). Both were banned in late 1983 by the West German government as Nazi successor-organizations. The example of Kühnen allows us to draw all the relevant connections that elucidate the interplay between the Nazi International, the ideological and tactical overlapping of left and right extremist groups, and the Green movement.

In the early 1970s, after the traditional right extremist organizations like the NPD ceased to be effective, Kühnen began to build a new National Socialist shock troop, which first made its appearance as the Hansa-Bund, and later on as the ANS. After a few street provocations the group went over into terrorist operations, robbing a bank in Hamburg and attacking a group of Dutch soldiers during a maneuver at the military drill grounds at Bergen-Hohe. Kühnen, Uwe Rohwer, and four other ANS members were caught and convicted in 1978. Rohwer and Kühnen are disciples of various old Nazis whose connections reach directly into the higher echelons of the Nazi International, as exemplied by Gelli and Genoud. Kühnen's enthusiastic backers included the former Luftwaffe colonel Hans-Ulrich Rudel, who belongs to Genoud's circle of friends. "Kühnen is a vanguard in many respects. Ninety-nine percent of what he says and does is right," Rudel raved.

Other "old warriors" in Kühnen's immediate circle are Otto-Ernst Remer and Willi Krämer. Remer likewise belongs to the hard-core of the Nazi International. During the war he commanded the Berlin Guard Battalion, which was largely responsible for putting down the attempted putsch against Hitler on July 20, 1944. After the war Remer was a functionary of the banned Socialist Reich Party (SRP) and constantly commuted between the Mideast and his illegal existence in the Federal Republic. Since 1981 he has emerged from obscurity and has appeared at various international meetings of old Nazi associations in Luxembourg and Alsace. Since the spring of 1983 he has repeatedly made public appearances with Kühnen.

Willi Krämer also comes out of the SRP, and was Joseph Goebbels' adjutant during the war. Krämer has been named honorary chairman of the ANS/ NA.

Another "old boy" and glowing admirer of Kühnen, who nominally comes out of a completely different corner, is the "left-wing" poet Erich Fried. It has become increasingly evident that there is a communality on the "left" and "right" scene which is not only ideological, but which extends to manifold organizational and logistical relationships.

Fried came from a Viennese Jewish family which in 1938 emigrated to England. In the 1950s, Fried was working as a political commentator for the BBC. In the mid-1960s, his anti-Vietnam War poems earned him a reputation as the "poet of the extra-parliamentary opposition." Fried, who defines himself as a "leftist anti-Zionist," suddenly joined up with the Baader-Meinhof and RAF sympathizers. By 1971 he was describing political measures against RAF sympathizers as "Nazi methods." The darling of *taz* and the entire scene from left-alternative-Green to terrorist, Fried suddenly began to enthuse about the Nazi-terrorist Kühnen. In the spring of 1983 he offered to do a joint television appearance with Kühnen, which was only prevented at the last minute by a Jewish representative of the Radio Commission.

Fried talked about Kühnen in the following terms: "Sure he's a neo-fascist; he just doesn't know enough yet, but he is subjectively a very honest person; his fascism is revolutionary, just as Mussolini's fascism in the Salô Republic and the Peronists' fascism was revolutionary.... For him the Americans are the main danger for Germany, and on this we can only agree with him." Fried went on to state that Kühnen was "a together person" who has "charisma." Minor "slip-ups," such as his hostility to foreigners, could be ironed out. Fried explained that Kühnen even lives next to a Turkish family, and gets along splendidly with their children. Kühnen, according to Fried, is a "left fascist," a "social revolutionary," who represents the same current as the old left SA grouping.

Such remarks might be shocking, but for those familiar with the "scene" they are perfectly coherent. Already in 1979 "Red Danny," Daniel Cohn-Bendit, veteran of the Frankfurt anarcho-terrorist scene, had taken the public position that one cannot simply dismiss the neo-Nazis' "revolutionary potential."

Unity between Brown and Red 'Environmentalists'

During the same time period, the Communist Alliance (KB-Nord), one of the key organizations in the anarchist-autonomist spectrum, began to integrate Punkers, decorated with swastikas and runic SS letters, into their violent riots. In 1979 a tract by the old Nazi Erwin Schönborn, entitled "Green Correspondence," was published, large sections of which read like one of the Greens' pamphlets. Its demands included: "Action for protection of environment, nature and animals"; "ecology before economy"; "the fight against nuclear weapons, the instruments of the holocaust"; "for peace and humanity against the global arms-race insanity"; "political solidarity with the Islamic green revolution." Schönborn's co-authors, Walter Kexel and Dieter

Sporleder, later became terrorist bombers who were arrested during the latter half of 1983 for a series of brutal attacks against American GIs. And the list of these overlaps between the left and right radical scene could be infinitely extended. Old Nazis such as Per Engdahl in Sweden and Gaston Guy Amaudruz in Switzerland repeatedly underline these links. Engdahl is a leading light among the successors to the fascist Malmö International, which in the 1950s was already trying to find a common platform between the diverse neo-Nazi organizations. Engdahl once said: "I totally agree with the environmentalist movement. Traditionally the theme of environmental protection was a theme of the right, but now the left has taken it over." Genoud's confidant Amaudruz has repeatedly expressed the same views with almost identical words.

Calls for a common struggle of the left and right were also evident in 1977 during the climax of the demonstrations against the nuclear plant at Brockdorf, West Germany. The National-Socialist terrorist Manfred Roeder wrote at the time:

> We must bring things to a boil as we did at Brockdorf. Brockdorf was the beacon and the ray of hope on the horizon. The soul of the people is boiling over. The democratic rabble is starting to tremble. We have waited years for this situation. Finally the hour is come! Brockdorf is the Achilles heel of democracy! The time is ripe to strike!

Rejoicing over the Red Army Fraction's assassination of West German Attorney General Siegfried Buback, Roeder exclaimed that "Buback has not only persecuted me and other patriots, but he has also tolerated two different kinds of law. We must feel sympathy for those who persecute German soldiers and patriots! There he lies, he who would destroy us, buried in the earth!" At another point he stated: "No longer are the police our helpers and friends. I am fighting shoulder to shoulder with the anarchists and the left."

Michael Kühnen made this liaison clear in a lengthy interview with the *Deutsche Allgemeine Sonntagsblatt* in February 1982. He described the Munich shootout with the Busse group as "an incident that I'm already thinking of as a Stammheim in reverse. That is, I'm convinced that these events in Munich will boomerang just like it happened at Stuttgart-Stammheim with the RAF comrades. Here we're dealing with a police attack. . . ." Asked about the possibility of an action unity between National Socialists and Communists, as occurred off and on during the 1930s, Kühnen's words were:

The readiness to do something like that [is] more marked in left circles than it is in right circles. Once, for example, I offered the KBW in Hanover, as well as the Communist Alliance in Hamburg on the occasion of the municipal elections, a direct or indirect moratorium so as not to disperse our forces, because I have always said that these guys are against the system, too, in their own way. The first thing is to weaken the system. . . . I see on the left—the alternatives, the peace movement, the antinuclear movement—people who for very honorable reasons are against certain aspects of this system. And here I think that action unity is possible. . . . And it's not difficult for me to

imagine young National Socialists jointly dem-
onstrating as easily against the [Frankfurt airport's] West Runway as they would against
speculation in housing construction.

But these relationships are not merely on the
level of declarations of intent. It can be proven that
this red-brown partnership is reflected with increasing frequency in organizational and personnel
overlaps.

For example, it was already known in 1981 that
Udo Reinhard, an activist of the Green Alternative
Citizens List (GABL) in Hanover, was also a member of the National Revolutionary organization
NRAO/SdV. Moreover, Reinhardt was friends with
one of the National Socialist terrorists who were
killed in the Munich police shootout with members
of the Busse group. A better known case is that of
Werner Vogel, the Green member of parliament
who turned out to be an old Nazi official but who
nevertheless continued to enjoy the support of the
greater part of the Greens. But this is not surprising, since the "environmentalist movement" was
from its inception largely the work of old Nazis.

The example of Kühnen can serve as a case study
for the development of tendencies within neo-Nazi
layers. But more than that, Kühnen's group ex-
hibits a dangerous recruitment potential for violent
terrorist acts. Kühnen's following is increasing particularly among the proto-fascist "Skinheads" and
violence-prone soccer fan clubs and rock bands. For
example, fan clubs are being formed with names
like "Zyklon-B" and "Borussenfront" (a take-off on
the name of a Dortmund soccer team, with the
double-S written in the old SS runic characters).
Kühnen is also playing a considerable role in making international contacts in the United States and

France. There is also collaboration with old Nazis like Schönborn, Christophersen, Roeder, Remer, and Amaudruz, etc., who have little organizational relevance today, but who provide backup for the young Nazis with their wealth of intelligence, international connections, money, and logistics.

An interesting glimpse into the activities of Nazi-oriented terrorist groups and their associations is provided by the group around Odfried Hepp, whose members include Walter Kexel, Hans-Peter Frass, Hans Sporleder, Helge Blasche and Ulrich Tillman. This group has gotten over a half million deutschmarks by robbing banks, and has taken responsibility for the December 1982 attacks against American GIs. Three members of this organization come out of "new right" groups such as the Hoffman paramilitary group or the VSDB/PdA (Busse group). Furthermore, Hepp's people completed a course at a Lebanese training camp, which professionally qualified them in weaponry and explosives. In the estimation of French experts, this group is particularly dangerous because they are said to have international contacts. Kexel and Tillman were arrested in the English city of Poole, notably in the home of a former SAS major.

In 1982 this group circulated a paper entitled "Parting with Hitlerism," which announced a formal split with the Kühnen group, which was labeled the "National Socialist chaotics" and "Hitler-fascists." The paper, however, reveals very strong leanings toward the National Bolshevist ideology of Henning Eichberg's *Wir Selbst* group, which puts heavy emphasis on the National Revolutionary Ernst Niekisch. The paper includes the following:

Our goal is not to turn back the wheel of history and to resurrect a state on the Hitler

model, but rather to lead a non-dogmatic liberation struggle, which guarantees the survival of our people. In this struggle against
Americanism we welcome everyone who, like
us, has recognized that we will have a chance
only if the activist youth within left and right
circles overcome their dogmas and join up
with the liberation struggle. We in the FRG
will also, of course, heartily welcome anti-
Americans from other countries who wish to
take part in our struggle. In conclusion we
wish to emphasize once more that we are neither "left" nor "right," and we wish to establish
neither an American-style federal state nor
another Soviet republic. . . . But under no circumstances must we fail to appreciate the anti-
bourgeois-capitalist driving power of Bolshevism, and it is our desire and will to live, as a
neutral Germany, in peace and friendship with
Soviet Russia.

The declaration concludes with the slogan: "Forward in the anti-imperialist liberation struggle!"

As is usually the case in West Germany, investigations into this extremely strident group seem
to have petered out into "lone-culprit" theories.
The first results of a special commission of the Hesse
State Criminal Office (LKA) consisted of the
groundbreaking discovery that the group had re-
sorted to crime primarily because of "avarice"! The
commission claimed that this "small Hessian group"
could not be ascertained to have had contact with
supraregional or international right extremist
movements. When, following their arrest, the
group's weapons depot was discovered near Dietz-
enbach, located only one hundred meters from one

of the RAF's weapons depots, near where the RAF terrorists Schulz and Mohnhaupt were also arrested, the LKA was just as quick to explain that there was no collaboration between left and right extremists—the reaction of most German authorities whenever key points are touched in the structure of terrorism and organized crime.

Afterword

Even before this book goes to print, everything points to the likelihood that public interest in it will be great. In the course of a television broadcast for the May 26, 1984 European Parliament elections, I mentioned the imminent publication of the book, and briefly indicated its contents. The large number of telephone calls received by myself and my associates in the days following the broadcast, leads me to conclude that the book could very well become a best-seller.

"I've always thought there was a lot more behind Hitler," was the most frequent comment heard from these callers. Their many questions about who really brought Hitler to power, seems to confirm my suspicion that this is indeed the Gordian knot which must be cut if we are ever to rediscover a true German identity.

But West German readers will not be the only ones to appreciate the liberating effects of this book. The founding members of the Schiller Institute in the United States are committed to publishing an

English-language edition by June of this year. At this very moment, when the same circles who saw Hitler as their best alternative are involved in an attempt to decouple Western Europe from the United States, we have an obligation to set the historical record straight. Germany's history is not what Hollywood has ever alleged it to be.

The Schiller Institute is planning a publication series on German-American history. These studies will place special emphasis on a positive redefinition of the Atlantic Alliance, not only in the field of military strategy, but also in economics, science, and culture.

Such an initiative has come not a moment too soon. The international financial and debt crisis is speeding toward a complete collapse, which this time will be considerably worse than the Great Crash of 1931. But for the first time, now there exist ideas and politically organized forces capable of solving the crisis, within the framework of a reorganization of the world monetary system. Whether or not this opportunity will be seized, depends to a large extent on whether we have truly learned from our past.

We hope at any rate that the reader of this book, having gained new insights and perspectives, will decide to join in the work of the Schiller Institute. It was a long, hard fall from Friedrich Schiller's high ideal of humanity, to the barbaric world-view of an Adolf Hitler. But should it not also be possible for us to set into motion a movement in the opposite direction, if we joyfully apply ourselves to that task?

Helga Zepp-LaRouche
Virginia, May 31, 1984

Principles of the Schiller Institute

1. The purpose of the Schiller Institute is to counterpose to the multiple tendencies toward decoupling Western Europe from the United States a positive conception for the maintenance and revitalization of the Western alliance. Its members commit themselves to the idea of returning to the spirit of the American Revolution, the German classics, and the Liberation Wars against Napoleon, and to proceed from that basis to find solutions to the present problems.

2. The Schiller Institute sees as its task to newly define the interest of the Western alliance, namely in the humanist tradition of Nicolaus of Cusa, Leibniz, and William Penn, and to work for a more just world order in which national sovereign republics are united as a community of principle of mutual help and development. The members of the Schiller Institute regard themselves as world citizens and patriots alike, in the sense that Friedrich Schiller used these notions.

3. It is not without reason that the Western alliance has been afflicted with the present crisis. To elaborate those causes of the crisis and to redesign the areas of positive collaboration are included tasks of the Institute. The following departments shall be created to this end:

I. Department for military cooperation. Subsumed areas: Topics of military history from Lazare Carnot, Scharnhorst, Gneisenau to MacArthur, et al. The alliance in the era of the doctrine of Mutually Assured Survival.

II. Department for economic cooperation. Subsumed areas: The economic theory of Alexander Hamilton, the "American System" of Political Economy, Friedrich List, the Careys, etc. Common future economic tasks of the alliance.

III. Department for scientific and technological cooperation. Subsumed areas: The physical principles in the work of Gauss, Riemann, Cantor. Future areas of scientific cooperation.

IV. Department for the study of the common historical and cultural roots of Western Europe and the United States. Subsumed areas: The significance of the Weimar Classics, Schiller, Beethoven, and Franklin's European networks. The influence of German culture in America. Historical developments in the eighteenth, nineteenth and twentieth centuries.

4. The Institute shall carry the name of Schiller because no one has combined the idea of republican freedom and the idea of poetical beauty more effectively than Friedrich Schiller. For Schiller as for the members of this Institute, the greatest work of art is building political freedom.